T0296437

PURELY FUNCTIONAL DATA STRUCTURES

Most books on data structures assume an imperative language like C or C++. However, data structures for these languages do not always translate well to functional languages such as Standard ML, Haskell, or Scheme. This book describes data structures from the point of view of functional languages, with examples, and presents design techniques so that programmers can develop their own functional data structures. It includes both classical data structures, such as red-black trees and binomial queues, and a host of new data structures developed exclusively for functional languages. All source code is given in Standard ML and Haskell, and most of the programs can easily be adapted to other functional languages.

This handy reference for professional programmers working with functional languages can also be used as a tutorial or for self-study.

PURELY FUNCTIONAL
DATA STRUCTURES

CHRIS OKASAKI
COLUMBIA UNIVERSITY

CAMBRIDGE
UNIVERSITY PRESS

CAMBRIDGE
UNIVERSITY PRESS

University Printing House, Cambridge CB2 8BS, United Kingdom

One Liberty Plaza, 20th Floor, New York, NY 10006, USA

477 Williamstown Road, Port Melbourne, VIC 3207, Australia

314–321, 3rd Floor, Plot 3, Splendor Forum, Jasola District Centre, New Delhi – 110025, India

79 Anson Road, #06–04/06, Singapore 079906

Cambridge University Press is part of the University of Cambridge.

It furthers the University's mission by disseminating knowledge in the pursuit of education, learning and research at the highest international levels of excellence.

First published 1998
First paperback edition 1999
Reprinted 2020

Printed in the United Kingdom by TJ International Ltd. Padstow Cornwall

A catalog record for this book is available from the British library

library of Congress Cataloging in Publication data is available

ISBN 978 0 521 63124 2 hardback
ISBN 978 0 521 66350 2 paperback

Contents

Preface

I first began programming in Standard ML in 1989. I had always enjoyed implementing efficient data structures, so I immediately set about translating some of my favorites into Standard ML. For some data structures, this was quite easy, and to my great delight, the resulting code was often both much clearer and much more concise than previous versions I had written in C or Pascal or Ada. However, the experience was not always so pleasant. Time after time, I found myself wanting to use destructive updates, which are discouraged in Standard ML and forbidden in many other functional languages. I sought advice in the existing literature, but found only a handful of papers. Gradually, I realized that this was unexplored territory, and began to search for new ways of doing things.

Eight years later, I am still searching. There are still many examples of data structures that I just do not know how to implement efficiently in a functional language. But along the way, I have learned many lessons about what *does* work in functional languages. This book is an attempt to codify these lessons. I hope that it will serve as both a reference for functional programmers and as a text for those wanting to learn more about data structures in a functional setting.

Standard ML Although the data structures in this book can be implemented in practically any functional language, I will use Standard ML for all my examples. The main advantages of Standard ML, at least for presentational purposes, are (1) that it is a strict language, which greatly simplifies reasoning about how much time a given algorithm will take, and (2) that it has an excellent module system that is ideally suited for describing these kinds of abstract data types. However, users of other languages, such as Haskell or Lisp, should find it quite easy to adapt these examples to their particular environments. (I provide Haskell translations of most of the examples in an appendix.) Even

C or Java programmers should find it relatively straightforward to implement these data structures, although C's lack of automatic garbage collection can sometimes prove painful.

For those readers who are not familiar with Standard ML, I recommend Paulson's *ML for the Working Programmer* [Pau96] or Ullman's *Elements of ML Programming* [Ull94] as introductions to the language.

Other Prerequisites This book is not intended as a first introduction to data structures in general. I assume that the reader is reasonably familiar with basic abstract data types such as stacks, queues, heaps (priority queues), and finite maps (dictionaries). I also assume familiarity with the basics of algorithm analysis, especially "big-Oh" notation (e.g., $O(n \log n)$). These topics are frequently taught in the second course for computer science majors.

Acknowledgments My understanding of functional data structures has been greatly enriched by discussions with many people over the years. I would particularly like to thank Peter Lee, Henry Baker, Gerth Brodal, Bob Harper, Haim Kaplan, Graeme Moss, Simon Peyton Jones, and Bob Tarjan.

1

Introduction

When a C programmer needs an efficient data structure for a particular problem, he or she can often simply look one up in any of a number of good textbooks or handbooks. Unfortunately, programmers in functional languages such as Standard ML or Haskell do not have this luxury. Although most of these books purport to be language-independent, they are unfortunately language-independent only in the sense of Henry Ford: Programmers can use any language they want, as long as it's imperative.† To rectify this imbalance, this book describes data structures from a functional point of view. We use Standard ML for all our examples, but the programs are easily translated into other functional languages such as Haskell or Lisp. We include Haskell versions of our programs in Appendix A.

1.1 Functional vs. Imperative Data Structures

The methodological benefits of functional languages are well known [Bac78, Hug89, HJ94], but still the vast majority of programs are written in imperative languages such as C. This apparent contradiction is easily explained by the fact that functional languages have historically been slower than their more traditional cousins, but this gap is narrowing. Impressive advances have been made across a wide front, from basic compiler technology to sophisticated analyses and optimizations. However, there is one aspect of functional programming that no amount of cleverness on the part of the compiler writer is likely to mitigate — the use of inferior or inappropriate data structures. Unfortunately, the existing literature has relatively little advice to offer on this subject.

Why should functional data structures be any more difficult to design and implement than imperative ones? There are two basic problems. First, from

† Henry Ford once said of the available colors for his Model T automobile, "[Customers] can have any color they want, as long as it's black."

1

the point of view of designing and implementing efficient data structures, functional programming's stricture against destructive updates (i.e., assignments) is a staggering handicap, tantamount to confiscating a master chef's knives. Like knives, destructive updates can be dangerous when misused, but tremendously effective when used properly. Imperative data structures often rely on assignments in crucial ways, and so different solutions must be found for functional programs.

The second difficulty is that functional data structures are expected to be more flexible than their imperative counterparts. In particular, when we update an imperative data structure we typically accept that the old version of the data structure will no longer be available, but, when we update a functional data structure, we expect that both the old and new versions of the data structure will be available for further processing. A data structure that supports multiple versions is called *persistent* while a data structure that allows only a single version at a time is called *ephemeral* [DSST89]. Functional programming languages have the curious property that *all* data structures are automatically persistent. Imperative data structures are typically ephemeral, but when a persistent data structure is required, imperative programmers are not surprised if the persistent data structure is more complicated and perhaps even asymptotically less efficient than an equivalent ephemeral data structure.

Furthermore, theoreticians have established lower bounds suggesting that functional programming languages may be fundamentally less efficient than imperative languages in some situations [BAG92, Pip96]. In light of all these points, functional data structures sometimes seem like the dancing bear, of whom it is said, "the amazing thing is not that [he] dances so well, but that [he] dances at all!" In practice, however, the situation is not nearly so bleak. As we shall see, it is often possible to devise functional data structures that are asymptotically as efficient as the best imperative solutions.

1.2 Strict vs. Lazy Evaluation

Most (sequential) functional programming languages can be classified as either *strict* or *lazy*, according to their order of evaluation. Which is superior is a topic debated with sometimes religious fervor by functional programmers. The difference between the two evaluation orders is most apparent in their treatment of arguments to functions. In strict languages, the arguments to a function are evaluated before the body of the function. In lazy languages, arguments are evaluated in a demand-driven fashion; they are initially passed in unevaluated form and are evaluated only when (and if!) the computation needs the results to continue. Furthermore, once a given argument is evaluated, the value of that argument is cached so that, if it is ever needed again, it can be looked up rather than recomputed. This caching is known as *memoization* [Mic68].

Each evaluation order has its advantages and disadvantages, but strict evaluation is clearly superior in at least one area: ease of reasoning about asymptotic complexity. In strict languages, exactly which subexpressions will be evaluated, and when, is for the most part syntactically apparent. Thus, reasoning about the running time of a given program is relatively straightforward. However, in lazy languages, even experts frequently have difficulty predicting when, or even if, a given subexpression will be evaluated. Programmers in such languages are often reduced to pretending the language is actually strict to make even gross estimates of running time!

Both evaluation orders have implications for the design and analysis of data structures. As we shall see, strict languages can describe worst-case data structures, but not amortized ones, and lazy languages can describe amortized data structures, but not worst-case ones. To be able to describe both kinds of data structures, we need a programming language that supports both evaluation orders. We achieve this by extending Standard ML with lazy evaluation primitives as described in Chapter 4.

1.3 Terminology

Any discussion of data structures is fraught with the potential for confusion, because the term *data structure* has at least four distinct, but related, meanings.

- *An abstract data type (that is, a type and a collection of functions on that type).* We will refer to this as an *abstraction*.
- *A concrete realization of an abstract data type.* We will refer to this as an *implementation*, but note that an implementation need not be actualized as code — a concrete design is sufficient.
- *An instance of a data type, such as a particular list or tree.* We will refer to such an instance generically as an *object* or a *version*. However, particular data types often have their own nomenclature. For example, we will refer to stack or queue objects simply as stacks or queues.
- *A unique identity that is invariant under updates.* For example, in a stack-based interpreter, we often speak informally about "the stack" as if there were only one stack, rather than different versions at different times. We will refer to this identity as a *persistent identity*. This issue mainly arises in the context of persistent data structures; when we speak of different versions of the same data structure, we mean that the different versions share a common persistent identity.

Roughly speaking, abstractions correspond to signatures in Standard ML, implementations to structures or functors, and objects or versions to values. There is no good analogue for persistent identities in Standard ML.†

The term *operation* is similarly overloaded, meaning both the functions supplied by an abstract data type and applications of those functions. We reserve the term *operation* for the latter meaning, and use the terms *function* or *operator* for the former.

1.4 Approach

Rather than attempting to catalog efficient data structures for every purpose (a hopeless task!), we instead concentrate on a handful of general techniques for designing efficient functional data structures and illustrate each technique with one or more implementations of fundamental abstractions such as sequences, heaps (priority queues), and search structures. Once you understand the techniques involved, you can easily adapt existing data structures to your particular needs, or even design new data structures from scratch.

1.5 Overview

This book is structured in three parts. The first part (Chapters 2 and 3) serves as an introduction to functional data structures.

- Chapter 2 describes how functional data structures achieve persistence.
- Chapter 3 examines three familiar data structures—leftist heaps, binomial heaps, and red-black trees—and shows how they can be implemented in Standard ML.

The second part (Chapters 4–7) concerns the relationship between lazy evaluation and amortization.

- Chapter 4 sets the stage by briefly reviewing the basic concepts of lazy evaluation and introducing the notation we use for describing lazy computations in Standard ML.
- Chapter 5 reviews the basic techniques of amortization and explains why these techniques are not appropriate for analyzing persistent data structures.

---

† The persistent identity of an ephemeral data structure can be reified as a reference cell, but this approach is insufficient for modelling the persistent identity of a persistent data structure.

- Chapter 6 describes the mediating role lazy evaluation plays in combining amortization and persistence, and gives two methods for analyzing the amortized cost of data structures implemented with lazy evaluation.
- Chapter 7 illustrates the power of combining strict and lazy evaluation in a single language. It describes how one can often derive a worst-case data structure from an amortized data structure by systematically scheduling the premature execution of lazy components.

The third part of the book (Chapters 8–11) explores a handful of general techniques for designing functional data structures.

- Chapter 8 describes *lazy rebuilding*, a lazy variant of *global rebuilding* [Ove83]. Lazy rebuilding is significantly simpler than global rebuilding, but yields amortized rather than worst-case bounds. Combining lazy rebuilding with the scheduling techniques of Chapter 7 often restores the worst-case bounds.
- Chapter 9 explores *numerical representations*, which are implementations designed in analogy to representations of numbers (typically binary numbers). In this model, designing efficient insertion and deletion routines corresponds to choosing variants of binary numbers in which adding or subtracting one take constant time.
- Chapter 10 examines *data-structural bootstrapping* [Buc93]. This technique comes in three flavors: *structural decomposition*, in which unbounded solutions are bootstrapped from bounded solutions; *structural abstraction*, in which efficient solutions are bootstrapped from inefficient solutions; and *bootstrapping to aggregate types*, in which implementations with atomic elements are bootstrapped to implementations with aggregate elements.
- Chapter 11 describes *implicit recursive slowdown*, a lazy variant of the *recursive-slowdown* technique of Kaplan and Tarjan [KT95]. As with lazy rebuilding, implicit recursive slowdown is significantly simpler than recursive slowdown, but yields amortized rather than worst-case bounds. Again, we can often recover the worst-case bounds using scheduling.

Finally, Appendix A includes Haskell translations of most of the implementations in this book.

2

Persistence

A distinctive property of functional data structures is that they are always *persistent*—updating a functional data structure does not destroy the existing version, but rather creates a new version that coexists with the old one. Persistence is achieved by *copying* the affected nodes of a data structure and making all changes in the copy rather than in the original. Because nodes are never modified directly, all nodes that are unaffected by an update can be *shared* between the old and new versions of the data structure without worrying that a change in one version will inadvertently be visible to the other.

In this chapter, we examine the details of copying and sharing for two simple data structures: lists and binary search trees.

2.1 Lists

We begin with simple linked lists, which are common in imperative programming and ubiquitous in functional programming. The core functions supported by lists are essentially those of the stack abstraction, which is described as a Standard ML signature in Figure 2.1. Lists and stacks can be implemented trivially using either the built-in type of lists (Figure 2.2) or a custom datatype (Figure 2.3).

Remark The signature in Figure 2.1 uses list nomenclature (cons, head, tail) rather than stack nomenclature (push, top, pop), because we regard stacks as an instance of the general class of sequences. Other instances include *queues*, *double-ended queues*, and *catenable lists*. We use consistent naming conventions for functions in all of these abstractions, so that different implementations can be substituted for each other with a minimum of fuss. ◇

Another common function on lists that we might consider adding to this signature is ++, which catenates (i.e., appends) two lists. In an imperative setting,

7

```
signature STACK =
sig
  type α Stack

  val empty   : α Stack
  val isEmpty : α Stack → bool

  val cons  : α × α Stack → α Stack
  val head  : α Stack → α          (* raises EMPTY if stack is empty *)
  val tail  : α Stack → α Stack    (* raises EMPTY if stack is empty *)
end
```

Figure 2.1. Signature for stacks.

```
structure List : STACK =
struct
  type α Stack = α list

  val empty = [ ]
  fun isEmpty s = null s

  fun cons (x, s) = x :: s
  fun head s = hd s
  fun tail s = tl s
end
```

Figure 2.2. Implementation of stacks using the built-in type of lists.

```
structure CustomStack : STACK =
struct
  datatype α Stack = NIL | CONS of α × α Stack

  val empty = NIL
  fun isEmpty NIL = true | isEmpty _ = false

  fun cons (x, s) = CONS (x, s)
  fun head NIL = raise EMPTY
    | head (CONS (x, s)) = x
  fun tail NIL = raise EMPTY
    | tail (CONS (x, s)) = s
end
```

Figure 2.3. Implementation of stacks using a custom datatype.

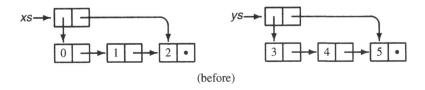

(before)

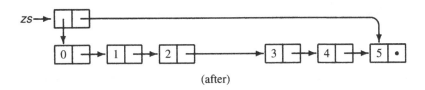

(after)

Figure 2.4. Executing *zs* = *xs* ++ *ys* in an imperative setting. Note that this operation destroys the argument lists, *xs* and *ys*.

this function can easily be supported in $O(1)$ time by maintaining pointers to both the first and last cell in each list. Then ++ simply modifies the last cell of the first list to point to the first cell of the second list. The result of this operation is shown pictorially in Figure 2.4. Note that this operation *destroys* both of its arguments—after executing *zs* = *xs* ++ *ys*, neither *xs* nor *ys* can be used again.

In a functional setting, we cannot destructively modify the last cell of the first list in this way. Instead, we *copy* the cell and modify the tail pointer of the copy. Then we copy the second-to-last cell and modify its tail to point to the copy of the last cell. We continue in this fashion until we have copied the entire list. This process can be implemented generically as

fun *xs* ++ *ys* = **if** isEmpty *xs* **then** *ys* **else** cons (head *xs*, tail *xs* ++ *ys*)

If we have access to the underlying representation (say, Standard ML's built-in lists), then we can rewrite this function using pattern matching as

fun [] ++ *ys* = *ys*
| (*x* :: *xs*) ++ *ys* = *x* :: (*xs* ++ *ys*)

Figure 2.5 illustrates the result of catenating two lists. Note that after the oper-

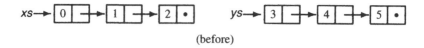

(before)

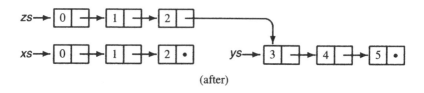

(after)

Figure 2.5. Executing *zs* = *xs* ++ *ys* in a functional setting. Notice that the argument lists, *xs* and *ys*, are unaffected by the operation.

ation, we are free to continue using the old lists, *xs* and *ys*, as well as the new list, *zs*. Thus, we get persistence, but at the cost of $O(n)$ copying.†

Although this is undeniably a lot of copying, notice that we did not have to copy the second list, *ys*. Instead, these nodes are shared between *ys* and *zs*. Another function that illustrates these twin concepts of copying and sharing is update, which changes the value of a node at a given index in the list. This function can be implemented as

```
fun update ([ ], i, y) = raise SUBSCRIPT
  | update (x :: xs, 0, y) = y :: xs
  | update (x :: xs, i, y) = x :: update (xs, i−1, y)
```

Here we do not copy the entire argument list. Rather, we copy only the node to be modified (node *i*) and all those nodes that contain direct or indirect pointers to node *i*. In other words, to modify a single node, we copy all the nodes on the path from the root to the node in question. All nodes that are not on this path are shared between the original version and the updated version. Figure 2.6 shows the results of updating the third node of a five-node list; the first three nodes are copied and the last two nodes are shared.

Remark This style of programming is greatly simplified by automatic garbage collection. It is crucial to reclaim the space of copies that are no longer needed, but the pervasive sharing of nodes makes manual garbage collection awkward.

---

† In Chapters 10 and 11, we will see how to support ++ in $O(1)$ time without sacrificing persistence.

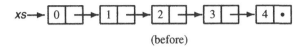

(before)

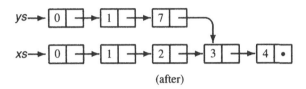

(after)

Figure 2.6. Executing *ys* = update(*xs*, 2, 7). Note the sharing between *xs* and *ys*.

Exercise 2.1 Write a function suffixes of type α list $\rightarrow$ α list list that takes a list *xs* and returns a list of all the suffixes of *xs* in decreasing order of length. For example,

suffixes [1,2,3,4] = [[1,2,3,4], [2,3,4], [3,4], [4], []]

Show that the resulting list of suffixes can be generated in $O(n)$ time and represented in $O(n)$ space.

2.2 Binary Search Trees

More complicated patterns of sharing are possible when there is more than one pointer field per node. Binary search trees provide a good example of this kind of sharing.

Binary search trees are binary trees with elements stored at the interior nodes in *symmetric order*, meaning that the element at any given node is greater than each element in its left subtree and less than each element in its right subtree. We represent binary search trees in Standard ML with the following type:

datatype Tree = E | T **of** Tree × Elem × Tree

where Elem is some fixed type of totally-ordered elements.

Remark Binary search trees are not polymorphic in the type of elements because they cannot accept arbitrary types as elements—only types that are equipped with a total ordering relation are suitable. However, this does not mean that we must re-implement binary search trees for each different element

```
signature SET =
sig
  type Elem
  type Set

  val empty   : Set
  val insert  : Elem × Set → Set
  val member : Elem × Set → bool
end
```

Figure 2.7. Signature for sets.

type. Instead, we make the type of elements and its attendant comparison functions parameters of the *functor* that implements binary search trees (see Figure 2.9). ◇

We will use this representation to implement sets. However, it can easily be adapted to support other abstractions (e.g., finite maps) or fancier functions (e.g., find the ith smallest element) by augmenting the T constructor with extra fields.

Figure 2.7 describes a minimal signature for sets. This signature contains a value for the empty set and functions for inserting a new element and testing for membership. A more realistic implementation would probably include many additional functions, such as deleting an element or enumerating all elements.

The member function searches a tree by comparing the query element with the element at the root. If the query element is smaller than the root element, then we recursively search the left subtree. If the query element is larger than the root element, then we recursively search the right subtree. Otherwise the query element is equal to the element at the root, so we return true. If we ever reach the empty node, then the query element is not an element of the set, so we return false. This strategy is implemented as follows:

```
fun member (x, E) = false
  | member (x, T (a, y, b)) =
    if x < y then member (x, a)
    else if x > y then member (x, b)
    else true
```

Remark For simplicity, we have assumed that the comparison functions are named < and >. However, when these functions are passed as parameters to a functor, as they will be in Figure 2.9, it is often more convenient to use names such as lt or leq, and reserve < and > for comparing integers and other primitive types. ◇

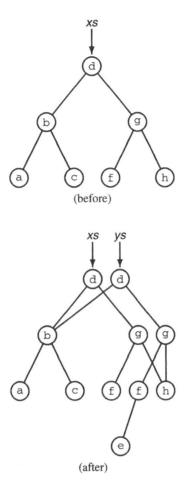

Figure 2.8. Execution of *ys* = insert (" e ", *xs*). Once again, notice the sharing between *xs* and *ys*.

The insert function searches the tree using the same strategy as member, except that it copies every node along the way. When it finally reaches an empty node, it replaces the empty node with a node containing the new element.

```
fun insert (x, E) = T (E, x, E)
  | insert (x, s as T (a, y, b)) =
     if x < y then T (insert (x, a), y, b)
     else if x > y then T (a, y, insert (x, b))
     else s
```

Figure 2.8 illustrates a typical insertion. Every node that is copied shares one

```
signature ORDERED =
  (* a totally ordered type and its comparison functions *)
sig
  type T

  val eq  : T × T → bool
  val lt  : T × T → bool
  val leq : T × T → bool
end

functor UnbalancedSet (Element : ORDERED) : SET =
struct
  type Elem = Element.T
  datatype Tree = E | T of Tree × Elem × Tree
  type Set = Tree

  val empty = E

  fun member (x, E) = false
    | member (x, T (a, y, b)) =
        if Element.lt (x, y) then member (x, a)
        else if Element.lt (y, x) then member (x, b)
        else true

  fun insert (x, E) = T (E, x, E)
    | insert (x, s as T (a, y, b)) =
        if Element.lt (x, y) then T (insert (x, a), y, b)
        else if Element.lt (y, x) then T (a, y, insert (x, b))
        else s
end
```

Figure 2.9. Implementation of binary search trees as a Standard ML functor.

subtree with the original tree—the subtree that was not on the search path. For most trees, this search path contains only a tiny fraction of the nodes in the tree. The vast majority of nodes reside in the shared subtrees.

Figure 2.9 shows how binary search trees might be implemented as a Standard ML functor. This functor takes the element type and its associated comparison functions as parameters. Because these same parameters will often be used by other functors as well (see, for example, Exercise 2.6), we package them in a structure matching the ORDERED signature.

Exercise 2.2 (Andersson [And91]) In the worst case, member performs approximately $2d$ comparisons, where d is the depth of the tree. Rewrite member to take no more than $d + 1$ comparisons by keeping track of a candidate element that *might* be equal to the query element (say, the last element for which

$<$ returned false or $\leq$ returned true) and checking for equality only when you hit the bottom of the tree.

Exercise 2.3 Inserting an existing element into a binary search tree copies the entire search path even though the copied nodes are indistinguishable from the originals. Rewrite insert using exceptions to avoid this copying. Establish only one handler per insertion rather than one handler per iteration.

Exercise 2.4 Combine the ideas of the previous two exercises to obtain a version of insert that performs no unnecessary copying and uses no more than $d + 1$ comparisons.

Exercise 2.5 Sharing can also be useful within a single object, not just between objects. For example, if the two subtrees of a given node are identical, then they can be represented by the same tree.

(a) Using this idea, write a function complete of type Elem × int → Tree where complete (x, d) creates a complete binary tree of depth d with x stored in every node. (Of course, this function makes no sense for the set abstraction, but it can be useful as an auxiliary function for other abstractions, such as bags.) This function should run in $O(d)$ time.

(b) Extend this function to create balanced trees of arbitrary size. These trees will not always be complete binary trees, but should be as balanced as possible: for any given node, the two subtrees should differ in size by at most one. This function should run in $O(\log n)$ time. (Hint: use a helper function create2 that, given a size m, creates a pair of trees, one of size m and one of size m+1.)

Exercise 2.6 Adapt the UnbalancedSet functor to support finite maps rather than sets. Figure 2.10 gives a minimal signature for finite maps. (Note that the NOTFOUND exception is not predefined in Standard ML—you will have to define it yourself. Although this exception could be made part of the FINITEMAP signature, with every implementation defining its own NOTFOUND exception, it is convenient for all finite maps to use the same exception.)

2.3 Chapter Notes

Myers [Mye82, Mye84] used copying and sharing to implement persistent binary search trees (in his case, AVL trees). Sarnak and Tarjan [ST86a] coined the term *path copying* for the general technique of implementing persistent

```
signature FINITEMAP =
sig
  type Key
  type α Map

  val empty  : α Map
  val bind    : Key × α × α Map → α Map
  val lookup : Key × α Map → α  (* raise NOTFOUND if key is not found *)
end
```

Figure 2.10. Signature for finite maps.

data structures by copying all affected nodes. Other general techniques for implementing persistent data structures have been proposed by Driscoll, Sarnak, Sleator, and Tarjan [DSST89] and Dietz [Die89], but these techniques are not purely functional.

3
Some Familiar Data Structures in a Functional Setting

Although many imperative data structures are difficult or impossible to adapt to a functional setting, some can be adapted quite easily. In this chapter, we review three data structures that are commonly taught in an imperative setting. The first, leftist heaps, is quite simple in either setting, but the other two, binomial queues and red-black trees, have a reputation for being rather complicated because imperative implementations of these data structures often degenerate into nightmares of pointer manipulations. In contrast, functional implementations of these data structures abstract away from troublesome pointer manipulations and directly reflect the high-level ideas. A bonus of implementing these data structures functionally is that we get persistence for free.

3.1 Leftist Heaps

Sets and finite maps typically support efficient access to arbitrary elements. But sometimes we need efficient access only to the *minimum* element. A data structure supporting this kind of access is called a *priority queue* or a *heap*. To avoid confusion with FIFO queues, we use the latter name. Figure 3.1 presents a simple signature for heaps.

Remark In comparing the signature for heaps with the signature for sets (Figure 2.7), we see that in the former the ordering relation on elements is included in the signature while in the latter it is not. This discrepancy is because the ordering relation is crucial to the semantics of heaps but not to the semantics of sets. On the other hand, one could justifiably argue that an *equality* relation is crucial to the semantics of sets and should be included in the signature. $\diamond$

Heaps are often implemented as *heap-ordered* trees, in which the element at each node is no larger than the elements at its children. Under this ordering, the minimum element in a tree is always at the root.

17

```
signature HEAP =
sig
  structure Elem : ORDERED

  type Heap

  val empty    : Heap
  val isEmpty  : Heap → bool

  val insert   : Elem.T × Heap → Heap
  val merge    : Heap × Heap → Heap

  val findMin  : Heap → Elem.T   (* raises EMPTY if heap is empty *)
  val deleteMin : Heap → Heap    (* raises EMPTY if heap is empty *)
end
```

Figure 3.1. Signature for heaps (priority queues).

Leftist heaps [Cra72, Knu73a] are heap-ordered binary trees that satisfy the *leftist property*: the rank of any left child is at least as large as the rank of its right sibling. The rank of a node is defined to be the length of its *right spine* (i.e., the rightmost path from the node in question to an empty node). A simple consequence of the leftist property is that the right spine of any node is always the shortest path to an empty node.

Exercise 3.1 Prove that the right spine of a leftist heap of size n contains at most $\lfloor \log(n + 1) \rfloor$ elements. (All logarithms in this book are base 2 unless otherwise indicated.)   ◇

Given some structure Elem of ordered elements, we represent leftist heaps as binary trees decorated with rank information.

```
datatype Heap = E | T of int × Elem.T × Heap × Heap
```

Note that the elements along the right spine of a leftist heap (in fact, along any path through a heap-ordered tree) are stored in sorted order. The key insight behind leftist heaps is that two heaps can be merged by merging their right spines as you would merge two sorted lists, and then swapping the children of nodes along this path as necessary to restore the leftist property. This can be implemented as follows:

```
fun merge (h, E) = h
  | merge (E, h) = h
  | merge (h₁ as T (_, x, a₁, b₁), h₂ as T (_, y, a₂, b₂)) =
      if Elem.leq (x, y) then makeT (x, a₁, merge (b₁, h₂))
      else makeT (y, a₂, merge (h₁, b₂))
```

where makeT is a helper function that calculates the rank of a T node and swaps its children if necessary.

```
fun rank E = 0
  | rank (T (r, _, _, _)) = r
fun makeT (x, a, b) = if rank a ≥ rank b then T (rank b + 1, x, a, b)
                      else T (rank a + 1, x, b, a)
```

Because the length of each right spine is at most logarithmic, merge runs in $O(\log n)$ time.

Now that we have an efficient merge function, the remaining functions are trivial: insert creates a new singleton tree and merges it with the existing heap, findMin returns the root element, and deleteMin discards the root element and merges its children.

```
fun insert (x, h) = merge (T (1, x, E, E), h)
fun findMin (T (_, x, a, b)) = x
fun deleteMin (T (_, x, a, b)) = merge (a, b)
```

Since merge takes $O(\log n)$ time, so do insert and deleteMin. findMin clearly runs in $O(1)$ time. The complete implementation of leftist heaps is given in Figure 3.2 as a functor that takes the structure of ordered elements as a parameter.

Remark To avoid cluttering our examples with minor details, we usually ignore error cases when presenting code fragments. For example, the above code fragments do not describe the behavior of findMin or deleteMin on empty heaps. We always include the error cases when presenting complete implementations, as in Figure 3.2.

Exercise 3.2 Define insert directly rather than via a call to merge.

Exercise 3.3 Implement a function fromList of type Elem.T list → Heap that produces a leftist heap from an unordered list of elements by first converting each element into a singleton heap and then merging the heaps until only one heap remains. Instead of merging the heaps in one right-to-left or left-to-right pass using foldr or foldl, merge the heaps in $\lceil \log n \rceil$ passes, where each pass merges adjacent pairs of heaps. Show that fromList takes only $O(n)$ time.

Exercise 3.4 (Cho and Sahni [CS96]) Weight-biased leftist heaps are an alternative to leftist heaps that replace the leftist property with the *weight-biased leftist property*: the size of any left child is at least as large as the size of its right sibling.

```
functor LeftistHeap (Element : ORDERED) : HEAP =
struct
  structure Elem = Element

  datatype Heap = E | T of int × Elem.T × Heap × Heap

  fun rank E = 0
    | rank (T (r, _, _, _)) = r
  fun makeT (x, a, b) = if rank a ≥ rank b then T (rank b + 1, x, a, b)
                        else T (rank a + 1, x, b, a)

  val empty = E
  fun isEmpty E = true | isEmpty _ = false

  fun merge (h, E) = h
    | merge (E, h) = h
    | merge (h₁ as T (_, x, a₁, b₁), h₂ as T (_, y, a₂, b₂)) =
        if Elem.leq (x, y) then makeT (x, a₁, merge (b₁, h₂))
        else makeT (y, a₂, merge (h₁, b₂))
  fun insert (x, h) = merge (T (1, x, E, E), h)

  fun findMin E = raise EMPTY
    | findMin (T (_, x, a, b)) = x
  fun deleteMin E = raise EMPTY
    | deleteMin (T (_, x, a, b)) = merge (a, b)
end
```

Figure 3.2. Leftist heaps.

(a) Prove that the right spine of a weight-biased leftist heap contains at most $\lfloor \log(n + 1) \rfloor$ elements.

(b) Modify the implementation in Figure 3.2 to obtain weight-biased leftist heaps.

(c) Currently, merge operates in two passes: a top-down pass consisting of calls to merge, and a bottom-up pass consisting of calls to the helper function makeT. Modify merge for weight-biased leftist heaps to operate in a single, top-down pass.

(d) What advantages would the top-down version of merge have in a lazy environment? In a concurrent environment?

3.2 Binomial Heaps

Another common implementation of heaps is binomial queues [Vui78, Bro78], which we call *binomial heaps* to avoid confusion with FIFO queues. Binomial heaps are more complicated than leftist heaps, and at first appear to offer no compensatory advantages. However, in later chapters, we will see ways in

Rank 0   Rank 1   Rank 2   Rank 3

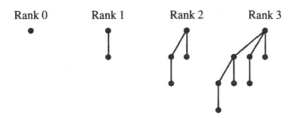

Figure 3.3. Binomial trees of ranks 0–3.

which insert and merge can be made to run in $O(1)$ time for various flavors of binomial heaps.

Binomial heaps are composed of more primitive objects known as binomial trees. Binomial trees are inductively defined as follows:

- A binomial tree of rank 0 is a singleton node.
- A binomial tree of rank $r + 1$ is formed by *linking* two binomial trees of rank r, making one tree the leftmost child of the other.

From this definition, it is easy to see that a binomial tree of rank r contains exactly 2^r nodes. There is a second, equivalent definition of binomial trees that is sometimes more convenient: a binomial tree of rank r is a node with r children $t_1 \ldots t_r$, where each t_i is a binomial tree of rank $r - i$. Figure 3.3 illustrates binomial trees of ranks 0 through 3.

We represent a node in a binomial tree as an element and a list of children. For convenience, we also annotate each node with its rank.

datatype Tree = Node **of** int × Elem.T × Tree list

Each list of children is maintained in decreasing order of rank, and elements are stored in heap order. We maintain heap order by always linking trees with larger roots under trees with smaller roots.

```
fun link (t₁ as Node (r, x₁, c₁), t₂ as Node (_, x₂, c₂)) =
    if Elem.leq (x₁, x₂) then Node (r+1, x₁, t₂ :: c₁)
    else Node (r+1, x₂, t₁ :: c₂)
```

We always link trees of equal rank.

Now, a binomial heap is a collection of heap-ordered binomial trees in which no two trees have the same rank. This collection is represented as a list of trees in increasing order of rank.

type Heap = Tree list

Because each binomial tree contains 2^r elements and no two trees have the same rank, the trees in a binomial heap of size n correspond exactly to the ones in the binary representation of n. For example, the binary representation of 21 is 10101 so a binomial heap of size 21 would contain one tree of rank 0, one tree of rank 2, and one tree of rank 4 (of sizes 1, 4, and 16, respectively). Note that, just as the binary representation of n contains at most $\lfloor \log(n+1) \rfloor$ ones, a binomial heap of size n contains at most $\lfloor \log(n+1) \rfloor$ trees.

We are now ready to describe the functions on binomial heaps. We begin with insert and merge, which are defined in loose analogy to incrementing or adding binary numbers. (We will tighten this analogy in Chapter 9.) To insert a new element into a heap, we first create a new singleton tree (i.e., a binomial tree of rank 0). We then step through the existing trees in increasing order of rank until we find a missing rank, linking trees of equal rank as we go. Each link corresponds to a carry in binary arithmetic.

```
fun rank (Node (r, x, c)) = r
fun insTree (t, [ ]) = [t]
  | insTree (t, ts as t' :: ts') =
      if rank t < rank t' then t :: ts else insTree (link (t, t'), ts')
fun insert (x, ts) = insTree (Node (0, x, [ ]), ts)
```

The worst case is insertion into a heap of size $n = 2^k - 1$, requiring a total of k links and $O(k) = O(\log n)$ time.

To merge two heaps, we step through both lists of trees in increasing order of rank, linking trees of equal rank as we go. Again, each link corresponds to a carry in binary arithmetic.

```
fun merge (ts₁, [ ]) = ts₁
  | merge ([ ], ts₂) = ts₂
  | merge (ts₁ as t₁ :: ts₁', ts₂ as t₂ :: ts₂') =
      if rank t₁ < rank t₂ then t₁ :: merge (ts₁', ts₂)
      else if rank t₂ < rank t₁ then t₂ :: merge (ts₁, ts₂')
      else insTree (link (t₁, t₂), merge (ts₁', ts₂'))
```

Both findMin and deleteMin call an auxiliary function removeMinTree that finds the tree with the minimum root and removes it from the list, returning both the tree and the remaining list.

```
fun removeMinTree [t] = (t, [ ])
  | removeMinTree (t :: ts) =
      let val (t', ts') = removeMinTree ts
      in if Elem.leq (root t, root t') then (t, ts) else (t', t :: ts') end
```

Now, findMin simply returns the root of the extracted tree.

```
fun findMin ts = let val (t, _) = removeMinTree ts in root t end
```

The deleteMin function is a little trickier. After discarding the root of the extracted tree, we must somehow return the children of the discarded node to the remaining list of trees. Note that each list of children is *almost* a valid binomial heap. Each is a collection of heap-ordered binomial trees of unique rank, but in decreasing rather than increasing order of rank. Thus, we convert the list of children into a valid binomial heap by reversing it and then merge this list with the remaining trees.

fun deleteMin *ts* = **let val** (Node (_, *x*, *ts*$_1$), *ts*$_2$) = removeMinTree *ts*
　　　　　　　in merge (rev *ts*$_1$, *ts*$_2$) **end**

The complete implementation of binomial heaps is shown in Figure 3.4. All four major operations require $O(\log n)$ time in the worst case.

Exercise 3.5 Define findMin directly rather than via a call to removeMinTree.

Exercise 3.6 Most of the rank annotations in this representation of binomial heaps are redundant because we know that the children of a node of rank r have ranks $r - 1, \ldots, 0$. Thus, we can remove the rank annotations from each node and instead pair each tree at the top-level with its rank, i.e.,

datatype Tree = Node **of** Elem × Tree list
type Heap = (int × Tree) list

Reimplement binomial heaps with this new representation.

Exercise 3.7 One clear advantage of leftist heaps over binomial heaps is that findMin takes only $O(1)$ time, rather than $O(\log n)$ time. The following functor skeleton improves the running time of findMin to $O(1)$ by storing the minimum element separately from the rest of the heap.

functor ExplicitMin (H : HEAP) : HEAP =
struct
　　structure Elem = H.Elem
　　datatype Heap = E | NE **of** Elem.T × H.Heap
　　　...
end

Note that this functor is not specific to binomial heaps, but rather takes any implementation of heaps as a parameter. Complete this functor so that findMin takes $O(1)$ time, and insert, merge, and deleteMin take $O(\log n)$ time (assuming that all four take $O(\log n)$ time or better for the underlying implementation H).

```
functor BinomialHeap (Element : ORDERED) : HEAP =
struct
  structure Elem = Element

  datatype Tree = Node of int × Elem.T × Tree list
  type Heap = Tree list

  val empty = [ ]
  fun isEmpty ts = null ts

  fun rank (Node (r, x, c)) = r
  fun root (Node (r, x, c)) = x
  fun link (t₁ as Node (r, x₁, c₁), t₂ as Node (_, x₂, c₂)) =
      if Elem.leq (x₁, x₂) then Node (r+1, x₁, t₂ :: c₁)
      else Node (r+1, x₂, t₁ :: c₂)
  fun insTree (t, [ ]) = [t]
    | insTree (t, ts as t′ :: ts′) =
        if rank t < rank t′ then t :: ts else insTree (link (t, t′), ts′)

  fun insert (x, ts) = insTree (Node (0, x, [ ]), ts)
  fun merge (ts₁, [ ]) = ts₁
    | merge ([ ], ts₂) = ts₂
    | merge (ts₁ as t₁ :: ts₁′, ts₂ as t₂ :: ts₂′) =
        if rank t₁ < rank t₂ then t₁ :: merge (ts₁′, ts₂)
        else if rank t₂ < rank t₁ then t₂ :: merge (ts₁, ts₂′)
        else insTree (link (t₁, t₂), merge (ts₁′, ts₂′))

  fun removeMinTree [ ] = raise EMPTY
    | removeMinTree [t] = (t, [ ])
    | removeMinTree (t :: ts) =
        let val (t′, ts′) = removeMinTree ts
        in if Elem.leq (root t, root t′) then (t, ts) else (t′, t :: ts′) end

  fun findMin ts = let val (t, _) = removeMinTree ts in root t end
  fun deleteMin ts =
      let val (Node (_, x, ts₁), ts₂) = removeMinTree ts
      in merge (rev ts₁, ts₂) end
end
```

Figure 3.4. Binomial heaps.

3.3 Red-Black Trees

In Section 2.2, we introduced binary search trees. Although these trees work very well on random or unordered data, they perform very poorly on ordered data, for which any individual operation might take up to $O(n)$ time. The solution to this problem is to keep each tree approximately balanced. Then no individual operation takes more than $O(\log n)$ time. Red-black trees [GS78] are one of the most popular families of balanced binary search trees.

A red-black tree is a binary search tree in which every node is colored either red or black. We augment the type of binary search trees from Section 2.2 with a color field.

datatype Color = R | B
datatype Tree = E | T **of** Color × Tree × Elem × Tree

All empty nodes are considered to be black, so the empty constructor E does not need a color field.

We insist that every red-black tree satisfy the following two balance invariants:

Invariant 1. No red node has a red child.
Invariant 2. Every path from the root to an empty node contains the same number of black nodes.

Taken together, these two invariants guarantee that the longest possible path in a red-black tree, one with alternating black and red nodes, is no more than twice as long as the shortest possible path, one with black nodes only.

Exercise 3.8 Prove that the maximum depth of a node in a red-black tree of size n is at most $2\lfloor \log(n+1) \rfloor$. ◇

The member function on red-black trees ignores the color fields. Except for a wildcard in the T case, it is identical to the member function on unbalanced search trees.

```
fun member (x, E) = false
  | member (x, T (_, a, y, b)) =
    if x < y then member (x, a)
    else if x > y then member (x, b)
    else true
```

The insert function is more interesting because it must maintain the two balance invariants.

```
fun insert (x, s) =
    let fun ins E = T (R, E, x, E)
          | ins (s as T (color, a, y, b)) =
            if x < y then balance (color, ins a, y, b)
            else if x > y then balance (color, a, y, ins b)
            else s
        val T (_, a, y, b) = ins s   (* guaranteed to be non-empty *)
    in T (B, a, y, b) end
```

This function extends the insert function for unbalanced search trees in three significant ways. First, when we create a new node in the ins E case, we initially color it red. Second, we force the final root to be black, regardless of the color returned by ins. Finally, we replace the calls to the T constructor in the $x < y$ and $x > y$ cases with calls to the balance function. The balance function acts just like the T constructor except that it massages its arguments as necessary to enforce the balance invariants.

Coloring the new node red maintains Invariant 2, but violates Invariant 1 whenever the parent of the new node is red. We allow a single red-red violation at a time, and percolate this violation up the search path toward the root during rebalancing. The balance function detects and repairs each red-red violation when it processes the black parent of the red node with a red child. This black-red-red path can occur in any of four configurations, depending on whether each red node is a left or right child. However, the solution is the same in every case: rewrite the black-red-red path as a red node with two black children, as illustrated in Figure 3.5. This transformation can be coded as follows:

```
fun balance (B,T (R,T (R,a,x,b),y,c),z,d) = T (R,T (B,a,x,b),y,T (B,c,z,d))
  | balance (B,T (R,a,x,T (R,b,y,c)),z,d) = T (R,T (B,a,x,b),y,T (B,c,z,d))
  | balance (B,a,x,T (R,T (R,b,y,c),z,d)) = T (R,T (B,a,x,b),y,T (B,c,z,d))
  | balance (B,a,x,T (R,b,y,T (R,c,z,d))) = T (R,T (B,a,x,b),y,T (B,c,z,d))
  | balance body = T body
```

It is routine to verify that the red-black balance invariants both hold for the resulting (sub)tree.

Remark   Notice that the right-hand sides of the first four clauses are identical. Some implementations of Standard ML, notably Standard ML of New Jersey, support a feature known as *or-patterns* that allows multiple clauses with identical right-hand sides to be collapsed into a single clause [FB97]. Using or-patterns, the balance function might be rewritten

```
fun balance ( (B,T (R,T (R,a,x,b),y,c),z,d)
            | (B,T (R,a,x,T (R,b,y,c)),z,d)
            | (B,a,x,T (R,T (R,b,y,c),z,d))
            | (B,a,x,T (R,b,y,T (R,c,z,d))) ) = T (R,T (B,a,x,b),y,T (B,c,z,d))
  | balance body = T body
```

$\diamond$

After balancing a given subtree, the red root of that subtree might now be the child of another red node. Thus, we continue balancing all the way to the top of the tree. At the very top of the tree, we might end up with a red node with a red child, but with no black parent. We handle this case by always recoloring the root to be black.

This implementation of red-black trees is summarized in Figure 3.6.

Hint to Practitioners: Even without optimization, this implementation of balanced binary search trees is one of the fastest around. With appropriate optimizations, such as Exercises 2.2 and 3.10, it really flies!

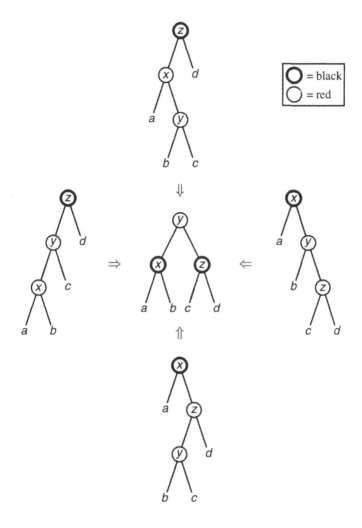

Figure 3.5. Eliminating red nodes with red parents.

Remark One of the reasons this implementation is so much simpler than typical presentations of red-black trees (e.g., Chapter 14 of [CLR90]) is that it uses subtly different rebalancing transformations. Imperative implementations typically split the four dangerous cases considered here into eight cases, according to the color of the sibling of the red node with a red child. Knowing the color of the red parent's sibling allows the transformations to use fewer assignments in some cases and to terminate rebalancing early in others. However, in a func-

```
functor RedBlackSet (Element : ORDERED) : SET =
struct
  type Elem = Element.T

  datatype Color = R | B
  datatype Tree = E | T of Color × Tree × Elem × Tree
  type Set = Tree

  val empty = E

  fun member (x, E) = false
    | member (x, T (_, a, y, b)) =
      if Element.lt (x, y) then member (x, a)
      else if Element.lt (y, x) then member (x, b)
      else true

  fun balance (B,T (R,T (R,a,x,b),y,c),z,d) = T (R,T (B,a,x,b),y,T (B,c,z,d))
    | balance (B,T (R,a,x,T (R,b,y,c)),z,d) = T (R,T (B,a,x,b),y,T (B,c,z,d))
    | balance (B,a,x,T (R,T (R,b,y,c),z,d)) = T (R,T (B,a,x,b),y,T (B,c,z,d))
    | balance (B,a,x,T (R,b,y,T (R,c,z,d))) = T (R,T (B,a,x,b),y,T (B,c,z,d))
    | balance body = T body

  fun insert (x, s) =
      let fun ins E = T (R, E, x, E)
            | ins (s as T (color, a, y, b)) =
              if Element.lt (x, y) then balance (color, ins a, y, b)
              else if Element.lt (y, x) then balance (color, a, y, ins b)
              else s

          val T (_, a, y, b) = ins s   (* guaranteed to be non-empty *)
      in T (B, a, y, b) end
end
```

Figure 3.6. Red black trees.

tional setting, where we are copying the nodes in question anyway, we cannot reduce the number of assignments in this fashion, nor can we terminate copying early, so there is no point is using the more complicated transformations.

Exercise 3.9 Write a function fromOrdList of type Elem list → Tree that converts a sorted list with no duplicates into a red-black tree. Your function should run in $O(n)$ time.

Exercise 3.10 The balance function currently performs several unnecessary tests. For example, when the ins function recurses on the left child, there is no need for balance to test for red-red violations involving the right child.

(a) Split balance into two functions, lbalance and rbalance, that test for violations involving the left child and right child, respectively. Replace the calls to balance in ins with calls to either lbalance or rbalance.

(b) Extending the same logic one step further, one of the remaining tests on the grandchildren is also unnecessary. Rewrite ins so that it never tests the color of nodes not on the search path.

3.4 Chapter Notes

Núñez, Palao, and Peña [NPP95] and King [Kin94] describe similar implementations in Haskell of leftist heaps and binomial heaps, respectively. Red-black trees have not previously appeared in the functional programming literature, but several other kinds of balanced binary search trees have, including AVL trees [Mye82, Mye84, BW88, NPP95], 2-3 trees [Rea92], and weight-balanced trees [Ada93].

Knuth [Knu73a] originally introduced leftist heaps as a simplification of a data structure by Crane [Cra72]. Vuillemin [Vui78] invented binomial heaps; Brown [Bro78] examined many of the properties of this elegant data structure. Guibas and Sedgewick [GS78] proposed red-black trees as a general framework for describing many other kinds of balanced trees.

4

Lazy Evaluation

Lazy evaluation is the default evaluation strategy of many functional programming languages (although not of Standard ML). This strategy has two essential properties. First, the evaluation of a given expression is delayed, or *suspended*, until its result is needed. Second, the first time a suspended expression is evaluated, the result is *memoized* (i.e., cached) so that, if it is ever needed again, it can be looked up rather than recomputed. Both aspects of lazy evaluation are algorithmically useful.

In this chapter, we introduce a convenient notation for lazy evaluation and illustrate this notation by developing a simple streams package. We will use both lazy evaluation and streams extensively in later chapters.

4.1 $-notation

Unfortunately, the definition of Standard ML [MTHM97] does not include support for lazy evaluation, so each compiler is free to provide its own set of lazy evaluation primitives. We present here one such set of primitives, called $-notation. Translating programs written with $-notation into other notations for lazy evaluation should be straightforward.

In $-notation, we introduce a new type α susp to represent suspensions. This type has a single, unary constructor called $. To a first approximation, α susp and $ behave as if defined by the ordinary datatype declaration

datatype α susp = $ **of** α

We create a new suspension of type τ susp by writing e, where e is an expression of type τ. Similarly, we extract the contents of an existing suspension by matching against the pattern p. If the pattern p matches values of type τ, then p matches suspensions of type τ susp.

The main difference between $ and ordinary constructors is that $ does not

31

immediately evaluate its argument. Instead, it saves whatever information it will need to resume the evaluation of the argument expression at a later time. (Typically, this information consists of a code pointer together with the values of the free variables in the expression.) The argument expression is not evaluated until and unless the suspension is matched against a pattern of the form p. At that time, the argument expression is evaluated and the result is memoized. Then the result is matched against the pattern p. If the suspension is later matched against another pattern of the form p', the memoized value of the suspension is looked up and matched against p'.

The \$ constructor is also parsed differently from ordinary constructors. First, the scope of the \$ constructor extends as far to the right as possible. Thus, for example, the expression \$*f x* parses as \$(*f x*) rather than (\$*f*) *x*, and the pattern \$Cons (*x, xs*) parses as \$(Cons (*x, xs*)) rather than (\$Cons) (*x, xs*). Second, \$ does not constitute a valid expression by itself—it must always be accompanied by an argument.

As an example of \$-notation, consider the following program fragment:

val *s* = \$primes 1000000   (* *fast* *)
...
val \$*x* = *s*   (* *slow* *)
...
val \$*y* = *s*   (* *fast* *)
...

This program computes the one millionth prime. The first line, which simply creates a new suspension, runs very quickly. The second line actually computes the prime by evaluating the suspension. Depending on the algorithm for computing primes, it might take a long time. The third line looks up the memoized value and also runs very quickly.

As a second example, consider the fragment

let val *s* = \$primes 1000000
in 15 **end**

This program never demands the contents of the suspension, and so never evaluates primes 1000000.

Although we can program all the examples of lazy evaluation in this book using only \$-expressions and \$-patterns, two forms of syntactic sugar will be convenient. The first is the force operator, defined as

fun force (\$*x*) = *x*

This is useful for extracting the contents of a suspension in the middle of an expression, where it might be awkward to introduce a pattern matching construct.

The second form of syntactic sugar is useful for writing certain kinds of lazy functions. For example, consider the following function for addition of suspended integers:

fun plus ($m, $n) = $m+n

Although this function seems perfectly reasonable, it is in fact not the function that we probably intended. The problem is that it forces both of its arguments too early. In particular, it forces its arguments when plus is applied, rather than when the suspension created by plus is forced. One way to get the desired behavior is to explicitly delay the pattern matching, as in

fun plus (x, y) = $**case** (x, y) **of** ($m, $n) $\Rightarrow$ m+n

However, this idiom is common enough that we provide syntactic sugar for it, writing

fun lazy f $p = e$

instead of

fun f x = $**case** x **of** $p \Rightarrow$ force e

The extra force ensures that the **lazy** keyword has no effect on the type of a function (assuming that the result was a susp type to begin with), so we can add or remove the annotation without changing the function text in any other way. Now we can write the desired function for addition of suspended integers simply as

fun lazy plus ($m, $n) = $m+n

Expanding this syntactic sugar yields

fun plus (x, y) = $**case** (x, y) **of** ($m, $n) $\Rightarrow$ force ($m+n$)

which is exactly same as the hand-written version above except for the extra force and $ around the m+n. This force and $ would be optimized away by a good compiler since force (e) is equivalent to e for any e.

The plus function uses the **lazy** annotation to delay pattern matching, so that $-patterns are not matched prematurely. However, the **lazy** annotation is also useful when the right-hand side of the function is an expression that returns a suspension as the result of a possibly long and involved computation. Using the **lazy** annotation in this situation delays the execution of the expensive computation from the time the function is applied until the time that its resulting suspension is forced. We will see several functions in the next section that use the **lazy** annotation in this fashion.

The syntax and semantics of $-notation are formally defined in [Oka96a].

4.2 Streams

As an extended example of lazy evaluation and $-notation in Standard ML, we next develop a small streams package. These streams will be used in several of the data structures in subsequent chapters.

Streams (also known as lazy lists) are similar to ordinary lists, except that every cell is systematically suspended. The type of streams is

datatype α StreamCell = NIL | CONS **of** $\alpha \times \alpha$ Stream
withtype α Stream = α StreamCell susp

A simple stream containing the elements 1, 2, and 3 could be written

$$\text{\$CONS (1, \$CONS (2, \$CONS (3, \$NIL)))}$$

It is illuminating to contrast streams with suspended lists of type α list susp. The computations represented by the latter type are inherently *monolithic*—once begun by forcing the suspended list, they run to completion. The computations represented by streams, on the other hand, are often *incremental*—forcing a stream executes only enough of the computation to produce the outermost cell and suspends the rest. This behavior is common among datatypes such as streams that contain nested suspensions.

To see this difference in behavior more clearly, consider the append function, written $s + t$. On suspended lists, this function might be written

fun $s + t$ = $(force s @ force t)

or, equivalently,

fun lazy (xs) + (ys) = $($xs$ @ ys)

The suspension produced by this function forces both arguments and then appends the two lists, producing the entire result. Hence, this suspension is monolithic. We also say that the function is monolithic. On streams, the append function is written

fun lazy ($NIL) + t = t
        | ($CONS ($x$, s)) + t = $CONS ($x$, $s + t$)

This function immediately returns a suspension, which, when forced, demands the first cell of the left stream by matching against a $-pattern. If this cell is a CONS, then we construct the result from x and $s + t$. Because of the **lazy** annotation, the recursive call simply creates another suspension, without doing any extra work. Hence, the computation described by this function is incremental; it produces the first cell of the result and delays the rest. We also say that the function is incremental.

Another incremental function is take, which extracts the first *n* elements of a stream.

```
fun lazy take (0, s) = $NIL
       | take (n, $NIL) = $NIL
       | take (n, $CONS (x, s)) = $CONS (x, take (n−1, s))
```

As with ++, the recursive call to take (*n*−1, *s*) immediately returns a suspension, rather than executing the rest of the function.

However, consider the function to delete the first *n* elements of a stream, which could be written

```
fun lazy drop (0, s) = s
       | drop (n, $NIL) = $NIL
       | drop (n, $CONS (x, s)) = drop (n−1, s)
```

or more efficiently as

```
fun lazy drop (n, s) = let fun drop' (0, s) = s
                             | drop' (n, $NIL) = $NIL
                             | drop' (n, $CONS (x, s)) = drop' (n−1, s)
                       in drop' (n, s) end
```

This function is monolithic because the recursive calls to drop' are never delayed—calculating the first cell of the result requires executing the entire function. Here we use the **lazy** annotation to delay the initial call to drop' rather than to delay pattern matching.

Exercise 4.1 Use the fact that force ($*e*) is equivalent to *e* to show that these two definitions of drop are equivalent. ◇

Another common monolithic stream function is reverse.

```
fun lazy reverse s =
       let fun reverse' ($NIL, r) = r
             | reverse' ($CONS (x, s), r) = reverse' (s, $CONS (x, r))
       in reverse' (s, $NIL) end
```

Here the recursive calls to reverse' are never delayed, but note that each recursive call creates a new suspension of the form $CONS (*x*, *r*). It might seem then that reverse does not in fact do all of its work at once. However, suspensions such as these, whose bodies contain only a few constructors and variables, with no function applications, are called *trivial*. Trivial suspensions are delayed, not for any algorithmic purpose, but rather to make the types work out. We can consider the body of a trivial suspension to be executed at the time the

```
signature STREAM =
sig
    datatype α StreamCell = NIL | CONS of α × α Stream
    withtype α Stream = α StreamCell susp

    val ++     : α Stream × α Stream → α Stream     (* stream append *)
    val take   : int × α Stream → α Stream
    val drop   : int × α Stream → α Stream
    val reverse : α Stream → α Stream
end

structure Stream : STREAM =
struct
    datatype α StreamCell = NIL | CONS of α × α Stream
    withtype α Stream = α StreamCell susp

    fun lazy ($NIL) ++ t = t
          | ($CONS (x, s)) ++ t = $CONS (x, s ++ t)
    fun lazy take (0, s) = $NIL
          | take (n, $NIL) = $NIL
          | take (n, $CONS (x, s)) = $CONS (x, take (n−1, s))
    fun lazy drop (n, s) =
          let fun drop' (0, s) = s
                | drop' (n, $NIL) = $NIL
                | drop' (n, $CONS (x, s)) = drop' (n−1, s)
          in drop' (n, s) end
    fun lazy reverse s =
          let fun reverse' ($NIL, r) = r
                | reverse' ($CONS (x, s), r) = reverse' (s, $CONS (x, r))
          in reverse' (s, $NIL) end
end
```

Figure 4.1. A small streams package.

suspension is created. In fact, a reasonable compiler optimization is to create such suspensions in already-memoized form. Either way, forcing a trivial suspension never takes more than $O(1)$ time.

Although monolithic stream functions such as drop and reverse are common, incremental functions such as ++ and take are the *raison d'être* of streams. Each suspension carries a small but significant overhead, so for maximum efficiency laziness should be used only when there is a good reason to do so. If the only uses of lazy lists in a given application are monolithic, then that application should use simple suspended lists rather than streams.

Figure 4.1 summarizes these stream functions as a Standard ML module. Note that this module does not export functions such as isEmpty and cons, as one might expect. Instead, we deliberately expose the internal representation in order to support pattern matching on streams.

Exercise 4.2 Implement insertion sort on streams. Show that extracting the first k elements of sort xs takes only $O(n \cdot k)$ time, where n is the length of xs, rather than $O(n^2)$ time, as might be expected of insertion sort.

4.3 Chapter Notes

Lazy Evaluation Wadsworth [Wad71] introduced lazy evaluation as an optimization of normal-order reduction in the lambda calculus. Vuillemin [Vui74] later showed that, under certain restricted conditions, lazy evaluation is an optimal evaluation strategy. The formal semantics of lazy evaluation has been studied extensively [Jos89, Lau93, OLT94, AFM+95].

Streams Landin introduced streams in [Lan65], but without memoization. Friedman and Wise [FW76] and Henderson and Morris [HM76] extended Landin's streams with memoization.

Memoization Michie [Mic68] coined the term memoization to denote the augmentation of functions with a cache of argument–result pairs. The argument field is dropped when memoizing suspensions by regarding suspensions as nullary functions—that is, functions with zero arguments. Hughes [Hug85] later applied memoization, in the original sense of Michie, to functional programs.

Algorithmics Both components of lazy evaluation—delaying computations and memoizing the results—have a long history in algorithm design, although not always in combination. The idea of delaying the execution of potentially expensive computations (often deletions) is used to good effect in hash tables [WV86], priority queues [ST86b, FT87], and search trees [DSST89]. Memoization, on the other hand, is the basic principle of such techniques as dynamic programming [Bel57] and path compression [HU73, TvL84].

5

Fundamentals of Amortization

Over the past fifteen years, amortization has become a powerful tool in the design and analysis of data structures. Implementations with good amortized bounds are often simpler and faster than implementations with comparable worst-case bounds. In this chapter, we review the basic techniques of amortization and illustrate these ideas with a simple implementation of FIFO queues and several implementations of heaps.

Unfortunately, the simple view of amortization presented in this chapter breaks in the presence of persistence—these data structures may be extremely inefficient when used persistently. In practice, however, many applications do not require persistence, and for those applications, the implementations presented in this chapter are excellent choices. In the next chapter, we will see how to reconcile the notions of amortization and persistence using lazy evaluation.

5.1 Techniques of Amortized Analysis

The notion of amortization arises from the following observation. Given a sequence of operations, we may wish to know the running time of the entire sequence, but not care about the running time of any individual operation. For instance, given a sequence of n operations, we may wish to bound the total running time of the sequence by $O(n)$ without insisting that every individual operation run in $O(1)$ time. We might be satisfied if a few operations run in $O(\log n)$ or even $O(n)$ time, provided the total cost of the sequence is only $O(n)$. This freedom opens up a wide design space of possible solutions, and often yields new solutions that are simpler and faster than worst-case solutions with equivalent bounds.

To prove an amortized bound, one defines the amortized cost of each operation and then proves that, for any sequence of operations, the total amortized cost of the operations is an upper bound on the total actual cost, i.e.,

$$\sum_{i=1}^{m} a_i \geq \sum_{i=1}^{m} t_i$$

where a_i is the amortized cost of operation i, t_i is the actual cost of operation i, and m is the total number of operations. Usually, in fact, one proves a slightly stronger result: that at any intermediate stage in a sequence of operations, the accumulated amortized cost is an upper bound on the accumulated actual cost, i.e.,

$$\sum_{i=1}^{j} a_i \geq \sum_{i=1}^{j} t_i$$

for any j. The difference between the accumulated amortized costs and the accumulated actual costs is called the *accumulated savings*. Thus, the accumulated amortized costs are an upper bound on the accumulated actual costs whenever the accumulated savings is non-negative.

Amortization allows for occasional operations to have actual costs that exceed their amortized costs. Such operations are called *expensive*. Operations whose actual costs are less than their amortized costs are called *cheap*. Expensive operations decrease the accumulated savings and cheap operations increase it. The key to proving amortized bounds is to show that expensive operations occur only when the accumulated savings are sufficient to cover the remaining cost.

Tarjan [Tar85] describes two techniques for analyzing amortized data structures: the *banker's method* and the *physicist's method*. In the banker's method, the accumulated savings are represented as *credits* that are associated with individual locations in the data structure. These credits are used to pay for future accesses to these locations. The amortized cost of any operation is defined to be the actual cost of the operation plus the credits allocated by the operation minus the credits spent by the operation, i.e.,

$$a_i = t_i + c_i - \bar{c}_i$$

where c_i is the number of credits allocated by operation i and $\bar{c}_i$ is the number of credits spent by operation i. Every credit must be allocated before it is spent, and no credit may be spent more than once. Therefore, $\sum c_i \geq \sum \bar{c}_i$, which in turn guarantees that $\sum a_i \geq \sum t_i$, as desired. Proofs using the banker's method typically define a *credit invariant* that regulates the distribution of credits in such a way that, whenever an expensive operation might occur, sufficient credits have been allocated in the right locations to cover its cost.

In the physicist's method, one describes a function Φ that maps each object d to a real number called the *potential* of d. The function Φ is typically chosen so that the potential is initially zero and is always non-negative. Then, the potential represents a lower bound on the accumulated savings.

Let d_i be the output of operation i and the input of operation $i+1$. Then, the amortized cost of operation i is defined to be the actual cost plus the change in potential between d_{i-1} and d_i, i.e.,

$$a_i = t_i + \Phi(d_i) - \Phi(d_{i-1})$$

The accumulated actual costs of the sequence of operations are

$$
\begin{aligned}
\sum_{i=1}^{j} t_i &= \sum_{i=1}^{j} (a_i + \Phi(d_{i-1}) - \Phi(d_i)) \\
&= \sum_{i=1}^{j} a_i + \sum_{i=1}^{j} (\Phi(d_{i-1}) - \Phi(d_i)) \\
&= \sum_{i=1}^{j} a_i + \Phi(d_0) - \Phi(d_j)
\end{aligned}
$$

Sums such as $\sum(\Phi(d_{i-1}) - \Phi(d_i))$, where alternating positive and negative terms cancel each other out, are called *telescoping series*. Provided Φ is chosen in such a way that $\Phi(d_0)$ is zero and $\Phi(d_j)$ is non-negative, then $\Phi(d_j) \geq \Phi(d_0)$ and $\sum a_i \geq \sum t_i$, so the accumulated amortized costs are an upper bound on the accumulated actual costs, as desired.

Remark This is a somewhat simplified view of the physicist's method. In real analyses, one often encounters situations that are difficult to fit into the framework as described. For example, what about functions that take or return more than one object? However, this simplified view suffices to illustrate the relevant issues. $\diamond$

Clearly, the two methods are very similar. We can convert the banker's method to the physicist's method by ignoring locations and taking the potential to be the total number of credits in the object, as indicated by the credit invariant. Similarly, we can convert the physicist's method to the banker's method by converting potential to credits, and placing all credits on the root. It is perhaps surprising that the knowledge of locations in the banker's method offers no extra power, but the two methods are in fact equivalent [Tar85, Sch92]. The physicist's method is usually simpler, but it is occasionally convenient to take locations into account.

Note that both credits and potential are analysis tools only; neither actually appears in the program text (except maybe in comments).

```
signature QUEUE =
sig
    type α Queue

    val empty   : α Queue
    val isEmpty : α Queue → bool

    val snoc   : α Queue × α → α Queue
    val head   : α Queue → α          (* raises EMPTY if queue is empty *)
    val tail   : α Queue → α Queue    (* raises EMPTY if queue is empty *)
end
```

Figure 5.1. Signature for queues.

(Etymological note: snoc is cons spelled backward and means "cons on the right".)

5.2 Queues

We next illustrate the banker's and physicist's methods by analyzing a simple functional implementation of the FIFO queue abstraction, as specified by the signature in Figure 5.1.

The most common implementation of queues in a purely functional setting is as a pair of lists, f and r, where f contains the front elements of the queue in the correct order and r contains the rear elements of the queue in reverse order. For example, a queue containing the integers $1 \ldots 6$ might be represented by the lists $f = [1,2,3]$ and $r = [6,5,4]$. This representation is described by the following type:

type α Queue = α list × α list

In this representation, the head of the queue is the first element of f, so head and tail return and remove this element, respectively.

```
fun head (x :: f, r) = x
fun tail (x :: f, r) = (f, r)
```

Similarly, the last element of the queue is the first element of r, so snoc simply adds a new element to r.

```
fun snoc ((f, r), x) = (f, x :: r)
```

Elements are added to r and removed from f, so they must somehow migrate from one list to the other. This migration is accomplished by reversing r and installing the result as the new f whenever f would otherwise become empty, simultaneously setting the new r to [ ]. The goal is to maintain the invariant that f is empty only if r is also empty (i.e., the entire queue is empty). Note that, if f were empty when r was not, then the first element of the queue would be

```
structure BatchedQueue : QUEUE =
struct
  type α Queue = α list × α list

  val empty = ([ ], [ ])
  fun isEmpty (f, r) = null f

  fun checkf ([ ], r) = (rev r, [ ])
    | checkf q = q

  fun snoc ((f, r), x) = checkf (f, x :: r)

  fun head ([ ], _) = raise EMPTY
    | head (x :: f, r) = x
  fun tail ([ ], _) = raise EMPTY
    | tail (x :: f, r) = checkf (f, r)
end
```

Figure 5.2. A common implementation of purely functional queues.

the last element of r, which would take $O(n)$ time to access. By maintaining this invariant, we guarantee that head can always find the first element in $O(1)$ time.

snoc and tail must now detect those cases that would otherwise result in a violation of the invariant, and change their behavior accordingly.

```
fun snoc (([ ], _), x) = ([x], [ ])
  | snoc ((f, r), x) = (f, x :: r)
fun tail ([x], r) = (rev r, [ ])
  | tail (x :: f, r) = (f, r)
```

Note the use of the wildcard in the first clause of snoc. In this case, the r field is irrelevant because we know by the invariant that if f is [ ], then so is r.

A slightly cleaner way to write these functions is to consolidate into a single function checkf those parts of snoc and tail that are devoted to maintaining the invariant. checkf replaces f with rev r when f is empty, and otherwise does nothing.

```
fun checkf ([ ], r) = (rev r, [ ])
  | checkf q = q
fun snoc ((f, r), x) = checkf (f, x :: r)
fun tail (x :: f, r) = checkf (f, r)
```

The complete code for this implementation is shown in Figure 5.2. snoc and head run in $O(1)$ worst-case time, but tail takes $O(n)$ time in the worst-case. However, we can show that snoc and tail both take $O(1)$ amortized time using either the banker's method or the physicist's method.

Using the banker's method, we maintain a credit invariant that every element in the rear list is associated with a single credit. Every snoc into a non-empty queue takes one actual step and allocates a credit to the new element of the rear list, for an amortized cost of two. Every tail that does not reverse the rear list takes one actual step and neither allocates nor spends any credits, for an amortized cost of one. Finally, every tail that does reverse the rear list takes $m + 1$ actual steps, where m is the length of the rear list, and spends the m credits contained by that list, for an amortized cost of $m + 1 - m = 1$.

Using the physicist's method, we define the potential function Φ to be the length of the rear list. Then every snoc into a non-empty queue takes one actual step and increases the potential by one, for an amortized cost of two. Every tail that does not reverse the rear list takes one actual step and leaves the potential unchanged, for an amortized cost of one. Finally, every tail that does reverse the rear list takes $m + 1$ actual steps and sets the new rear list to [ ], decreasing the potential by m, for an amortized cost of $m + 1 - m = 1$.

In this simple example, the proofs are virtually identical. Even so, the physicist's method is slightly simpler for the following reason. Using the banker's method, we must first choose a credit invariant, and then decide for each function when to allocate or spend credits. The credit invariant provides guidance in this decision, but does not make it automatic. For instance, should snoc allocate one credit and spend none, or allocate two credits and spend one? The net effect is the same, so this freedom is just one more potential source of confusion. On the other hand, using the physicist's method, we have only one decision to make—the choice of the potential function. After that, the analysis is mere calculation, with no more freedom of choice.

> **Hint to Practitioners:** These queues cannot be beat for applications that do not require persistence and for which amortized bounds are acceptable.

Exercise 5.1 (Hoogerwoord [Hoo92]) This design can easily be extended to support the *double-ended queue*, or *deque*, abstraction, which allows reads and writes to both ends of the queue (see Figure 5.3). The invariant is updated to be symmetric in its treatment of *f* and *r*: both are required to be non-empty whenever the deque contains two or more elements. When one list becomes empty, we split the other list in half and reverse one of the halves.

(a) Implement this version of deques.

(b) Prove that each operation takes $O(1)$ amortized time using the potential function $\Phi(f, r) = abs(|f| - |r|)$, where *abs* is the absolute value function.

```
signature DEQUE =
sig
  type α Queue

  val empty   : α Queue
  val isEmpty : α Queue → bool

  (* insert, inspect, and remove the front element *)
  val cons   : α × α Queue → α Queue
  val head   : α Queue → α         (* raises EMPTY if queue is empty *)
  val tail   : α Queue → α Queue (* raises EMPTY if queue is empty *)

  (* insert, inspect, and remove the rear element *)
  val snoc   : α Queue × α → α Queue
  val last   : α Queue → α         (* raises EMPTY if queue is empty *)
  val init   : α Queue → α Queue (* raises EMPTY if queue is empty *)
end
```

Figure 5.3. Signature for double-ended queues.

5.3 Binomial Heaps

In Section 3.2, we showed that insert on binomial heaps runs in $O(\log n)$ worst-case time. Here, we prove that insert actually runs in $O(1)$ amortized time.

We use the physicist's method. Define the potential of a binomial heap to be the number of trees in the heap. Recall that this is equivalent to the number of ones in the binary representation of n, the number of elements in the heap. Now, a call to insert takes $k + 1$ steps where k is the number of calls to link. If there were initially t trees in the heap, then after the insertion, there are $t - k + 1$ trees. Thus, the change in potential is $(t - k + 1) - t = 1 - k$ and the amortized cost of the insertion is $(k + 1) + (1 - k) = 2$.

Exercise 5.2 Repeat this proof using the banker's method.   ◇

To be complete, we must also show that the amortized costs of merge and deleteMin are still $O(\log n)$. deleteMin poses no particular problem, but merge requires a minor extension to the physicist's method. Previously, we defined the amortized cost of an operation to be

$$a = t + \Phi(d_{out}) - \Phi(d_{in})$$

where d_{in} is the input to the operation and d_{out} is the output. However, if an operation takes or returns more than one object, then we generalize this rule to

$$a = t + \sum_{d \in Out} \Phi(d) - \sum_{d \in In} \Phi(d)$$

where *In* is the set of inputs and *Out* is the set of outputs. For the purposes of this rule, we consider only inputs and outputs of the type(s) being analyzed.

Exercise 5.3 Prove that the amortized costs of merge and deleteMin are still $O(\log n)$.

5.4 Splay Heaps

Splay trees [ST85] are perhaps the most famous and successful of all amortized data structures. Splay trees are a close relative of balanced binary search trees, but they maintain no explicit balance information. Instead, every operation blindly restructures the tree using some simple transformations that tend to increase balance. Although any individual operation can take as much as $O(n)$ time, we will show that every operation runs in $O(\log n)$ amortized time.

A major difference between splay trees and balanced binary search trees such as the red-black trees of Section 3.3 is that splay trees are restructured even during queries (e.g., member) instead of only during updates (e.g., insert). This property makes it awkward to use splay trees to implement abstractions such as sets or finite maps in a purely functional setting, because the query would have to return the new tree along with the answer.† For some abstractions, however, the queries are limited enough to avoid these problems. A good example is the heap abstraction, where the only interesting query is findMin. In fact, as we will see, splay trees make an excellent implementation of heaps.

The representation of splay trees is identical to that of unbalanced binary search trees.

datatype Tree = E | T **of** Tree × Elem.T × Tree

Unlike the unbalanced binary search trees of Section 2.2, however, we allow duplicate elements within a single tree. This is not a fundamental difference between splay trees and unbalanced binary search trees; rather, it reflects a difference between the set abstraction and the heap abstraction.

Consider the following strategy for implementing insert: partition the existing tree into two subtrees, one containing all the elements smaller than or equal to the new element and one containing all the elements bigger than the new element, and then construct a new node from the new element and the two subtrees. Unlike insertion into ordinary binary search trees, this procedure adds the new element at the root of the tree rather than at the leaves. The code for insert is simply

---

† In a language like Standard ML, it is possible to store the root of each splay tree in a ref cell, and then update the ref cell after each query, but this is not purely functional.

fun insert (*x*, *t*) = T (smaller (*x*, *t*), *x*, bigger (*x*, *t*))

where smaller and bigger extract the appropriate subtrees. In analogy to the partitioning phase of quicksort, we call the new element the *pivot*.

We could implement bigger naively as

```
fun bigger (pivot, E) = E
  | bigger (pivot, T (a, x, b)) =
    if x ≤ pivot then bigger (pivot, b)
    else T (bigger (pivot, a), x, b)
```

but this makes no attempt to restructure the tree to make it more balanced. Instead, we use a very simple restructuring heuristic: every time we follow two left branches in a row, we rotate those two nodes.

```
fun bigger (pivot, E) = E
  | bigger (pivot, T (a, x, b)) =
    if x ≤ pivot then bigger (pivot, b)
    else case a of
           E ⇒ T (E, x, b)
         | T (a₁, y, a₂) ⇒
             if y ≤ pivot then T (bigger (pivot, a₂), x, b)
             else T (bigger (pivot, a₁), y, T (a₂, x, b))
```

Figure 5.4 illustrates the effect of bigger on a very unbalanced tree. Although still not balanced in the usual sense, the new tree is much more balanced than the original tree; the depth of every node has been reduced by about half, from d to $\lfloor d/2 \rfloor$ or $\lfloor d/2 \rfloor + 1$. Of course, we cannot always halve the depth of every node in the tree, but we can always halve the depth of every node along the search path. In fact, this is the guiding principle of splay trees: search paths should be restructured to reduce the depth of every node in the path by about half.

Exercise 5.4 Implement smaller. Keep in mind that smaller should retain equal elements (but do not make a separate test for equality!). ◇

Notice that smaller and bigger both traverse the same search path. Rather than duplicating this traversal, we can combine smaller and bigger into a single function called partition that returns the results of both as a pair. This function is straightforward, but somewhat tedious.

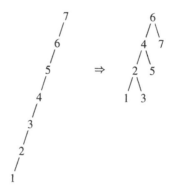

Figure 5.4. Calling bigger with a pivot element of 0.

```
fun partition (pivot, E) = (E, E)
  | partition (pivot, t as T (a, x, b)) =
      if x ≤ pivot then
        case b of
          E ⇒ (t, E)
        | T (b₁, y, b₂) ⇒
            if y ≤ pivot then
              let val (small, big) = partition (pivot, b₂)
              in (T (T (a, x, b₁), y, small), big) end
            else
              let val (small, big) = partition (pivot, b₁)
              in (T (a, x, small), T (big, y, b₂)) end
      else
        case a of
          E ⇒ (E, t)
        | T (a₁, y, a₂) ⇒
            if y ≤ pivot then
              let val (small, big) = partition (pivot, a₂)
              in (T (a₁, y, small), T (big, x, b)) end
            else
              let val (small, big) = partition (pivot, a₁)
              in (small, T (big, y, T (a₂, x, b))) end
```

Remark This function is not exactly equivalent to smaller and bigger because of phase differences: partition always processes nodes in pairs whereas smaller and bigger sometimes process only a single node. Thus, smaller and bigger sometimes rotate different pairs of nodes than partition. However, these differences are inconsequential.   ◇

Next, we consider findMin and deleteMin. The minimum element in a splay tree is stored in the leftmost T node. Finding this node is trivial.

```
fun findMin (T (E, x, b)) = x
  | findMin (T (a, x, b)) = findMin a
```

deleteMin should discard the minimum node, and at the same time, restructure the tree in the same style as bigger. Since we always take the left branch, there is no need for comparisons.

```
fun deleteMin (T (E, x, b)) = b
  | deleteMin (T (T (E, x, b), y, c)) = T (b, y, c)
  | deleteMin (T (T (a, x, b), y, c)) = T (deleteMin a, x, T (b, y, c))
```

Figure 5.5 summarizes this implementation of splay trees. For completeness, we have included the merge function on splay trees even though it is rather inefficient, taking up to $O(n)$ time for many inputs.

Next, we show that insert runs in $O(\log n)$ time. Let $\#t$ denote the size of t plus one and note that if $t = T(a, x, b)$ then $\#t = \#a + \#b$. Define the potential $\phi(t)$ of an individual node to be $\log(\#t)$ and the potential $\Phi(t)$ of an entire tree be the sum of potentials of all the individual nodes in the tree. We will need the following elementary fact about logarithms:

Lemma 5.1 *For all positive x, y, z such that $y + z \leq x$,*

$$1 + \log y + \log z < 2 \log x$$

Proof Without loss of generality, assume that $y \leq z$. Then $y \leq x/2$ and $z < x$, so $1 + \log y \leq \log x$ and $\log z < \log x$. □

Let $\mathcal{T}(t)$ denote the actual cost of calling partition on tree t, defined as the total number of recursive calls to partition. Let $\mathcal{A}(t)$ denote the amortized cost of calling partition on t, defined as

$$\mathcal{A}(T) = \mathcal{T}(t) + \Phi(a) + \Phi(b) - \Phi(t)$$

where a and b are the subtrees returned by *partition*.

Theorem 5.2 $\mathcal{A}(t) \leq 1 + 2\phi(t) = 1 + 2\log(\sharp t)$.

Proof There are two interesting cases, called the zig-zig case and the zig-zag case, depending on whether a particular call to partition follows two left branches (symmetrically, two right branches) or a left branch followed by a right branch (symmetrically, a right branch followed by a left branch).

For the zig-zig case, assume that the original tree and the resulting trees have the shapes

```
functor SplayHeap (Element : ORDERED) : HEAP =
struct
  structure Elem = Element

  datatype Heap = E | T of Heap × Elem.T × Heap

  val empty = E
  fun isEmpty E = true | isEmpty _ = false

  fun partition (pivot, E) = (E, E)
    | partition (pivot, t as T (a, x, b)) =
      if Elem.leq (x, pivot) then
        case b of
          E ⇒ (t, E)
        | T (b₁, y, b₂) ⇒
            if Elem.leq (y, pivot) then
              let val (small, big) = partition (pivot, b₂)
              in (T (T (a, x, b₁), y, small), big) end
            else
              let val (small, big) = partition (pivot, b₁)
              in (T (a, x, small), T (big, y, b₂)) end
      else
        case a of
          E ⇒ (E, t)
        | T (a₁, y, a₂) ⇒
            if Elem.leq (y, pivot) then
              let val (small, big) = partition (pivot, a₂)
              in (T (a₁, y, small), T (big, x, b)) end
            else
              let val (small, big) = partition (pivot, a₁)
              in (small, T (big, y, T (a₂, x, b))) end
  fun insert (x, t) = let val (a, b) = partition (x, t) in T (a, x, b) end
  fun merge (E, t) = t
    | merge (T (a, x, b), t) =
      let val (ta, tb) = partition (x, t)
      in T (merge (ta, a), x, merge (tb, b)) end

  fun findMin E = raise EMPTY
    | findMin (T (E, x, b)) = x
    | findMin (T (a, x, b)) = findMin a
  fun deleteMin E = raise EMPTY
    | deleteMin (T (E, x, b)) = b
    | deleteMin (T (T (E, x, b), y, c)) = T (b, y, c)
    | deleteMin (T (T (a, x, b), y, c)) = T (deleteMin a, x, T (b, y, c))
end
```

Figure 5.5. Implementation of heaps using splay trees.

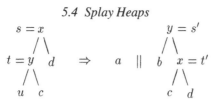

where a and b are the results of partition (*pivot*, u). Then,

$$\mathcal{A}(s)$$
$$= \quad \{ \text{ definition of } \mathcal{A} \ \}$$
$$\mathcal{T}(s) + \Phi(a) + \Phi(s') - \Phi(s)$$
$$= \quad \{ \ \mathcal{T}(s) = 1 + \mathcal{T}(u) \ \}$$
$$1 + \mathcal{T}(u) + \Phi(a) + \Phi(s') - \Phi(s)$$
$$= \quad \{ \ \mathcal{T}(u) = \mathcal{A}(u) - \Phi(a) - \Phi(b) + \Phi(u) \ \}$$
$$1 + \mathcal{A}(u) - \Phi(a) - \Phi(b) + \Phi(u) + \Phi(a) + \Phi(s') - \Phi(s)$$
$$= \quad \{ \text{ expand } \Phi(s') \text{ and } \Phi(s) \text{ and simplify } \}$$
$$1 + \mathcal{A}(u) + \phi(s') + \phi(t') - \phi(s) - \phi(t)$$
$$\leq \quad \{ \text{ inductive hypothesis: } \mathcal{A}(u) \leq 1 + 2\phi(u) \ \}$$
$$2 + 2\phi(u) + \phi(s') + \phi(t') - \phi(s) - \phi(t)$$
$$< \quad \{ \ \phi(u) < \phi(t) \text{ and } \phi(s') \leq \phi(s) \ \}$$
$$2 + \phi(u) + \phi(t')$$
$$< \quad \{ \ \sharp u + \sharp t' < \sharp s \text{ and Lemma 5.1 } \}$$
$$1 + 2\phi(s)$$

The proof of the zig-zag case is left as an exercise.   □

Exercise 5.5 Prove the zig-zag case.   ◇

The additional cost of insert over that of partition is one actual step plus the change in potential between the two subtrees returned by partition and the final tree. This change in potential is simply ϕ of the new root. Since the amortized cost of partition is bounded by $1 + 2\log(\sharp t)$, the amortized cost of insert is bounded by $2 + 2\log(\sharp t) + \log(\sharp t + 1) \approx 2 + 3\log(\sharp t)$.

Exercise 5.6 Prove that deleteMin also runs in $O(\log n)$ time.   ◇

Now, what about findMin? For a very unbalanced tree, findMin might take up to $O(n)$ time. But since findMin does not do any restructuring and therefore causes no change in potential, there is no way to amortize this cost! However, since findMin takes time proportional to deleteMin, if we double the charged cost of deleteMin then we can essentially run findMin for free once per call to deleteMin. This suffices for those applications that always call findMin and deleteMin together. However, some applications may call findMin several times per call to deleteMin. For those applications, we would not use the SplayHeap functor directly, but rather would use the SplayHeap functor in conjunction with the ExplicitMin functor of Exercise 3.7. Recall that the purpose of the ExplicitMin functor was to make findMin run in $O(1)$ time. The insert and deleteMin functions would still run in $O(\log n)$ amortized time.

Hint to Practitioners: Splay trees, perhaps in combination with the ExplicitMin functor, are the fastest known implementation of heaps for most applications that do not depend on persistence and that do not call the merge function.

A particularly pleasant feature of splay trees is that they naturally adapt to any order that happens to be present in the input data. For example, using splay heaps to sort an already sorted list takes only $O(n)$ time rather than $O(n \log n)$ time [MEP96]. Leftist heaps also share this property, but only for decreasing sequences. Splay heaps excel on both increasing and decreasing sequences, as well as on sequences that are only partially sorted.

Exercise 5.7 Write a sorting function that inserts elements into a splay tree and then performs an inorder traversal of the tree, dumping the elements into a list. Show that this function takes only $O(n)$ time on an already sorted list.

5.5 Pairing Heaps

Pairing heaps [FSST86] are one of those data structures that drive theoreticians crazy. On the one hand, pairing heaps are simple to implement and perform extremely well in practice. On the other hand, they have resisted analysis for over ten years!

Pairing heaps are heap-ordered multiway trees, as defined by the following datatype:

datatype Heap = E | T **of** Elem.T × Heap list

We allow only well-formed trees, in which E never occurs in the child list of a T node.

Since these trees are heap-ordered, the findMin function is trivial.

fun findMin (T (*x, hs*)) = *x*

The merge and insert functions are not much harder. merge makes the tree with the larger root the leftmost child of the tree with the smaller root. insert first creates a new singleton tree and then immediately calls merge.

```
fun merge (h, E) = h
  | merge (E, h) = h
  | merge (h₁ as T (x, hs₁), h₂ as T (y, hs₂)) =
     if Elem.leq (x, y) then T (x, h₂ :: hs₁) else T (y, h₁ :: hs₂)
fun insert (x, h) = merge (T (x, []), h)
```

Pairing heaps get their name from the deleteMin operation. deleteMin discards the root and then merges the children in two passes. The first pass merges children in pairs from left to right (i.e., the first child with the second, the third with the fourth, and so on). The second pass merges the resulting trees from right to left. These two passes can be coded concisely as

```
fun mergePairs [] = E
  | mergePairs [h] = h
  | mergePairs (h₁ :: h₂ :: hs) = merge (merge (h₁, h₂), mergePairs hs)
```

Then, deleteMin is simply

```
fun deleteMin (T (x, hs)) = mergePairs hs
```

The complete implementation appears in Figure 5.6.

Now, it is easy to see that findMin, insert, and merge all run in $O(1)$ worst-case time. However, deleteMin can take up to $O(n)$ time in the worst case. By drawing an analogy to splay trees (see Exercise 5.8), we can show that insert, merge, and deleteMin all run in $O(\log n)$ amortized time. It has been conjectured that insert and merge actually run in $O(1)$ amortized time [FSST86], but no one has yet been able to prove or disprove this claim.

Hint to Practitioners: Pairing heaps are almost as fast in practice as splay heaps for applications that do not use the merge function, and much faster for applications that do. Like splay heaps, however, they should be used only for applications that do not take advantage of persistence.

Exercise 5.8 Binary trees are often more convenient than multiway trees. Fortunately, there is an easy way to represent any multiway tree as a binary tree. Simply convert every multiway node into a binary node whose left child represents the leftmost child of the multiway node and whose right child represents the sibling to the immediate right of the multiway node. If either the leftmost child or the right sibling of the multiway node is missing, then the corresponding field in the binary node is empty. (Note that this implies that the right child of the root is always empty in the binary representation.) Applying this transformation to pairing heaps yields half-ordered binary trees in which the element at each node is no greater than any element in its left subtree.

```
functor PairingHeap (Element : ORDERED) : HEAP =
struct
    structure Elem = Element

    datatype Heap = E | T of Elem.T × Heap list

    val empty = E
    fun isEmpty E = true | isEmpty _ = false

    fun merge (h, E) = h
      | merge (E, h) = h
      | merge (h₁ as T (x, hs₁), h₂ as T (y, hs₂)) =
            if Elem.leq (x, y) then T (x, h₂ :: hs₁) else T (y, h₁ :: hs₂)
    fun insert (x, h) = merge (T (x, []), h)

    fun mergePairs [ ] = E
      | mergePairs [h] = h
      | mergePairs (h₁ :: h₂ :: hs) = merge (merge (h₁, h₂), mergePairs hs)

    fun findMin E = raise EMPTY
      | findMin (T (x, hs)) = x
    fun deleteMin E = raise EMPTY
      | deleteMin (T (x, hs)) = mergePairs hs
end
```

Figure 5.6. Pairing heaps.

(a) Write a function toBinary that converts pairing heaps from the existing representation into the type

datatype BinTree = E' | T' **of** Elem.T × BinTree × BinTree

(b) Reimplement pairing heaps using this new representation.

(c) Adapt the analysis of splay trees to prove that deleteMin and merge run in $O(\log n)$ amortized time for this new representation (and hence for the old representation as well). Use the same potential function as for splay trees.

5.6 The Bad News

As we have seen, amortized data structures are often tremendously effective in practice. Unfortunately, the analyses in this chapter implicitly assume that the data structures in question are used ephemerally (i.e., in a single-threaded fashion). What happens if we try to use one of these data structures persistently?

Consider the queues of Section 5.2. Let q be the result of inserting n elements into an initially empty queue, so that the front list of q contains a single element and the rear list contains $n - 1$ elements. Now, suppose we use q persistently by taking its tail n times. Each call of tail q takes n actual steps. The total actual cost of this sequence of operations, including the time to build q, is $n^2 + n$. If the operations truly took $O(1)$ amortized time each, then the total actual cost would be only $O(n)$. Clearly, using these queues persistently invalidates the $O(1)$ amortized time bounds proved in Section 5.2. Where do these proofs go wrong?

In both cases, a fundamental requirement of the analysis is violated by persistent data structures. The banker's method requires that no credit be spent more than once, while the physicist's method requires that the output of one operation be the input of the next operation (or, more generally, that no output be used as input more than once). Now, consider the second call to tail q in the example above. The first call to tail q spends all the credits on the rear list of q, leaving none to pay for the second and subsequent calls, so the banker's method breaks. And the second call to tail q reuses q rather than the output of the first call, so the physicist's method breaks.

Both these failures reflect the inherent weakness of any accounting system based on accumulated savings—that savings can only be spent once. The traditional methods of amortization operate by accumulating savings (as either credits or potential) for future use. This works well in an ephemeral setting, where every operation has only a single logical future. But with persistence, an operation might have multiple logical futures, each competing to spend the same savings.

In the next chapter, we will clarify what we mean by the "logical future" of an operation, and show how to reconcile amortization and persistence using lazy evaluation.

Exercise 5.9 Give examples of sequences of operations for which binomial heaps, splay heaps, and pairing heaps take much longer than indicated by their amortized bounds.

5.7 Chapter Notes

The techniques of amortization presented in this chapter were developed by Sleator and Tarjan [ST85, ST86b] and popularized by Tarjan [Tar85]. Schoenmakers [Sch92] has shown how to systematically derive amortized bounds in a functional setting without persistence.

Gries [Gri81, pages 250–251] and Hood and Melville [HM81] first proposed the queues in Section 5.2. Burton [Bur82] proposed a similar implementation, but without the restriction that the front list be non-empty whenever the queue is non-empty. Burton combines head and tail into a single function, and so does not require this restriction to support head efficiently.

Several empirical studies have shown that splay heaps [Jon86] and pairing heaps [MS91, Lia92] are among the fastest of all heap implementations. Stasko and Vitter [SV87] have confirmed the conjectured $O(1)$ amortized bound on insert for a variant of pairing heaps.

6
Amortization and Persistence via Lazy Evaluation

The previous chapter introduced the idea of amortization and gave several examples of data structures with good amortized bounds. However, for each these data structures, the amortized bounds break in the presence of persistence. In this chapter, we demonstrate how lazy evaluation can mediate the conflict between amortization and persistence, and adapt both the banker's and physicist's methods to account for lazy evaluation. We then illustrate the use of these new methods on several amortized data structures that use lazy evaluation internally.

6.1 Execution Traces and Logical Time

In the previous chapter, we saw that traditional methods of amortization break in the presence of persistence because they assume a unique future, in which the accumulated savings will be spent at most once. However, with persistence, multiple logical futures might all try to spend the same savings. But what exactly do we mean by the "logical future" of an operation?

We model logical time with *execution traces*, which give an abstract view of the history of a computation. An execution trace is a directed graph whose nodes represent operations of interest, usually just update operations on the data type in question. An edge from v to v' indicates that operation v' uses some result of operation v. The *logical history* of operation v, denoted $\hat{v}$, is the set of all operations on which the result of v depends (including v itself). In other words, $\hat{v}$ is the set of all nodes w such that there exists a path (possibly of length 0) from w to v. A *logical future* of a node v is any path from v to a terminal node (i.e., a node with out-degree zero). If there is more than one such path, then node v has multiple logical futures. We sometimes refer to the logical history or logical future of an object, meaning the logical history or logical future of the operation that created the object.

Exercise 6.1 Draw an execution trace for the following set of operations. Annotate each node in the trace with the number of logical futures at that node.

val a = snoc (empty, 0)
val b = snoc (a, 1)
val c = tail b
val d = snoc (b, 2)
val e = c ++ d
val f = tail c
val g = snoc (d, 3)

$\diamondsuit$

Execution traces generalize the notion of *version graphs* [DSST89], which are often used to model the histories of persistent data structures. In a version graph, nodes represent the various versions of a single persistent identity and edges represent dependencies between versions. Thus, version graphs model the results of operations and execution traces model the operations themselves. Execution traces are often more convenient for combining the histories of several persistent identities (perhaps not even of the same type) or for reasoning about operations that do not return a new version (e.g., queries) or that return several results (e.g., splitting a list into two sublists).

For ephemeral data structures, the out-degree of every node in a version graph or execution trace is typically restricted to be at most one, reflecting the limitation that objects can be updated at most once. To model various flavors of persistence, version graphs allow the out-degree of every node to be unbounded, but make other restrictions. For instance, version graphs are often limited to be trees (forests) by restricting the in-degree of every node to be at most one. Other version graphs allow in-degrees of greater than one, but forbid cycles, making every graph a dag. We make none of these restrictions on execution traces for persistent data structures. Nodes with in-degree greater than one correspond to operations that take more than one argument, such as list catenation or set union. Cycles arise from recursively defined objects, which are supported by many lazy languages. We even allow multiple edges between a single pair of nodes, as might occur if a list is catenated with itself.

We will use execution traces in Section 6.3.1 when we extend the banker's method to cope with persistence.

6.2 Reconciling Amortization and Persistence

In this section, we show how the banker's and physicist's methods can be repaired by replacing the notion of accumulated savings with accumulated debt, where debt measures the cost of unevaluated lazy computations. The intuition is that, although savings can only be spent once, it does no harm to pay off debt more than once.

6.2.1 The Role of Lazy Evaluation

Recall that an *expensive* operation is one whose actual costs are greater than its (desired) amortized costs. For example, suppose some application f x is expensive. With persistence, a malicious adversary might call f x arbitrarily often. (Note that each operation is a new logical future of x.) If each operation takes the same amount of time, then the amortized bounds degrade to the worst-case bounds. Hence, we must find a way to guarantee that if the first application of f to x is expensive, then subsequent applications of f to x will not be.

Without side-effects, this is impossible under call-by-value (i.e., strict evaluation) or call-by-name (i.e., lazy evaluation without memoization), because every application of f to x takes exactly the same amount of time. Therefore, amortization cannot be usefully combined with persistence in languages supporting only these evaluation orders.

But now consider call-by-need (i.e., lazy evaluation with memoization). If x contains some suspended component that is needed by f, then the first application of f to x forces the (potentially expensive) evaluation of that component and memoizes the result. Subsequent operations may then access the memoized result directly. This is exactly the desired behavior!

Remark   In retrospect, the relationship between lazy evaluation and amortization is not surprising. Lazy evaluation can be viewed as a form of self-modification, and amortization often involves self-modification[ST85, ST86b]. However, lazy evaluation is a particularly disciplined form of self-modification — not all forms of self-modification typically used in amortized ephemeral data structures can be encoded as lazy evaluation. In particular, splay trees do not appear to be amenable to this technique.

6.2.2 A Framework for Analyzing Lazy Data Structures

We have just shown that lazy evaluation is necessary to implement amortized data structures purely functionally. Unfortunately, analyzing the running times of programs involving lazy evaluation is notoriously difficult. Historically, the most common technique for analyzing lazy programs has been to pretend that they are actually strict. However, this technique is completely inadequate for analyzing lazy amortized data structures. We next describe a basic framework to support such analyses. In the remainder of this chapter, we adapt the banker's and physicist's methods to this framework, yielding both the first techniques for analyzing persistent amortized data structures and the first practical techniques for analyzing non-trivial lazy programs.

We classify the costs of any given operation into several categories. First, the *unshared cost* of an operation is the actual time it would take to execute the operation under the assumption that every suspension in the system at the beginning of the operation has already been forced and memoized (i.e., under the assumption that force always takes $O(1)$ time, except for those suspensions that are created and forced within the same operation). The *shared cost* of an operation is the time that it would take to execute every suspension created but not evaluated by the operation (under the same assumption as above). The *complete cost* of an operation is the sum of its shared and unshared costs. Note that the complete cost is what the actual cost of the operation would be if lazy evaluation were replaced with strict evaluation.

We further partition the total shared costs of a sequence of operations into realized and unrealized costs. *Realized costs* are the shared costs for suspensions that are executed during the overall computation. *Unrealized costs* are the shared costs for suspensions that are never executed. The *total actual cost* of a sequence of operations is the sum of the unshared costs and the realized shared costs—unrealized costs do not contribute to the actual cost. Note that the amount that any particular operation contributes to the total actual cost is at least its unshared cost, and at most its complete cost, depending on how much of its shared cost is realized.

We account for shared costs using the notion of *accumulated debt*. Initially, the accumulated debt is zero, but every time a suspension is created, we increase the accumulated debt by the shared cost of the suspension (and any nested suspensions). Each operation then pays off a portion of the accumulated debt. The *amortized cost* of an operation is the unshared cost of the operation plus the amount of accumulated debt paid off by the operation. We are not allowed to force a suspension until the debt associated with the suspension is entirely paid off.

Remark   An amortized analysis based on the notion of accumulated debt works a lot like a *layaway plan*. In a layaway plan, you find something—a diamond ring, say—that you want to buy, but that you can't afford to pay for yet. You agree on a price with the jewelry store and ask them to set the ring aside in your name. You then make regular payments, and receive the ring only when it is entirely paid off.

In analyzing a lazy data structure, you find a computation that you can't afford to execute yet. You create a suspension for the computation, and assign the suspension an amount of debt proportional to its shared cost. You then pay off the debt a little at a time. Finally, when the debt is entirely paid off, you are allowed to execute the suspension. ◇

There are three important moments in the life cycle of a suspension: when it is created, when it is entirely paid off, and when it is executed. The proof obligation is to show that the second moment precedes the third. If every suspension is paid off before it is forced, then the total amount of debt that has been paid off is an upper bound on the realized shared costs, and therefore the total amortized cost (i.e., the total unshared cost plus the total amount of debt that has been paid off) is an upper bound on the total actual cost (i.e., the total unshared cost plus the realized shared costs). We will formalize this argument in Section 6.3.1.

One of the most difficult problems in analyzing the running time of lazy programs is reasoning about the interactions of multiple logical futures. We avoid this problem by reasoning about each logical future *as if it were the only one*. From the point of view of the operation that creates a suspension, any logical future that forces the suspension must itself pay for the suspension. If two logical futures wish to force the same suspension, then both must pay for the suspension individually—they may not cooperate and each pay only a portion of the debt. An alternative view of this restriction is that we are allowed to force a suspension *only when the debt for that suspension has been paid off within the logical history of the current operation*. Using this method, we sometimes pay off a debt more than once, thereby overestimating the total time required for a particular computation, but this does no harm and is a small price to pay for the simplicity of the resulting analyses.

6.3 The Banker's Method

We adapt the banker's method to account for accumulated debt rather than accumulated savings by replacing credits with debits. Each debit represents a constant amount of suspended work. When we initially suspend a given computation, we create a number of debits proportional to its shared cost and associate each debit with a location in the object. The choice of location for each debit depends on the nature of the computation. If the computation is *monolithic* (i.e., once begun, it runs to completion), then all debits are usually assigned to the root of the result. On the other hand, if the computation is *incremental* (i.e., decomposable into fragments that may be executed independently), then the debits may be distributed among the roots of the partial results.

The amortized cost of an operation is the unshared cost of the operation plus the number of debits discharged by the operation. Note that the number of debits created by an operation is *not* included in its amortized cost. The order in which debits should be discharged depends on how the object will be accessed; debits on nodes likely to be accessed soon should be discharged first. To prove an amortized bound, we must show that, whenever we access a location (possibly triggering the execution of a suspension), all debits associated with that location have already been discharged (and hence the suspended computation has been entirely paid off). This guarantees that the total number of debits discharged by a sequence of operations is an upper bound on the realized shared costs of the operations. The total amortized costs are therefore an upper bound on the total actual costs. Debits leftover at the end of the computation correspond to unrealized shared costs, and are irrelevant to the total actual costs.

Incremental functions play an important role in the banker's method because they allow debits to be dispersed to different locations in a data structure, each corresponding to a nested suspension. Then, each location can be accessed as soon as its debits are discharged, without waiting for the debits at other locations to be discharged. In practice, this means that the initial partial results of an incremental computation can be paid for very quickly, and that subsequent partial results may be paid for as they are needed. Monolithic functions, on the other hand, are much less flexible. The programmer must anticipate when the result of an expensive monolithic computation will be needed, and set up the computation far enough in advance to be able to discharge all its debits by the time its result is needed.

6.3.1 Justifying the Banker's Method

In this section, we justify the claim that the total amortized cost is an upper bound on the total actual cost. The total amortized cost is the total unshared cost plus the total number of debits discharged (counting duplicates); the total actual cost is the total unshared cost plus the realized shared costs. Therefore, we must show that the total number of debits discharged is an upper bound on the realized shared costs.

We can view the banker's method abstractly as a graph labelling problem, using the execution traces of Section 6.1. The problem is to label every node in a trace with three (multi)sets, $s(v)$, $a(v)$, and $r(v)$, such that

$$(\text{I}) \qquad v \neq v' \Rightarrow s(v) \cap s(v') = \emptyset$$
$$(\text{II}) \qquad a(v) \subseteq \bigcup_{w \in \hat{v}} s(w)$$
$$(\text{III}) \qquad r(v) \subseteq \bigcup_{w \in \hat{v}} a(w)$$

$s(v)$ is a set, but $a(v)$ and $r(v)$ may be multisets (i.e., may contain duplicates). Conditions II and III ignore duplicates.

$s(v)$ is the set of debits allocated by operation v. Condition I states that no debit may be allocated more than once. $a(v)$ is the multiset of debits discharged by v. Condition II insists that no debit may be discharged before it is created, or more specifically, that an operation can only discharge debits that appear in its logical history. Finally, $r(v)$ is the multiset of debits *realized* by v—that is, the multiset of debits corresponding to the suspensions forced by v. Condition III requires that no debit may be realized before it is discharged, or more specifically, that no debit may realized unless it has been discharged within the logical history of the current operation.

Why are $a(v)$ and $r(v)$ multisets rather than sets? Because a single operation might discharge the same debits more than once or realize the same debits more than once (by forcing the same suspensions more than once). Although we never deliberately discharge the same debit more than once, it could happen if we were to combine a single object with itself. For example, suppose in some analysis of a list catenation function, we discharge a few debits from the first argument and a few debits from the second argument. If we then catenate a list with itself, we might discharge the same few debits twice.

Given this abstract view of the banker's method, we can easily measure various costs of a computation. Let V be the set of all nodes in the execution trace. Then, the total shared cost is $\sum_{v \in V} |s(v)|$ and the total number of debits discharged is $\sum_{v \in V} |a(v)|$. Because of memoization, the realized shared cost is not $\sum_{v \in V} |r(v)|$, but rather $|\bigcup_{v \in V} r(v)|$, where $\bigcup$ discards duplicates. Thus, a suspension that is forced multiple times contributes only once to the actual cost. By Condition III, we know that $\bigcup_{v \in V} r(v) \subseteq \bigcup_{v \in V} a(v)$. Therefore,

$$\left| \bigcup_{v \in V} r(v) \right| \leq \left| \bigcup_{v \in V} a(v) \right| \leq \sum_{v \in V} |a(v)|$$

So the realized shared cost is bounded by the total number of debits discharged, and the total actual cost is bounded by the total amortized cost, as desired.

Remark This argument once again emphasizes the importance of memoization. Without memoization (i.e., if we were using call-by-name rather than call-by-need), the total realized cost would be $\sum_{v \in V} |r(v)|$, and there is no reason to expect this sum to be less than $\sum_{v \in V} |a(v)|$.

6.3.2 Example: Queues

We next develop an efficient persistent implementation of queues, and prove that every operation runs in $O(1)$ amortized time using the banker's method.

Based on the discussion in the previous section, we must somehow incorporate lazy evaluation into the design of the data structure, so we replace the pair of lists in the simple queues of Section 5.2 with a pair of streams.† To simplify later operations, we also explicitly track the lengths of the two streams.

type α Queue = int × α Stream × int × α Stream

The first integer is the length of the front stream and the second integer is the length of the rear stream. Note that a pleasant side effect of maintaining this length information is that we can trivially support a constant-time size function.

Now, waiting until the front list becomes empty to reverse the rear list does not leave sufficient time to pay for the reverse. Instead, we periodically *rotate* the queue by moving all the elements of the rear stream to the end of the front stream, replacing f with f ++ reverse r and setting the new rear stream to empty. Note that this transformation does not affect the relative ordering of the elements.

When should we rotate the queue? Recall that reverse is a monolithic function. We must therefore set up the computation far enough in advance to be able to discharge all its debits by the time its result is needed. The reverse computation takes $|r|$ steps, so we allocate $|r|$ debits to account for its cost. (For now we ignore the cost of the ++ operation). The earliest the reverse suspension could be forced is after $|f|$ applications of tail, so if we rotate the queue when $|r| \approx |f|$ and discharge one debit per operation, then we will have paid for the reverse by the time it is executed. In fact, we rotate the queue whenever r becomes one longer than f, thereby maintaining the invariant that $|f| \geq |r|$. Incidentally, this guarantees that f is empty only if r is also empty, as in the simple queues of Section 5.2. The major queue functions can now be written as follows:

```
fun snoc ((lenf, f, lenr, r) , x) = check (lenf, f, lenr+1, $CONS (x, r))
fun head (lenf, $CONS (x, f'), lenr, r) = x
fun tail (lenf, $CONS (x, f'), lenr, r) = check (lenf−1, f', lenr, r)
```

where the helper function check guarantees that $|f| \geq |r|$.

```
fun check (q as (lenf, f, lenr, r)) =
    if lenr ≤ lenf then q else (lenf+lenr, f ++ reverse r, 0, $NIL)
```

---

† Actually, it would be enough to replace only the front list with a stream, but we replace both for simplicity.

```
structure BankersQueue : QUEUE =
struct
  type α Queue = int × α Stream × int × α Stream

  val empty = (0, $NIL, 0, $NIL)
  fun isEmpty (lenf, _, _, _) = (lenf = 0)

  fun check (q as (lenf, f, lenr, r)) =
      if lenr ≤ lenf then q else (lenf+lenr, f ++ reverse r, 0, $NIL)

  fun snoc ((lenf, f, lenr, r), x) = check (lenf, f, lenr+1, $CONS (x, r))

  fun head (lenf, $NIL, lenr, r) = raise EMPTY
    | head (lenf, $CONS (x, f'), lenr, r) = x
  fun tail (lenf, $NIL, lenr, r) = raise EMPTY
    | tail (lenf, $CONS (x, f'), lenr, r) = check (lenf−1, f', lenr, r)
end
```

Figure 6.1. Amortized queues using the banker's method.

The complete code for this implementation appears in Figure 6.1.

To understand how this implementation deals efficiently with persistence, consider the following scenario. Let q_0 be some queue whose front and rear streams are both of length m, and let $q_i =$ tail q_{i-1}, for $0 < i \leq m + 1$. The queue is rotated during the first application of tail, and the reverse suspension created by the rotation is forced during the last application of tail. This reversal takes m steps, and its cost is amortized over the sequence $q_1 \ldots q_m$. (For now, we are concerned only with the cost of the reverse—we ignore the cost of the ++.)

Now, choose some branch point k, and repeat the calculation from q_k to q_{m+1}. (Note that q_k is used persistently.) Do this d times. How often is the reverse executed? It depends on whether the branch point k is before or after the rotation. Suppose k is after the rotation. In fact, suppose $k = m$ so that each of the repeated branches is a single tail. Each of these branches forces the reverse suspension, but they each force the *same* suspension, so the reverse is executed only once. Memoization is crucial here—without memoization, the reverse would be re-executed each time, for a total cost of $m(d+1)$ steps, with only $m + 1 + d$ operations over which to amortize this cost. For large d, this would result in an $O(m)$ amortized cost per operation, but memoization gives us an amortized cost of only $O(1)$ per operation.

It is possible to re-execute the reverse however. Simply take $k = 0$ (i.e., make the branch point just before the rotation). Then the first tail of each branch repeats the rotation and creates a new reverse suspension. This new suspension is forced in the last tail of each branch, executing the reverse. Because these are different suspensions, memoization does not help at all. The total cost of all the reversals is $m \cdot d$, but now we have $(m+1)(d+1)$ operations over which to amortize this cost, again yielding an amortized cost of $O(1)$ per operation. The key is that we duplicate work only when we also duplicate the sequence of operations over which to amortize the cost of that work.

This informal argument shows that these queues require only $O(1)$ amortized time per operation even when used persistently. We formalize this proof using the banker's method.

By inspection, the unshared cost of every queue operation is $O(1)$. Therefore, to show that the amortized cost of every queue operation is $O(1)$, we must prove that discharging $O(1)$ debits per operation suffices to pay off every suspension before it is forced. In fact, only snoc and tail discharge any debits.

Let $d(i)$ be the number of debits on the ith node of the front stream and let $D(i) = \sum_{j=0}^{i} d(j)$ be the cumulative number of debits on all nodes up to and including the ith node. We maintain the following *debit invariant*:

$$D(i) \leq \min(2i, |f| - |r|)$$

The $2i$ term guarantees that all debits on the first node of the front stream have been discharged (since $d(0) = D(0) \leq 2 \cdot 0 = 0$), so this node may be forced at will (for instance, by head or tail). The $|f| - |r|$ term guarantees that all debits in the entire queue have been discharged whenever the streams are of equal length, which happens just before the next rotation.

Theorem 6.1 snoc *and* tail *maintain the debit invariant by discharging one and two debits, respectively.*

Proof Every snoc that does not cause a rotation simply adds a new element to the rear stream, increasing $|r|$ by one and decreasing $|f| - |r|$ by one. This violates the invariant at any node for which $D(i)$ was previously equal to $|f| - |r|$. We can restore the invariant by discharging the first debit in the queue, which decreases every subsequent cumulative debit total by one. Similarly, every tail that does not cause a rotation simply removes an element from the front stream. This decreases $|f|$ by one (and hence $|f| - |r|$ by one), but, more importantly, it decreases the index i of every remaining node by one, which in turn decreases $2i$ by two. Discharging the first two debits in the queue restores the invariant. Finally, consider a snoc or tail that causes a rotation. Just before the rotation, we are guaranteed that all debits in the queue have been discharged, so, after the rotation, the only undischarged debits are those generated by the rotation itself. If $|f| = m$ and $|r| = m + 1$ at the time of the rotation, then we create m debits for the append and $m + 1$ debits for the reverse. The append function is incremental so we place one of its debits on each of the first m nodes. On the other hand, the reverse function is monolithic so we place all $m + 1$ of its debits on node m, the first node of the reversed stream. Thus, the debits are distributed such that

$$d(i) = \begin{cases} 1 & \text{if } i < m \\ m + 1 & \text{if } i = m \\ 0 & \text{if } i > m \end{cases} \quad \text{and} \quad D(i) = \begin{cases} i + 1 & \text{if } i < m \\ 2m + 1 & \text{if } i \geq m \end{cases}$$

This distribution violates the invariant at both node 0 and node m, but discharging the debit on node 0 restores the invariant at both locations.   □

The format of this argument is typical. Debits are distributed across several nodes for incremental functions, and all on the same node for monolithic functions. Debit invariants measure, not just the number of debits on a given node, but the number of debits along the path from the root to the given node. This reflects the fact that accessing a node requires first accessing all its ancestors. Therefore, the debits on all those nodes must be zero as well.

This data structure also illustrates a subtle point about nested suspensions— the debits for a nested suspension may be allocated, and even discharged, before the suspension is physically created. For example, consider how ++ works. The suspension for the second node in the stream is not physically created until the suspension for the first node is forced. However, because of memoization, the suspension for the second node will be shared whenever the suspension for the first node is shared. Therefore, we consider a nested suspension to be implicitly created at the time that its enclosing suspension is created. Furthermore, when considering debit arguments or otherwise reasoning about the shape of an object, we ignore whether a node has been physically created or not. Rather we reason about the shape of an object as if all nodes were in their final form, i.e., as if all suspensions in the object had been forced.

Exercise 6.2 Suppose we change the invariant from $|f| \geq |r|$ to $2|f| \geq |r|$.

(a) Prove that the $O(1)$ amortized bounds still hold.
(b) Compare the relative performance of the two implementations on a sequence of one hundred snocs followed by one hundred tails.

6.3.3 Debit Inheritance

We frequently create suspensions whose bodies force other, existing suspensions. We say that the new suspension *depends* on the older suspensions. In the queue example, the suspension created by reverse r depends on r, and the suspension created by f ++ reverse r depends on f. Whenever we force a suspension, we must be sure that we have discharged not only all the debits for that suspension, but also all the debits for any suspensions on which it depends. In the queue example, the debit invariant guarantees that we create new suspensions using ++ and reverse only when the existing suspensions have been entirely paid off. However, we will not always be so lucky.

When we create a suspension that depends on an existing suspension with undischarged debits, we reassign those debits to the new suspension. We say that the new suspension *inherits* the debits of the older suspension. We may not force the new suspension until we have discharged both the new suspension's own debits and the debits it inherited from the older suspension. The banker's method makes no distinction between the two sets of debits, treating them all as if they belong to the new suspension. We will use debit inheritance to analyze data structures in Chapters 9, 10, and 11.

Remark Debit inheritance assumes that there is no way to access the older suspension in the current object other than through the new suspension. For example, debit inheritance could not be used in analyzing the following function on pairs of streams:

fun reverseSnd (*xs, ys*) = (reverse *ys, ys*)

Here, we can force *ys* through either the first component of the pair or the second component of the pair. In such situations, we either duplicate the debits on *ys* and let the new suspension inherit the duplicates, or keep one copy of each debit and explicitly track the dependencies.

6.4 The Physicist's Method

Like the banker's method, the physicist's method can also be adapted to work with accumulated debt rather than accumulated savings. In the traditional physicist's method, one describes a potential function Φ that represents a lower bound on the accumulated savings. To work with debt instead of savings, we replace Φ with a function Ψ that maps each object to a potential representing an upper bound on the accumulated debt (or at least, an upper bound on this object's portion of the accumulated debt). Roughly speaking, the amortized cost of an operation is then the complete cost of the operation (i.e., the shared and unshared costs) minus the change in potential. Recall that an easy way to calculate the complete cost of an operation is to pretend that all computation is strict.

Any changes in the accumulated debt are reflected by changes in the potential. If an operation does not pay any shared costs, then the change in potential is equal to its shared cost, so the amortized cost of the operation is equal to its unshared cost. On the other hand if an operation does pay some of its shared cost, or shared costs of previous operations, then the change in potential is smaller than the shared cost (i.e., the accumulated debt increases by less than the shared cost), so the amortized cost of the operation is greater than its unshared cost. However, the amortized cost of an operation can never be less than its unshared cost, so the change in potential is not allowed to be more than the shared cost.

We can justify the physicist's method by relating it back to the banker's method. Recall that in the banker's method, the amortized cost of an operation was its unshared cost plus the number of debits discharged. In the physicist's method, the amortized cost is the complete cost minus the change in potential, or, in other words, the unshared cost plus the difference between the shared cost and the change in potential. If we consider one unit of potential to be equivalent to one debit, then the shared cost is the number of debits by which the accumulated debt could have increased, and the change in potential is the number of debits by which the accumulated debt did increase. The difference must have been made up by discharging some debits. Therefore, the amortized cost in the physicist's method can also be viewed as the unshared cost plus the number of debits discharged.

Sometimes, we wish to force a suspension in an object when the potential of the object is not zero. In that case, we add the object's potential to the amortized cost. This typically happens in queries, where the cost of forcing the suspension cannot be reflected by a change in potential because the operation does not return a new object.

The major difference between the banker's and physicist's methods is that, in the banker's method, we are allowed to force a suspension as soon as the debits for that suspension have been paid off, without waiting for the debits for other suspensions to be discharged, but in the physicist's method, we can force a shared suspension only when we have reduced the entire accumulated debt of an object, as measured by the potential, to zero. Since potential measures only the accumulated debt of an object as a whole and does not distinguish between different locations, we must pessimistically assume that the entire outstanding debt is associated with the particular suspension we wish to force. For this reason, the physicist's method appears to be less powerful than the banker's method. However, when it applies, the physicist's method tends to be much simpler than the banker's method.

Since the physicist's method cannot take advantage of the piecemeal execution of nested suspensions, there is no reason to prefer incremental functions over monolithic functions. In fact, a good hint that the physicist's method might be applicable is if all or most suspensions are monolithic.

6.4.1 Example: Binomial Heaps

In Chapter 5, we showed that the binomial heaps of Section 3.2 support insert in $O(1)$ amortized time. However, this bound degrades to $O(\log n)$ worst-case time if the heaps are used persistently. With lazy evaluation, we can restore the $O(1)$ amortized time bound such that it holds regardless of whether the heaps are used persistently.

The key is to change the representation of heaps from a list of trees to a suspended list of trees.

type Heap = Tree list susp

Then we can rewrite insert as

fun lazy insert (*x*, $ts) = $insTree (NODE (0, *x*, [ ]), *ts*)

or, equivalently, as

fun insert (*x*, *h*) = $insTree (NODE (0, *x*, [ ]), force *h*)

The remaining functions are equally easy to rewrite, and are shown in Figure 6.2.

Next, we analyze the amortized running time of insert. Since insert is monolithic, we use the physicist's method. First, we define the potential function to be $\Psi(h) = Z(|h|)$, where $Z(n)$ is the number of zeros in the (minimum length) binary representation of n. Next, we show that the amortized cost of inserting an element into a binomial heap of size n is two. Suppose that the lowest k digits in the binary representation of n are ones. Then the complete cost of insert is proportional to $k + 1$, eventually including k calls to link. Now, consider the change in potential. The lowest k digits change from ones to zeros and the next digit changes from zero to one, so the change in potential is $k - 1$. The amortized cost is therefore $(k + 1) - (k - 1) = 2$.

Remark Note that this proof is dual to the one given in Section 5.3. The potential was the number of ones in the binary representation of n; here it is the number of zeros. This reflects the dual nature of accumulated savings and accumulated debt.

Exercise 6.3 Prove that findMin, deleteMin, and merge also run in $O(\log n)$ amortized time.

```
functor LazyBinomialHeap (Element : ORDERED) : HEAP =
struct
    structure Elem = Element

    datatype Tree = NODE of int × Elem.T × Tree list
    type Heap = Tree list susp

    val empty = $[]
    fun isEmpty ($ts) = null ts

    fun rank (NODE (r, x, c)) = r
    fun root (NODE (r, x, c)) = x
    fun link (t₁ as NODE (r, x₁, c₁), t₂ as NODE (_, x₂, c₂)) =
        if Elem.leq (x₁, x₂) then NODE (r+1, x₁, t₂ :: c₁)
        else NODE (r+1, x₂, t₁ :: c₂)
    fun insTree (t, []) = [t]
      | insTree (t, ts as t' :: ts') =
        if rank t < rank t' then t :: ts else insTree (link (t, t'), ts')

    fun mrg (ts₁, []) = ts₁
      | mrg ([], ts₂) = ts₂
      | mrg (ts₁ as t₁ :: ts₁', ts₂ as t₂ :: ts₂') =
        if rank t₁ < rank t₂ then t₁ :: mrg (ts₁', ts₂)
        else if rank t₂ < rank t₁ then t₂ :: mrg (ts₁, ts₂')
        else insTree (link (t₁, t₂), mrg (ts₁', ts₂'))

    fun lazy insert (x, $ts) = $insTree (NODE (0, x, []), ts)
    fun lazy merge ($ts₁, $ts₂) = $mrg (ts₁, ts₂)

    fun removeMinTree [] = raise EMPTY
      | removeMinTree [t] = (t, [])
      | removeMinTree (t :: ts) =
        let val (t', ts') = removeMinTree ts
        in if Elem.leq (root t, root t') then (t, ts) else (t', t :: ts') end

    fun findMin ($ts) = let val (t, _) = removeMinTree ts in root t end
    fun lazy deleteMin ($ts) =
        let val (NODE (_, x, ts₁), ts₂) = removeMinTree ts
        in $mrg (rev ts₁, ts₂) end
end
```

Figure 6.2. Lazy binomial heaps.

Exercise 6.4 Suppose that we remove the **lazy** keyword from the definitions of merge and deleteMin, so that these functions evaluate their arguments immediately. Show that both functions still run in $O(\log n)$ amortized time.

Exercise 6.5 An unfortunate consequence of suspending the list of trees is that the running time of isEmpty degrades from $O(1)$ worst-case time to $O(\log n)$ amortized time. Restore the $O(1)$ running time of isEmpty by explicitly maintaining the size of every heap. Rather than modifying this implementation directly, implement a functor SizedHeap, similar to the ExplicitMin functor of Exercise 3.7, that transforms any implementation of heaps into one that explicitly maintains the size.

6.4.2 Example: Queues

We next adapt our implementation of queues to use the physicist's method. Again, we show that every operation takes only $O(1)$ amortized time.

Because there is no longer any reason to prefer incremental suspensions over monolithic suspensions, we use suspended lists instead of streams. In fact, the rear list need not be suspended at all, so we represent it with an ordinary list. Again, we explicitly track the lengths of the lists and guarantee that the front list is always at least as long as the rear list.

Since the front list is suspended, we cannot access its first element without executing the entire suspension. We therefore keep a working copy of a prefix of the front list to answer head queries. This working copy is represented as an ordinary list for efficient access, and is non-empty whenever the front list is non-empty. The final type is

type α Queue = α list $\times$ int $\times$ α list susp $\times$ int $\times$ α list

The major functions on queues may then be written

```
fun snoc ((w, lenf, f, lenr, r), x) = check (w, lenf, f, lenr+1, x :: r)
fun head (x :: w, lenf, f, lenr, r) = x
fun tail (x :: w, lenf, f, lenr, r) = check (w, lenf–1, $tl (force f), lenr, r)
```

The helper function check enforces two invariants: that r is no longer than f, and that w is non-empty whenever f is non-empty.

```
fun checkw ([ ], lenf, f, lenr, r) = (force f, lenf, f, lenr, r)
  | checkw q = q
fun check (q as (w, lenf, f, lenr, r)) =
      if lenr ≤ lenf then checkw q
      else let val f' = force f
           in checkw (f', lenf+lenr, $(f' @ rev r), 0, [ ]) end
```

The complete implementation of these queues appears in Figure 6.3.

To analyze these queues using the physicist's method, we choose a potential function Ψ in such a way that the potential is zero whenever we force the suspended list. This happens in two situations: when w becomes empty and when r becomes longer than f. We therefore choose Ψ to be

$$\Psi(q) = \min(2|w|, |f| - |r|)$$

```
structure PhysicistsQueue : QUEUE =
struct
  type α Queue = α list × int × α list susp × int × α list

  val empty = ([ ], 0, $[ ], 0, [ ])
  fun isEmpty (_, lenf, _, _, _) = (lenf = 0)

  fun checkw ([ ], lenf, f, lenr, r) = (force f, lenf, f, lenr, r)
    | checkw q = q
  fun check (q as (w, lenf, f, lenr, r)) =
      if lenr ≤ lenf then checkw q
      else let val f' = force f
           in checkw (f', lenf+lenr, $(f' @ rev r), 0, [ ]) end

  fun snoc ((w, lenf, f, lenr, r), x) = check (w, lenf, f, lenr+1, x :: r)

  fun head ([ ], lenf, f, lenr, r) = raise EMPTY
    | head (x :: w, lenf, f, lenr, r) = x
  fun tail ([ ], lenf, f, lenr, r) = raise EMPTY
    | tail (x :: w, lenf, f, lenr, r) = check (w, lenf−1, $tl (force f), lenr, r)
end
```

Figure 6.3. Amortized queues using the physicist's method.

Theorem 6.2 *The amortized costs of* snoc *and* tail *are at most two and four, respectively.*

Proof Every snoc that does not cause a rotation simply adds a new element to the rear list, increasing $|r|$ by one and decreasing $|f| - |r|$ by one. The complete cost of the snoc is one, and the decrease in potential is at most one, for an amortized cost of at most $1 - (-1) = 2$. Every tail that does not cause a rotation removes the first element from the working list and lazily removes the same element from the front list. This decreases $|w|$ by one and $|f| - |r|$ by one, which decreases the potential by at most two. The complete cost of tail is two, one for the unshared costs (including removing the first element from w) and one for the shared cost of lazily removing the head of f. The amortized cost is therefore at most $2 - (-2) = 4$.

Finally, consider a snoc or tail that causes a rotation. In the initial queue, $|f| = |r|$, so $\Psi = 0$. Just before the rotation, $|f| = m$ and $|r| = m + 1$. The shared cost of the rotation is $2m + 1$ and the potential of the resulting queue is $2m$. The amortized cost of snoc is thus $1 + (2m + 1) - 2m = 2$. The amortized cost of tail is $2 + (2m + 1) - 2m = 3$. (The difference is that tail must also account for the shared cost of removing the first element of f.)

□

```
signature SORTABLE =
sig
   structure Elem : ORDERED

   type Sortable

   val empty : Sortable
   val add    : Elem.T × Sortable → Sortable
   val sort   : Sortable → Elem.T list
end
```

Figure 6.4. Signature for sortable collections.

Exercise 6.6 Show why each of the following proposed "optimizations" actually breaks the $O(1)$ amortized time bounds. These examples illustrate common mistakes in designing persistent amortized data structures.

(a) Observe that check forces *f* during a rotation and installs the result in *w*. Wouldn't it be lazier, and therefore better, to never force *f* until *w* becomes empty?

(b) Observe that, during a tail, we replace *f* with $tl (force *f*). Creating and forcing suspensions have non-trivial overheads that, even if $O(1)$, can contribute to a large constant factor. Wouldn't it be lazier, and therefore better, to not change *f*, but instead to merely decrement *lenf* to indicate that the element has been removed?   ◇

6.4.3 Example: Bottom-Up Mergesort with Sharing

The majority of examples in the remaining chapters use the banker's method rather than the physicist's method. Therefore, we give one more example of the physicist's method here.

Imagine that you want to sort several similar lists, such as *xs* and *x* :: *xs*, or *xs* @ *zs* and *ys* @ *zs*. For efficiency, you wish to take advantage of the fact that these lists share common tails, so that you do not repeat the work of sorting those tails. We call an abstract data type for this problem a *sortable collection*. A signature for sortable collections is given in Figure 6.4.

Now, if we create a sortable collection *xs'* by adding each of the elements in *xs*, then we can sort both *xs* and *x* :: *xs* by calling sort *xs'* and sort (add (*x*, *xs'*)).

We could implement sortable collections as balanced binary search trees. Then add and sort would run in $O(\log n)$ worst-case time and $O(n)$ worst-case time, respectively. We achieve the same bounds, but in an amortized sense, using *bottom-up mergesort*.

Bottom-up mergesort first splits a list into n ordered segments, where each segment initially contains a single element. It then merges equal-sized segments in pairs until only one segment of each size remains. Finally, segments of unequal size are merged, from smallest to largest.

Suppose we take a snapshot just before the final cleanup phase. Then the sizes of all segments are distinct powers of 2, corresponding to the one bits of n. This is the representation we will use for sortable collections. Then similar collections share all the work of bottom-up mergesort except for the final cleanup phase merging unequal-sized segments. The complete representation is a suspended list of segments, each of which is list of elements, together with an integer representing the total size of the collection.

```
type Sortable = int × Elem.T list list susp
```

The individual segments are stored in increasing order of size, and the elements in each segment are stored in increasing order as determined by the comparison functions in the Elem structure.

The fundamental operation on segments is mrg, which merges two ordered lists.

```
fun mrg ([ ], ys) = ys
  | mrg (xs, [ ]) = xs
  | mrg (xs as x :: xs', ys as y :: ys') =
      if Elem.leq (x, y) then x :: mrg (xs', ys) else y :: mrg (xs, ys')
```

To add a new element, we create a new singleton segment. If the smallest existing segment is also a singleton, we merge the two segments and continue merging until the new segment is smaller than the smallest existing segment. This merging is controlled by the bits of the size field. If the lowest bit of size is zero, then we simply cons the new segment onto the segment list. If the lowest bit is one, then we merge the two segments and repeat. Of course, all this is done lazily.

```
fun add (x, (size, segs)) =
      let fun addSeg (seg, segs, size) =
            if size mod 2 = 0 then seg :: segs
            else addSeg (mrg (seg, hd segs), tl segs, size div 2)
      in (size+1, $addSeg ([x], force segs, size)) end
```

Finally, to sort a collection, we merge the segments from smallest to largest.

```
fun sort (size, segs) =
      let fun mrgAll (xs, [ ]) = xs
            | mrgAll (xs, seg :: segs) = mrgAll (mrg (xs, seg), segs)
      in mrgAll ([ ], force segs) end
```

Remark mrgAll can be viewed as computing

$$[\,] \bowtie s_1 \bowtie \cdots \bowtie s_m$$

where s_i is the ith segment and $\bowtie$ is left-associative, infix notation for mrg. This is a specific instance of a very common program schema, which can be written

$$c \oplus x_1 \oplus \cdots \oplus x_m$$

for any c and left-associative $\oplus$. Other instances of this schema include summing a list of integers ($c = 0$ and $\oplus = +$) or finding the maximum of a list of natural numbers ($c = 0$ and $\oplus = $ max). One of the greatest strengths of functional languages is the ability to define schemas like this as *higher-order functions* (i.e., functions that take functions as arguments or return functions as results). For example, the above schema might be written

```
fun foldl (f, c, [ ]) = c
  | foldl (f, c, x :: xs) = foldl (f, f (c, x), xs)
```

Then sort could be written

```
fun sort (size, segs) = foldl (mrg, [ ], force segs)
```

$\diamond$

The complete code for this implementation of sortable collections appears in Figure 6.5.

We show that add takes $O(\log n)$ amortized time and sort takes $O(n)$ amortized time using the physicist's method. We begin by defining the potential function Ψ, which is completely determined by the size of the collection:

$$\Psi(n) = 2n - 2\sum_{i=0}^{\infty} b_i(n \bmod 2^i + 1)$$

where b_i is the ith bit of n. Note that $\Psi(n)$ is bounded above by $2n$ and that $\Psi(n) = 0$ exactly when $n = 2^k - 1$ for some k.

Remark This potential function can be a little intimidating. It arises from considering each segment to have a potential proportional to its own size minus the sizes of all the smaller segments. The intuition is that the potential of a segment starts out big and gets smaller as more elements are added to the collection, reaching zero at the point just before the segment in question is merged with another segment. However, note that you do not need to understand the origins of a potential function to be able to calculate with it. $\diamond$

We first calculate the complete cost of add. Its unshared cost is one and its

```
functor BottomUpMergeSort (Element : ORDERED) : SORTABLE =
struct
  structure Elem = Element

  type Sortable = int × Elem.T list list susp

  fun mrg ([ ], ys) = ys
    | mrg (xs, [ ]) = xs
    | mrg (xs as x :: xs', ys as y :: ys') =
        if Elem.leq (x, y) then x :: mrg (xs', ys) else y :: mrg (xs, ys')

  val empty = (0, $[ ])
  fun add (x, (size, segs)) =
      let fun addSeg (seg, segs, size) =
          if size mod 2 = 0 then seg :: segs
          else addSeg (mrg (seg, hd segs), tl segs, size div 2)
      in (size+1, $addSeg ([x], force segs, size)) end
  fun sort (size, segs) =
      let fun mrgAll (xs, [ ]) = xs
        | mrgAll (xs, seg :: segs) = mrgAll (mrg (xs, seg), segs)
      in mrgAll ([ ], force segs) end
end
```

Figure 6.5. Sortable collections based on bottom-up mergesort.

shared cost is the cost of performing the merges in addSeg. Suppose that the lowest k bits of n are one (i.e., $b_i = 1$ for $i < k$ and $b_k = 0$). Then addSeg performs k merges. The first combines two lists of size 1, the second combines two lists of size 2, and so on. Since merging two lists of size m takes $2m$ steps, addSeg takes

$$(1 + 1) + (2 + 2) + \cdots + (2^{k-1} + 2^{k-1}) = 2(\sum_{i=0}^{k-1} 2^i) = 2(2^k - 1)$$

steps. The complete cost of add is therefore $2(2^k - 1) + 1 = 2^{k+1} - 1$.

Next, we calculate the change in potential. Let $n' = n + 1$ and let b'_i be the ith bit of n'. Then,

$$\Psi(n') - \Psi(n)$$
$$= 2n' - 2\sum_{i=0}^{\infty} b'_i(n' \bmod 2^i + 1) - (2n - 2\sum_{i=0}^{\infty} b_i(n \bmod 2^i + 1))$$
$$= 2 + 2\sum_{i=0}^{\infty} (b_i(n \bmod 2^i + 1) - b'_i(n' \bmod 2^i + 1))$$
$$= 2 + 2\sum_{i=0}^{\infty} \delta(i)$$

where $\delta(i) = b_i(n \bmod 2^i + 1) - b'_i(n' \bmod 2^i + 1)$. We consider three cases: $i < k$, $i = k$, and $i > k$.

- $(i < k)$: Since $b_i = 1$ and $b_i' = 0$, $\delta(k) = n \bmod 2^i + 1$. But $n \bmod 2^i = 2^i - 1$ so $\delta(k) = 2^i$.
- $(i = k)$: Since $b_k = 0$ and $b_k' = 1$, $\delta(k) = -(n' \bmod 2^k + 1)$. But $n' \bmod 2^k = 0$ so $\delta(k) = -1 = -b_k'$.
- $(i > k)$: Since $b_i' = b_i$, $\delta(k) = b_i'(n \bmod 2^i - n' \bmod 2^i)$. But $n' \bmod 2^i = (n+1) \bmod 2^i = n \bmod 2^i + 1$ so $\delta(i) = b_i'(-1) = -b_i'$.

Therefore,

$$
\begin{aligned}
\Psi(n') - \Psi(n) &= 2 + 2\sum_{i=0}^{\infty} \delta(i) \\
&= 2 + 2\sum_{i=0}^{k-1} 2^i + 2\sum_{i=k}^{\infty}(-b_i') \\
&= 2 + 2(2^k - 1) - 2\sum_{i=k}^{\infty} b_i' \\
&= 2^{k+1} - 2B'
\end{aligned}
$$

where B' is the number of one bits in n'. Then the amortized cost of add is

$$
(2^{k+1} - 1) - (2^{k+1} - 2B') = 2B' - 1
$$

Since B' is $O(\log n)$, so is the amortized cost of add.

Finally, we calculate the amortized cost of sort. The first action of sort is to force the suspended list of segments. Since the potential is not necessarily zero, this adds $\Psi(n)$ to the amortized cost of the operation. sort next merges the segments from smallest to largest. The worst case is when $n = 2^k - 1$, so that there is one segment of each size from 1 to 2^{k-1}. Merging these segments takes

$$
(1 + 2) + (1 + 2 + 4) + (1 + 2 + 4 + 8) + \cdots + (1 + 2 + \cdots + 2^{k-1})
$$

$$
= \sum_{i=1}^{k-1} \sum_{j=0}^{i} 2^j = \sum_{i=1}^{k-1}(2^{i+1} - 1) = (2^{k+1} - 4) - (k - 1) = 2n - k - 1
$$

steps altogether. The amortized cost of sort is therefore $O(n) + \Psi(n) = O(n)$.

Exercise 6.7 Change the representation from a suspended list of lists to a list of streams.

(a) Prove the bounds on add and sort using the banker's method.

(b) Write a function to extract the k smallest elements from a sortable collection. Prove that your function runs in no more than $O(k \log n)$ amortized time.

6.5 Lazy Pairing Heaps

Finally, we adapt the pairing heaps of Section 5.5 to cope with persistence. Unfortunately, analyzing the resulting data structure appears to be just as hard as analyzing the original. However, we conjecture that the new implementation is asymptotically as efficient in a persistent setting as the original implementation of pairing heaps is in an ephemeral setting.

Recall that, in the previous implementation of pairing heaps, the children of a node were represented as a Heap list. Deleting the minimum element threw away the root and then merged the children in pairs using the function

```
fun mergePairs [ ] = E
  | mergePairs [h] = h
  | mergePairs (h₁ :: h₂ :: hs) = merge (merge (h₁, h₂), mergePairs hs)
```

If we were to delete the minimum element of the same heap twice, mergePairs would be called twice, duplicating work and destroying any hope of amortized efficiency. To cope with persistence, we must prevent this duplicated work. We once again turn to lazy evaluation. Instead of a Heap list, we represent the children of a node as a Heap susp. The value of this suspension is equal to $mergePairs *cs*. Since mergePairs operates on pairs of children, we extend the suspension with two children at once. Therefore, we include an extra Heap field in each node to hold any partnerless children. If there are no partnerless children (i.e., if the number of children is even), then this extra field is empty. Since this field is in use only when the number of children is odd, we call it the *odd field*. The new datatype is thus

```
datatype Heap = E | T of Elem.T × Heap × Heap susp
```

The insert and findMin operations are almost unchanged.

```
fun insert (x, a) = merge (T (x, E, $E), a)
fun findMin (T (x, a, m)) = x
```

Previously, the merge operation was simple and the deleteMin operation was complex. Now, the situation is reversed—all the complexity of mergePairs has been shifted to merge, which sets up the appropriate suspensions. deleteMin simply forces the heap suspension and merges it with the odd field.

```
fun deleteMin (T (x, a, $b)) = merge (a, b)
```

We define merge in two steps. The first step checks for empty arguments and otherwise compares the two arguments to see which has the smaller root.

```
fun merge (a, E) = a
  | merge (E, b) = b
  | merge (a as T (x, _, _), b as T (y, _, _)) =
      if Elem.leq (x, y) then link (a, b) else link (b, a)
```

```
functor LazyPairingHeap (Element : ORDERED) : HEAP =
struct
   structure Elem = Element

   datatype Heap = E | T of Elem.T × Heap × Heap susp

   val empty = E
   fun isEmpty E = true | isEmpty _ = false

   fun merge (a, E) = a
     | merge (E, b) = b
     | merge (a as T (x, _, _), b as T (y, _, _)) =
          if Elem.leq (x, y) then link (a, b) else link (b, a)
   and link (T (x, E, m), a) = T (x, a, m)
     | link (T (x, b, m), a) = T (x, E, $merge (merge (a, b), force m))

   fun insert (x, a) = merge (T (x, E, $E), a)

   fun findMin E = raise EMPTY
     | findMin (T (x, a, m)) = x
   fun deleteMin E = raise EMPTY
     | deleteMin (T (x, a, $b)) = merge (a, b)
end
```

Figure 6.6. Persistent pairing heaps using lazy evaluation.

The second step, embodied in the link helper function, adds a new child to a node. If the odd field is empty, then this child is placed in the odd field.

```
fun link (T (x, E, m), a) = T (x, a, m)
```

Otherwise, the new child is paired with the child in the odd field, and both are added to the suspension. In other words, we extend the suspension $m = $mergePairs cs to $mergePairs ($a$ :: b :: cs). Observe that

$$\text{\$mergePairs } (a :: b :: cs)$$
$$\equiv \text{\$merge (merge } (a, b), \text{mergePairs } cs)$$
$$\equiv \text{\$merge (merge } (a, b), \text{force (\$mergePairs } cs))$$
$$\equiv \text{\$merge (merge } (a, b), \text{force } m)$$

so the second clause of link may be written

```
fun link (T (x, b, m), a) = T (x, E, $merge (merge (a, b), force m))
```

The complete code for this implementation appears in Figure 6.6.

Hint to Practitioners: Although it now deals gracefully with persistence, this implementation of pairing heaps is relatively slow in practice because of overheads associated with lazy evaluation. It shines, however, under heavily persistent usage, where we reap maximum benefit from memoization. It is also competitive in lazy languages, where all data structures pay the overheads of lazy evaluation regardless of whether they actually gain any benefit.

6.6 Chapter Notes

Debits Some analyses using the traditional banker's method, such as Tarjan's analysis of path compression [Tar83], include both credits and debits. Whenever an operation needs more credits than are currently available, it creates a credit–debit pair and immediately spends the credit. The debit remains as an obligation that must be fulfilled. Later, a surplus credit may be used to discharge the debit.† Any debits that remain at the end of the computation add to the total actual cost. Although there are some similarities between the two kinds of debits, there are also some clear differences. For instance, with the debits introduced in this chapter, any debits leftover at the end of the computation are silently discarded.

It is interesting that debits arise in Tarjan's analysis of path compression since path compression is essentially an application of memoization to the find function.

Amortization and Persistence Until this work, amortization and persistence were thought to be incompatible. Several researchers [DST94, Ram92] had noted that amortized data structures could not be made efficiently persistent using existing techniques for adding persistence to ephemeral data structures, such as [DSST89, Die89], for reasons similar to those cited in Section 5.6. Ironically, these techniques produce persistent data structures with amortized bounds, but the underlying data structure must be worst-case. (These techniques have other limitations as well. Most notably, they cannot be applied to data structures supporting functions that combine two or more versions. Examples of offending functions include list catenation and set union.)

The idea that lazy evaluation could reconcile amortization and persistence first appeared, in rudimentary form, in [Oka95c]. The theory and practice of this technique were further developed in [Oka95a, Oka96b].

---

† There is a clear analogy here to the spontaneous creation and mutual annihilation of particle–antiparticle pairs in physics. In fact, a better name for these debits might be "anticredits".

Amortization and Functional Data Structures In his thesis, Schoenmakers [Sch93] studies amortized data structures in a strict functional language, concentrating on formal derivations of amortized bounds using the traditional physicist's method. He avoids the problems of persistence by insisting that data structures only be used in a single-threaded fashion.

Queues and Binomial Heaps The queues in Section 6.3.2 and the lazy binomial heaps in Section 6.4.1 first appeared in [Oka96b]. The analysis of lazy binomial heaps can also be applied to King's implementation of binomial heaps [Kin94].

Time-Analysis of Lazy Programs Several researchers have developed theoretical frameworks for analyzing the time complexity of lazy programs [BH89, San90, San95, Wad88]. However, these frameworks are not yet mature enough to be useful in practice. One difficulty is that these frameworks are, in some ways, too general. In each of these systems, the cost of a program is calculated with respect to some context, which is a description of how the result of the program will be used. However, this approach is often inappropriate for a methodology of program development in which data structures are designed as abstract data types whose behavior, including time complexity, is specified in isolation. In contrast, our analyses prove results that are independent of context (i.e., that hold regardless of how the data structures are used).

7

Eliminating Amortization

Most of the time, we do not care whether a data structure has amortized bounds or worst-case bounds; our primary criteria for choosing one data structure over another are overall efficiency and simplicity of implementation (and perhaps availability of source code). However, in some application areas, it is important to bound the running times of individual operations, rather than sequences of operations. In these situations, a worst-case data structure will often be preferable to an amortized data structure, even if the amortized data structure is simpler and faster overall. Raman [Ram92] identifies several such application areas, including

- **Real-time systems:** In real-time systems, predictability is more important than raw speed [Sta88]. If an expensive operation causes the system to miss a hard deadline, it does not matter how many cheap operations finished well ahead of schedule.
- **Parallel systems:** If one processor in a synchronous system executes an expensive operation while the other processors execute cheap operations, then the other processors may sit idle until the slow processor finishes.
- **Interactive systems:** Interactive systems are similar to real-time systems — users often value consistency more than raw speed [But83]. For instance, users might prefer 100 1-second response times to 99 0.25-second response times and 1 25-second response time, even though the latter scenario is twice as fast.

Remark Raman also identified a fourth application area — persistent data structures. As discussed in the previous chapter, amortization was thought to be incompatible with persistence. But, of course, we now know this to be untrue. ◇

Does this mean that amortized data structures are of no interest to programmers in these areas? Not at all. Since amortized data structures are often simpler than worst-case data structures, it is sometimes easier to design an amortized data structure, and then convert it to a worst-case data structure, than to design a worst-case data structure from scratch.

In this chapter, we describe *scheduling* — a technique for converting lazy amortized data structures to worst-case data structures by systematically forcing lazy components in such a way that no suspension ever takes very long to execute. Scheduling extends every object with an extra component, called a *schedule*, that regulates the order in which the lazy components of that object are forced.

7.1 Scheduling

Amortized and worst-case data structures differ mainly in when the computations charged to a given operation occur. In a worst-case data structure, all computations charged to an operation occur during the operation. In an amortized data structure, some computations charged to an operation may actually occur during later operations. From this, we see that virtually all nominally worst-case data structures become amortized when implemented in an entirely lazy language because many computations are unnecessarily suspended. To describe true worst-case data structures, we therefore need a strict language. If we want to describe both amortized and worst-case data structures, we need a language that supports both lazy and strict evaluation. Given such a language, we can also consider an intriguing hybrid approach: worst-case data structures that use lazy evaluation internally. We obtain such data structures by beginning with lazy amortized data structures and modifying them in such a way that every operation runs in the allotted time.

In a lazy amortized data structure, any specific operation might take longer than the stated bounds. However, this only occurs when the operation forces a suspension that has been paid off, but that takes a long time to execute. To achieve worst-case bounds, we must guarantee that every suspension executes in no more than the allotted time.

Define the *intrinsic cost* of a suspension to be the amount of time it takes to force the suspension under the assumption that all other suspensions on which it depends have already been forced and memoized, and therefore each take only $O(1)$ time to execute. (This is similar to the definition of the unshared cost of an operation.) The first step in converting an amortized data structure to a worst-case data structure is to reduce the intrinsic cost of every suspension to less than the desired bounds. Usually, this involves rewriting expensive monolithic functions to make them incremental, either by changing the underlying algorithms slightly or by switching from a representation that supports only monolithic functions, such as suspended lists, to one that supports incremental functions as well, such as streams.

Even if every suspension has a small intrinsic cost, some suspensions might still take longer than the allotted time to execute. This happens when one suspension depends on another suspension, which in turn depends on a third, and so on. If none of the suspensions have been executed previously, then forcing the first suspension results in a cascade of forces. For example, consider the following computation:

$$(\cdots((s_1 \mathbin{+\mkern-10mu+} s_2) \mathbin{+\mkern-10mu+} s_3) \mathbin{+\mkern-10mu+} \cdots) \mathbin{+\mkern-10mu+} s_k$$

Forcing the suspension returned by the outermost $\mathbin{+\mkern-10mu+}$ triggers a chain reaction in which every $\mathbin{+\mkern-10mu+}$ executes a single step. Even though the outermost suspension has an $O(1)$ intrinsic cost, the total time required to force this suspension is $O(k)$ (or even more if the first node of s_1 is expensive to force for some other reason).

Remark Have you ever stood dominoes in a row so that each one knocks over the next? Even though the intrinsic cost of knocking over each domino is $O(1)$, the actual cost of knocking over the first domino might be much, much greater. $\diamond$

The second step in converting an amortized data structure to a worst-case data structure is to avoid cascading forces by arranging that, whenever we force a suspension, any other suspensions on which it depends have already been forced and memoized. Then, no suspension takes longer than its intrinsic cost to execute. We accomplish this by systematically *scheduling* the execution of each suspension so that each is ready by the time we need it. The trick is to regard paying off debt as a literal activity, and to force each suspension as it is paid for.

Remark In essence, scheduling is like knocking over a series of dominoes starting from the rear, so that, whenever one domino falls on another, the second domino has already been knocked over. Then the actual cost of knocking over each domino is small. $\diamond$

We extend every object with an extra component, called the *schedule*, that, at least conceptually, contains a pointer to every unevaluated suspension in the object. Some of the suspensions in the schedule may have already been evaluated in a different logical future, but forcing these suspensions a second time does no harm since it can only make an algorithm run faster than expected, not slower. Every operation, in addition to whatever other manipulations it performs on an object, forces the first few suspensions in the schedule. The exact number of suspensions forced is governed by the amortized analysis; typically, every suspension takes $O(1)$ time to execute, so we force a number of suspensions proportional to the amortized cost of the operation. Depending on the data structure, maintaining the schedule can be non-trivial. For this technique to apply, adding a new suspension to the schedule, or retrieving the next suspension to be forced, cannot require more time than the desired worst-case bounds.

7.2 Real-Time Queues

As an example of this technique, we convert the amortized banker's queues of Section 6.3.2 to worst-case queues. Queues such as these that support all operations in $O(1)$ worst-case time are called *real-time queues* [HM81].

In the original data structure, queues are rotated using ++ and reverse. Since reverse is monolithic, our first task is finding a way to perform rotations incrementally. This can be done by executing one step of the reverse for every step of the ++. We define a function rotate such that

$$\text{rotate } (xs, ys, a) \ \equiv \ xs \ ++ \text{ reverse } ys \ ++ \ a$$

Then

$$\text{rotate } (f, r, \$\text{N{\scriptsize IL}}) \ \equiv \ f \ ++ \text{ reverse } r$$

The extra argument, *a*, is called an *accumulating parameter* and is used to accumulate the partial results of reversing *ys*. It is initially empty.

Rotations occur when $|r| = |f| + 1$, so initially $|ys| = |xs| + 1$. This relationship is preserved throughout the rotation, so when *xs* is empty, *ys* contains a single element. The base case is therefore

```
rotate ($NIL, $CONS (y, $NIL), a)
  ≡ ($NIL) ++ reverse ($CONS (y, $NIL)) ++ a
  ≡ $CONS (y, a)
```

In the recursive case,

```
rotate ($CONS (x, xs), $CONS (y, ys), a)
  ≡ ($CONS (x, xs)) ++ reverse ($CONS (y, ys)) ++ a
  ≡ $CONS (x, xs ++ reverse ($CONS (y, ys)) ++ a)
  ≡ $CONS (x, xs ++ reverse ys ++ $CONS (y, a))
  ≡ $CONS (x, rotate (xs, ys, $CONS (y, a)))
```

Putting these cases together, we get

```
fun rotate ($NIL, $CONS (y, _), a) = $CONS (y, a)
  | rotate ($CONS (x, xs), $CONS (y, ys), a) =
     $CONS (x, rotate (xs, ys, $CONS (y, a)))
```

Note that the intrinsic cost of every suspension created by rotate is $O(1)$.

Exercise 7.1 Show that replacing f ++ reverse r with rotate $(f, r, \$NIL)$ in the banker's queues of Section 6.3.2 reduces the worst-case running times of snoc, head, and tail from $O(n)$ to $O(\log n)$. (Hint: Prove that the longest chain of dependencies between suspensions is $O(\log n)$.) If it makes your analysis simpler, you may delay the pattern matching in the rotate function by writing **fun lazy** instead of **fun** . ◇

Next, we add a schedule to the datatype. The original datatype was

type α Queue = int $\times$ α Stream $\times$ int $\times$ α Stream

We extend this type with a new field s of type α Stream that represents a schedule for forcing the nodes of f. We can think of s in two ways, either as a suffix of f or as a pointer to the first unevaluated suspension in f. To evaluate the next suspension in the schedule, we simply force s.

Besides adding s, we make two further changes to the datatype. First, to emphasize the fact that the nodes of r need not be scheduled, we change r from a stream to a list. This involves minor changes to rotate. Second, we eliminate the length fields. As we will see shortly, we no longer need the length fields to determine when r becomes longer than f — instead, we can obtain this information from the schedule. The new datatype is thus

type α Queue = α Stream $\times$ α list $\times$ α Stream

Remark The savings in space from using three-tuples instead of four-tuples can make this change in representation worthwhile even if we don't care about worst-case bounds. ◇

With this representation, the major queue functions are simply

```
fun snoc ((f, r, s), x) = exec (f, x :: r, s)
fun head ($CONS (x, f), r, s) = x
fun tail ($CONS (x, f), r, s) = exec (f, r, s)
```

The helper function **exec** executes the next suspension in the schedule and maintains the invariant that $|s| = |f| - |r|$ (which incidentally guarantees that $|f| \geq |r|$ since $|s|$ cannot be negative). snoc increases $|r|$ by one and tail decreases $|f|$ by one, so when exec is called, $|s| = |f| - |r| + 1$. If s is non-empty, then we restore the invariant simply by taking the tail of s. If s is empty, then

```
structure RealTimeQueue : QUEUE =
struct
  type α Queue = α Stream × α list × α Stream

  val empty = ($NIL, [ ], $NIL)
  fun isEmpty ($NIL, _, _) = true
    | isEmpty _ = false

  fun rotate ($NIL, y :: _, a) = $CONS (y, a)
    | rotate ($CONS (x, xs), y :: ys, a) =
        $CONS (x, rotate (xs, ys, $CONS (y, a)))

  fun exec (f, r, $CONS (x, s)) = (f, r, s)
    | exec (f, r, $NIL) = let val f' = rotate (f, r, $NIL) in (f', [ ], f') end

  fun snoc ((f, r, s), x) = exec (f, x :: r, s)

  fun head ($NIL, r, s) = raise EMPTY
    | head ($CONS (x, f), r, s) = x
  fun tail ($NIL, r, s) = raise EMPTY
    | tail ($CONS (x, f), r, s) = exec (f, r, s)
end
```

Figure 7.1. Real-time queues based on scheduling.

r is one longer than f, so we rotate the queue. In either case, the very act of pattern matching against s to determine whether or not it is empty forces and memoizes the next suspension in the schedule.

```
fun exec (f, r, $CONS (x, s)) = (f, r, s)
  | exec (f, r, $NIL) = let val f' = rotate (f, r, $NIL) in (f', [ ], f') end
```

The complete code for this implementation appears in Figure 7.1.

By inspection, every queue operation does only $O(1)$ work outside of forcing suspensions, and no operation forces more than three suspensions. Hence, to show that all queue operations run in $O(1)$ worst-case time, we must prove that no suspension takes more than $O(1)$ time to execute.

Only three forms of suspensions are created by the various queue functions.

- $NIL is created by empty and exec (in the initial call to rotate). This suspension is trivial and therefore executes in $O(1)$ time regardless of whether it has been forced and memoized previously.

- $CONS (y, a) is created in both lines of rotate and is also trivial.

- $CONS $(x,$ rotate $(xs, ys, $CONS $(y, a)))$ is created in the second line of rotate. This suspension allocates a CONS cell, builds a new suspension, and makes a recursive call to rotate, which pattern matches against the first node in xs and immediately creates another suspension. Of these actions, only the force inherent in the pattern match has even the possibility of taking more than $O(1)$ time. But note that xs is a suffix of the front stream that existed just before the previous rotation. The treatment of the schedule s guarantees that *every* node in that stream was forced and memoized prior to the rotation, so forcing this node again takes only $O(1)$ time.

Since every suspension executes in $O(1)$ time, every queue operation runs in $O(1)$ worst-case time.

> **Hint to Practitioners:** These queues are by far the simplest of the real-time implementations. They are also among the fastest known implementations—worst-case or amortized—for applications that use persistence heavily.

Exercise 7.2 Compute the size of a queue from the sizes of s and r. How much faster might such a function run than one that measures the sizes of f and r?

7.3 Binomial Heaps

We next return to the lazy binomial heaps from Section 6.4.1, and use scheduling to support insertions in $O(1)$ worst-case time. Recall that, in the earlier implementation, the representation of the heap was a Tree list susp, so insert was necessarily monolithic. Our first goal is to make insert incremental.

We begin by substituting streams for suspended lists in the type of heaps. The insert function calls the insTree helper function, which can now be written as follows:

```
fun lazy insTree (t, $NIL) = $CONS (t, $NIL)
   | insTree (t, ts as $CONS (t', ts')) =
       if rank t < rank t' then $CONS (t, ts)
       else insTree (link (t, t'), ts')
```

This function is still monolithic because it cannot return the first tree until it has performed all the links. To make this function incremental, we need a way for insTree to return a partial result after each iteration. We can achieve this by making the connection between binomial heaps and binary numbers more explicit. The trees in the heap correspond to the ones in the binary representation of the size of the heap. We extend this with an explicit representation of the zeros.

```
datatype Tree = NODE of Elem.T × Tree list
datatype Digit = ZERO | ONE of Tree
type Heap = Digit Stream
```

Note that we have eliminated the rank field in the NODE constructor because the rank of each tree is uniquely determined by its position: a tree in the ith digit has rank i, and the children of a rank r node have ranks $r-1, \ldots, 0$. In addition, we will insist that every non-empty digit stream end in a ONE.

Now insTree can be written

```
fun lazy insTree (t, $NIL) = $CONS (ONE t, $NIL)
       | insTree (t, $CONS (ZERO, ds)) = $CONS (ONE t, ds)
       | insTree (t, $CONS (ONE t', ds)) =
           $CONS (ZERO, insTree (link (t, t'), ds))
```

This function is properly incremental since each intermediate step returns a CONS cell containing a ZERO and a suspension for the rest of the computation. The final step always returns a ONE.

Next, we add a schedule to the datatype. The schedule is a list of jobs, where each job is a Digit Stream representing a call to insTree that has not yet been fully executed.

```
type Schedule = Digit Stream list
type Heap = Digit Stream × Schedule
```

To execute one step of the schedule, we force the head of the first job. If the result is a ONE, then this job is finished so we delete it from the schedule. If the result is a ZERO, then we put the rest of the job back in the schedule.

```
fun exec [ ] = [ ]
   | exec (($CONS (ONE t, _)) :: sched) = sched
   | exec (($CONS (ZERO, job)) :: sched) = job :: sched
```

Finally, we update insert to maintain the schedule. Since the amortized cost of insert was two, we guess that executing two steps per insert will be enough to force every suspension by the time it is needed.

```
fun insert (x, (ds, sched)) =
   let val ds' = insTree (NODE (x, [ ]), ds)
   in (ds', exec (exec (ds' :: sched))) end
```

To show that insert runs in $O(1)$ worst-case time, we need to show that exec runs in $O(1)$ worst-case time. In particular, we need to show that, whenever exec forces a suspension (by pattern matching against it), any other suspensions on which the first suspension depends have already been forced and memoized.

If we expand the **fun lazy** syntax in the definition of insTree and simplify slightly, we see that insTree produces a suspension equivalent to

$case *ds* **of**
    $NIL ⇒ CONS (ONE t, $NIL)
    | $CONS (ZERO, *ds'*) ⇒ CONS (ONE *t*, *ds'*)
    | $CONS (ONE *t'*, *ds'*) ⇒ CONS (ZERO, insTree (link (*t*, *t'*), *ds'*))

The suspension for each digit produced by insTree depends on the suspension for the previous digit at the same index. We prove that there is never more than one outstanding suspension per index of the digit stream and hence that no unevaluated suspension depends on another unevaluated suspension.

Define the *range* of a job in the schedule to be the collection of digits produced by the corresponding call to insTree. Each range comprises a possibly empty sequence of ZEROs followed by a ONE. We say that two ranges *overlap* if any of their digits have the same index within the stream of digits. Every unevaluated digit is in the range of some job in the schedule, so we need to prove that no two ranges overlap.

In fact, we prove a slightly stronger result. Define a *completed zero* to be a ZERO whose cell in the stream has already been evaluated and memoized.

Theorem 7.1 *Every valid heap contains at least two completed zeros prior to the first range in the schedule, and at least one completed zero between every two adjacent ranges in the schedule.*

Proof Let r_1 and r_2 be the first two ranges in the schedule. Let z_1 and z_2 be the two completed zeros before r_1, and let z_3 be the completed zero between r_1 and r_2. insert adds a new range r_0 to the front of the schedule and then immediately calls exec twice. Note that r_0 terminates in a ONE that replaces z_1. Let m be the number of ZEROs in r_0. There are three cases.

Case 1. $m = 0$. The only digit in r_0 is a ONE, so r_0 is eliminated by the first exec. The second exec forces the first digit of r_1. If this digit is ZERO, then it becomes the second completed zero (along with z_2) before the first range. If this digit is ONE, then r_1 is eliminated and r_2 becomes the new first range. The two completed zeros prior to r_2 are z_2 and z_3.

Case 2. $m = 1$. The two digits in r_0 are ZERO and ONE. These digits are immediately forced by the two execs, eliminating r_0. The leading ZERO replaces z_1 as one of the two completed zeros before r_1.

Case 3. $m \geq 2$. The first two digits of r_0 are both ZEROs. After the two calls to exec, these digits become the two completed zeros before the new first range (the rest of r_0). z_2 becomes the single completed zero between r_0 and r_1.

□

Exercise 7.3 Show that it does no harm to the running time of insert to remove the **lazy** annotation from the definition of insTree.   ◇

Adapting the remaining functions to the new types is fairly straightforward. The complete implementation is shown in Figure 7.2. Four points about this code deserve further comment. First, rather than trying to do something clever with the schedule, merge and deleteMin evaluate every suspension in the system (using the function normalize) and set the schedule to [ ]. Second, by Theorem 7.1, no heap contains more than $O(\log n)$ unevaluated suspensions, so forcing these suspensions during normalization or while searching for the minimum root does not affect the asymptotic running-times of merge, find-Min, or deleteMin, each of which runs in $O(\log n)$ worst-case time. Third, the helper function removeMinTree sometimes produces digit streams with trailing ZEROs, but these streams are either discarded by findMin or merged with a list of ONEs by deleteMin. Finally, deleteMin must do a little more work than in previous implementations to convert a list of children into a valid heap. In addition to reversing the list, deleteMin must add a ONE to every tree and then convert the list to a stream. If c is the list of children, then this whole process can be written

        listToStream (map ONE (rev c))

where

        fun listToStream [ ] = $NIL
          | listToStream (x :: xs) = $CONS (x, listToStream xs)
        fun map f [ ] = [ ]
          | map f (x :: xs) = (f x) :: (map f xs)

map is the standard function for applying another function (in this case, the ONE constructor) to every element of a list.

Exercise 7.4 Write an efficient, specialized version of mrg, called mrgWith-List, so that deleteMin can call

        mrgWithList (rev c, ds')

instead of

        mrg (listToStream (map ONE (rev c)), ds')

```
functor ScheduledBinomialHeap (Element : ORDERED) : HEAP =
struct
  structure Elem = Element

  datatype Tree = NODE of Elem.T × Tree list
  datatype Digit = ZERO | ONE of Tree
  type Schedule = Digit Stream list
  type Heap = Digit Stream × Schedule

  val empty = ($NIL, [])
  fun isEmpty ($NIL, _) = true | isEmpty _ = false

  fun link (t₁ as NODE (x₁, c₁), t₂ as NODE (x₂, c₂)) =
      if Elem.leq (x₁,x₂) then NODE (x₁, t₂ :: c₁) else NODE (x₂, t₁ :: c₂)
  fun insTree (t, $NIL) = $CONS (ONE t, $NIL)
    | insTree (t, $CONS (ZERO, ds)) = $CONS (ONE t, ds)
    | insTree (t, $CONS (ONE t', ds)) =
        $CONS (ZERO, insTree (link (t, t'), ds))
  fun mrg (ds₁, $NIL) = ds₁
    | mrg ($NIL, ds₂) = ds₂
    | mrg ($CONS (ZERO,ds₁), $CONS (d,ds₂)) = $CONS (d,mrg (ds₁,ds₂))
    | mrg ($CONS (d,ds₁), $CONS (ZERO,ds₂)) = $CONS (d,mrg (ds₁,ds₂))
    | mrg ($CONS (ONE t₁, ds₁), $CONS (ONE t₂, ds₂)) =
        $CONS (ZERO, insTree (link (t₁, t₂), mrg (ds₁, ds₂)))

  fun normalize (ds as $NIL) = ds
    | normalize (ds as $CONS (_, ds')) = (normalize ds'; ds)
  fun exec [] = []
    | exec (($CONS (ZERO, job)) :: sched) = job :: sched
    | exec (_ :: sched) = sched

  fun insert (x, (ds, sched)) =
      let val ds' = insTree (NODE (x, []), ds)
      in (ds', exec (exec (ds' :: sched))) end
  fun merge ((ds₁, _), (ds₂, _)) =
      let val ds = normalize (mrg (ds₁, ds₂)) in (ds, []) end

  fun removeMinTree ($NIL) = raise EMPTY
    | removeMinTree ($CONS (ONE t, $NIL)) = (t, $NIL)
    | removeMinTree ($CONS (ZERO, ds)) =
        let val (t',ds') = removeMinTree ds in (t',$CONS (ZERO,ds')) end
    | removeMinTree ($CONS (ONE (t as NODE (x, _)), ds)) =
        case removeMinTree ds of
          (t' as NODE (x', _), ds') ⇒
            if Elem.leq (x, x') then (t, $CONS (ZERO, ds))
            else (t', $CONS (ONE t, ds'))
  fun findMin (ds, _) =
      let val (NODE (x, _), _) = removeMinTree ds in x end
  fun deleteMin (ds, _) =
      let val (NODE (x, c), ds') = removeMinTree ds
          val ds'' = mrg (listToStream (map ONE (rev c)), ds')
      in (normalize ds'', []) end
end
```

Figure 7.2. Scheduled binomial heaps.

7.4 Bottom-Up Mergesort with Sharing

As a third example of scheduling, we modify the sortable collections from Section 6.4.3 to support add in $O(\log n)$ worst-case time and sort in $O(n)$ worst-case time.

The only use of lazy evaluation in the amortized implementation is the suspended call to addSeg in add. This suspension is monolithic, so the first task is to perform this computation incrementally. In fact, we need only make mrg incremental: since addSeg takes only $O(\log n)$ steps, we can afford to execute it strictly. We therefore represent segments as streams rather than lists, and eliminate the suspension on the collection of segments. The new type for the collection of segments is thus Elem.T Stream list rather than Elem.T list list susp.

Rewriting mrg, add, and sort to use this new type is straightforward, except that sort must convert the final sorted stream back to a list. This is accomplished by the streamToList conversion function.

```
fun streamToList ($NIL) = [ ]
  | streamToList ($CONS (x, xs)) = x :: streamToList xs
```

The new version of mrg, shown in Figure 7.3, performs one step of the merge at a time, with an $O(1)$ intrinsic cost per step. Our second goal is to execute enough merge steps per add to guarantee that any sortable collection contains only $O(n)$ unevaluated suspensions. Then sort executes at most $O(n)$ unevaluated suspensions in addition to its own $O(n)$ work. Executing these unevaluated suspensions takes at most $O(n)$ time, so sort takes only $O(n)$ time altogether.

In the amortized analysis, the amortized cost of add was approximately $2B'$, where B' is the number of one bits in $n' = n+1$. This suggests that add should execute two suspensions per one bit, or equivalently, two suspensions per segment. We maintain a separate schedule for each segment. Each schedule is a list of streams, each of which represents a call to mrg that has not yet been fully evaluated. The complete type is therefore

```
type Schedule = Elem.T Stream list
type Sortable = int × (Elem.T Stream × Schedule) list
```

To execute one merge step from a schedule, we call the function exec1.

```
fun exec1 [ ] = [ ]
  | exec1 (($NIL) :: sched) = exec1 sched
  | exec1 (($CONS (x, xs)) :: sched) = xs :: sched
```

In the second clause, we reach the end of one stream and execute the first step of the next stream. This cannot loop because only the first stream in a schedule can ever be empty. The function exec2 takes a segment and invokes exec1 twice on the schedule.

fun exec2 (*xs, sched*) = (*xs*, exec1 (exec1 *sched*))

Now, add calls exec2 on every segment, but it is also responsible for building the schedule for the new segment. If the lowest k bits of n are one, then adding a new element will trigger k merges, of the form

$$\left(\left(s_0 \bowtie s_1\right) \bowtie s_2\right) \bowtie \cdots \bowtie s_k$$

where s_0 is the new singleton segment and $s_1 \ldots s_k$ are the first k segments of the existing collection. The partial results of this computation are $s_1' \ldots s_k'$, where $s_1' = s_0 \bowtie s_1$ and $s_i' = s_{i-1}' \bowtie s_i$. Since the suspensions in s_i' depend on the suspensions in s_{i-1}', we must schedule the execution of s_{i-1}' before the execution of s_i'. The suspensions in s_i' also depend on the suspensions in s_i, but we guarantee that $s_1 \ldots s_k$ have been completely evaluated at the time of the call to add.

The final version of add, which creates the new schedule and executes two suspensions per segment, is

```
fun add (x, (size, segs)) =
    let fun addSeg (xs, segs, size, rsched) =
        if size mod 2 = 0 then (xs, rev rsched) :: segs
        else let val ((xs', []) :: segs') = segs
                 val xs'' = mrg (xs, xs')
             in addSeg (xs'', segs', size div 2, xs'' :: rsched) end
        val segs' = addSeg ($CONS (x, $NIL), segs, size, [])
    in (size+1, map exec2 segs') end
```

The accumulating parameter *rsched* collects the newly merged streams in reverse order. Therefore, we reverse it back to the correct order on the last step. The pattern match in line 4 asserts that the old schedule for that segment is empty, i.e., that it has already been completely executed. We will see shortly why this true.

The complete code for this implementation is shown in Figure 7.3. add has an unshared cost of $O(\log n)$ and sort has an unshared cost of $O(n)$, so to prove the desired worst-case bounds, we must show that the $O(\log n)$ suspensions forced by add take $O(1)$ time each, and that the $O(n)$ unevaluated suspensions forced by sort take $O(n)$ time altogether.

Every merge step forced by add (through exec2 and exec1) depends on two other streams. If the current step is part of the stream s_i', then it depends on the streams s_{i-1}' and s_i. The stream s_{i-1}' was scheduled before s_i', so s_{i-1}' has been completely evaluated by the time we begin evaluating s_i'. Furthermore, s_i was completely evaluated before the add that created s_i'. Since the intrinsic cost of each merge step is $O(1)$, and the suspensions forced by each step have

Eliminating Amortization

```
functor ScheduledBottomUpMergeSort (Element : ORDERED) : SORTABLE =
struct
    structure Elem = Element

    type Schedule = Elem.T Stream list
    type Sortable = int × (Elem.T Stream × Schedule) list

    fun lazy mrg ($NIL, ys) = ys
      | mrg (xs, $NIL) = xs
      | mrg (xs as $CONS (x, xs'), ys as $CONS (y, ys')) =
          if Elem.leq (x, y) then $CONS (x, mrg (xs', ys))
          else $CONS (y, mrg (xs, ys'))

    fun exec1 [] = []
      | exec1 (($NIL) :: sched) = exec1 sched
      | exec1 (($CONS (x, xs)) :: sched) = xs :: sched
    fun exec2 (xs, sched) = (xs, exec1 (exec1 sched))

    val empty = (0, [])
    fun add (x, (size, segs)) =
        let fun addSeg (xs, segs, size, rsched) =
                if size mod 2 = 0 then (xs, rev rsched) :: segs
                else let val ((xs', []) :: segs') = segs
                         val xs'' = mrg (xs, xs')
                     in addSeg (xs'', segs', size div 2, xs'' :: rsched)
            val segs' = addSeg ($CONS (x, $NIL), segs, size, [])
        in (size+1, map exec2 segs') end
    fun sort (size, segs) =
        let fun mrgAll (xs, []) = xs
              | mrgAll (xs, (xs', _) :: segs) = mrgAll (mrg (xs, xs'), segs)
        in streamToList (mrgAll ($NIL, segs)) end
end
```

Figure 7.3. Scheduled bottom-up mergesort.

already been forced and memoized, every merge step forced by add takes only
$O(1)$ worst-case time.

The following lemma establishes both that any segment involved in a merge
by addSeg has been completely evaluated and that the collection as a whole
contains at most $O(n)$ unevaluated suspensions.

Lemma 7.2 *In any sortable collection of size n, the schedule for a segment of
size $m = 2^k$ contains a total of at most $2m - 2(n \bmod m + 1)$ elements.*

Proof Consider a sortable collection of size n, where the lowest k bits of n are
ones (i.e., n can be written $c2^{k+1} + (2^k - 1)$, for some integer c). Then add
produces a new segment of size $m = 2^k$, whose schedule contains streams of
sizes $2, 4, 8, \ldots, 2^k$. The total size of this schedule is $2^{k+1} - 2 = 2m - 2$. After

executing two steps, the size of the schedule is $2m - 4$. The size of the new collection is $n' = n + 1 = c2^{k+1} + 2^k$. Since $2m - 4 < 2m - 2(n' \bmod m + 1) = 2m - 2$, the lemma holds for this segment.

Every segment of size m' larger than m is unaffected by the add, except for the execution of two steps from the segment's schedule. The size of the new schedule is bounded by

$$2m' - 2(n \bmod m' + 1) - 2 = 2m' - 2(n' \bmod m' + 1),$$

so the lemma holds for these segments as well. $\quad\square$

Now, whenever the k lowest bits of n are ones (i.e., whenever the next add will merge the first k segments), we know by Lemma 7.2 that, for any segment of size $m = 2^i$, where $i < k$, the number of elements in that segment's schedule is at most

$$2m - 2(n \bmod m + 1) = 2m - 2((m - 1) + 1) = 0$$

In other words, that segment has been completely evaluated.

Finally, the combined schedules for all segments comprise at most

$$2 \sum_{i=0}^{\infty} b_i(2^i - (n \bmod 2^i + 1)) = 2n - 2 \sum_{i=0}^{\infty} b_i(n \bmod 2^i + 1)$$

elements, where b_i is the ith bit of n. Note the similarity to the potential function from the physicist's analysis in Section 6.4.3. Since this total is bounded by $2n$, the collection as a whole contains only $O(n)$ unevaluated suspensions, and therefore sort runs in $O(n)$ worst-case time.

7.5 Chapter Notes

Eliminating Amortization Dietz and Raman [DR91, DR93, Ram92] have devised a framework for eliminating amortization based on *pebble games*, where the derived worst-case algorithms correspond to winning strategies in some game. Others have used ad hoc techniques similar to scheduling to eliminate amortization from specific data structures such as *implicit binomial queues* [CMP88] and *relaxed heaps* [DGST88]. The form of scheduling described here was first applied to queues in [Oka95c] and later generalized in [Oka96b].

Queues The queue implementation in Section 7.2 first appeared in [Oka95c]. Hood and Melville [HM81] presented the first purely functional implementation of real-time queues, based on a technique known as *global rebuild-*

ing [Ove83], which will be discussed further in the next chapter. Their implementation does not use lazy evaluation and is more complicated than ours.

8
Lazy Rebuilding

The remaining four chapters describe general techniques for designing functional data structures. We begin in this chapter with *lazy rebuilding*, a variant of *global rebuilding* [Ove83].

8.1 Batched Rebuilding

Many data structures obey balance invariants that guarantee efficient access. The canonical example is balanced binary search trees, which improve the worst-case running times of many tree operations from the $O(n)$ required by unbalanced trees to $O(\log n)$. One approach to maintaining a balance invariant is to rebalance the structure after every update. For most balanced structures, there is a notion of *perfect balance*, which is a configuration that minimizes the cost of subsequent operations. However, since it is usually too expensive to restore perfect balance after every update, most implementations settle for approximations of perfect balance that are at most a constant factor slower. Examples of this approach include AVL trees [AVL62] and red-black trees [GS78].

However, provided no update disturbs the balance too drastically, an attractive alternative is to postpone rebalancing until after a sequence of updates, and then to rebalance the entire structure, restoring it to perfect balance. We call this approach *batched rebuilding*. Batched rebuilding yields good amortized time bounds provided that (1) the data structure is not rebuilt too often, and (2) individual updates do not excessively degrade the performance of later operations. More precisely, condition (1) states that, if one hopes to achieve a bound of $O(f(n))$ amortized time per operation, and the rebuilding transformation requires $O(g(n))$ time, then the rebuilding transformation cannot be executed any more frequently than every $c \cdot g(n)/f(n)$ operations, for some constant c. For example, consider binary search trees. Rebuilding a tree to per-

99

fect balance takes $O(n)$ time, so if one wants each operation to take $O(\log n)$ amortized time, then the data structure must not be rebuilt more often than every $c \cdot n/\log n$ operations, for some constant c.

Assume that a data structure is to be rebuilt every $c \cdot g(n)/f(n)$ operations, and that an individual operation on a newly rebuilt data structure takes $O(f(n))$ time (worst-case or amortized). Then, condition (2) states that, after up to $c \cdot g(n)/f(n)$ updates to a newly rebuilt data structure, individual operations must still take only $O(f(n))$ time. In other words, the cost of an individual operation can only degrade by a constant factor. Update functions satisfying condition (2) are called *weak updates*.

For example, consider the following approach to implementing a delete function on binary search trees. Instead of physically removing the specified node from the tree, leave it in the tree but mark it as deleted. Then, whenever half the nodes in the tree have been deleted, make a global pass removing the deleted nodes and restoring the tree to perfect balance. Does this approach satisfy both conditions, assuming we want deletions to take $O(\log n)$ amortized time?

Suppose a tree contains n nodes, up to half of which are marked as deleted. Then removing the deleted nodes and restoring the tree to perfect balance takes $O(n)$ time. We execute the transformation only every $\frac{1}{2}n$ delete operations, so condition (1) is satisfied. In fact, condition (1) would allow us to rebuild the data structure even more often, as often as every $c \cdot n/\log n$ operations. The naive delete algorithm finds the desired node and marks it as deleted. This takes $O(\log n)$ time, even if up to half the nodes have been marked as deleted, so condition (2) is satisfied. Note that, even if half the nodes in the tree are marked as deleted, the average depth per active node is only about one greater than it would be if the deleted nodes had been physically removed. The extra depth degrades each operation by only a constant additive factor, whereas condition (2) allows for each operation to be degraded by a constant multiplicative factor. Hence, condition (2) would allow us to rebuild the data structure even less often.

In the above discussion, we described only deletions, but of course binary search trees typically support insertions as well. Unfortunately, insertions are not weak because they can create a deep path very quickly. However, a hybrid approach is possible, in which insertions are handled by local rebalancing after every update, as in AVL trees or red-black trees, but deletions are handled via batched rebuilding.

Exercise 8.1 Extend the red-black trees of Section 3.3 with a delete function using these ideas. Add a boolean field to the T constructor and maintain estimates of the numbers of valid and invalid elements in the tree. Assume for the purposes of these estimates that every insertion adds a new valid element and that every deletion invalidates a previously valid element. Correct the estimates during rebuilding. You will find Exercise 3.9 helpful in rebuilding the tree. ◇

As a second example of batched rebuilding, consider the batched queues of Section 5.2. The rebuilding transformation reverses the rear list into the front list, restoring the queue to a state of perfect balance in which every element is contained in the front list. As we have already seen, batched queues have good amortized efficiency, but only when used ephemerally. Under persistent usage, the amortized bounds degrade to the cost of the rebuilding transformation because it is possible to trigger the transformation arbitrarily often. In fact, this is true for all data structures based on batched rebuilding.

8.2 Global Rebuilding

Overmars [Ove83] describes a technique for eliminating the amortization from batched rebuilding. He calls this technique *global rebuilding*. The basic idea is to execute the rebuilding transformation incrementally, performing a few steps per normal operation. This can be usefully viewed as running the rebuilding transformation as a coroutine. The tricky part of global rebuilding is that the coroutine must be started early enough that it can finish by the time the rebuilt structure is needed.

Concretely, global rebuilding is accomplished by maintaining two copies of each object. The primary, or *working*, copy is the ordinary structure. The secondary copy is the one that is being gradually rebuilt. All queries and updates operate on the working copy. When the secondary copy is completed, it becomes the new working copy and the old working copy is discarded. A new secondary copy might be started immediately, or the object may carry on for a while without a secondary structure, before eventually starting the next rebuilding phase.

There is a further complication to handle updates that occur while the secondary copy is being rebuilt. The working copy will be updated in the normal fashion, but the secondary copy must be updated as well or the effect of the update will be lost when the secondary copy takes over. However, the secondary copy will not in general be represented in a form that can be efficiently updated. Thus, these updates to the secondary copy are buffered and executed, a few at a time, after the secondary copy has been rebuilt, but before it takes over as the working copy.

Global rebuilding can be implemented purely functionally, and has been several times. For example, the real-time queues of Hood and Melville [HM81] are based on this technique. Unlike batched rebuilding, global rebuilding has no problems with persistence. Since no one operation is particularly expensive, arbitrarily repeating operations has no effect on the time bounds. Unfortunately, global rebuilding is often quite complicated. In particular, representing the secondary copy, which amounts to capturing the intermediate state of a coroutine, can be quite messy.

8.2.1 Example: Hood–Melville Real-Time Queues

Hood and Melville's implementation of real-time queues [HM81] is similar in many ways to the real-time queues of Section 7.2. Both implementations maintain two lists representing the front and rear of the queue, respectively, and incrementally rotate elements from the rear list to the front list beginning when the rear list becomes one longer than the front list. The differences lie in the details of this incremental rotation.

First, consider how we might reverse a list in an incremental fashion by keeping two lists and gradually transferring elements from one to the other.

datatype α ReverseState = WORKING **of** α list $\times$ α list | DONE **of** α list

fun startReverse xs = WORKING $(xs, [\,])$

fun exec (WORKING $(x :: xs, xs')$) = WORKING $(xs, x :: xs')$
  | exec (WORKING $([\,], xs')$) = DONE xs'

To reverse a list xs, we first create a new state WORKING $(xs, [\,])$ and then repeatedly call exec until it returns DONE with the reversed list. Altogether, this takes $n + 1$ calls to exec, where n is the initial length of xs.

We can incrementally append two lists xs and ys by applying this trick twice. First we reverse xs to get xs', then we reverse xs' onto ys.

datatype α AppendState =
  REVERSING **of** α list $\times$ α list $\times$ α list
  | APPENDING **of** α list $\times$ α list
  | DONE **of** α list

fun startAppend (xs, ys) = REVERSING $(xs, [\,], ys)$

fun exec (REVERSING $(x :: xs, xs', ys)$) = REVERSING $(xs, x :: xs', ys)$
  | exec (REVERSING $([\,], xs', ys)$) = APPENDING (xs', ys)
  | exec (APPENDING $(x :: xs', ys)$) = APPENDING $(xs', x :: ys)$
  | exec (APPENDING $([\,], ys)$) = DONE ys

Altogether, this takes $2m + 2$ calls to exec, where m is the initial length of xs.

Now, to append f onto reverse r in this fashion, we perform a total of three reversals. First, we reverse f and r in parallel to get f' and r' and then we reverse f' onto r'. The following code assumes that r is initially one longer than f.

datatype α RotationState =
   REVERSING **of** α list $\times$ α list $\times$ α list $\times$ α list
   | APPENDING **of** α list $\times$ α list
   | DONE **of** α list

fun startRotation (f, r) = REVERSING $(f, [\,], r, [\,])$

fun exec (REVERSING $(x :: f, f', y :: r, r')$) = REVERSING $(f, x :: f', r, y :: r')$
   | exec (REVERSING $([\,], f', [y], r')$) = APPENDING $(f', y :: r')$
   | exec (APPENDING $(x :: f', r')$) = APPENDING $(f', x :: r')$
   | exec (APPENDING $([\,], r')$) = DONE r'

Again, this finishes after a total of $2m + 2$ calls to exec, where m is the initial length of f.

Unfortunately, there is a major problem with this method of performing rotations. If we only call exec a few times per call to snoc or tail, then by the time the rotation finishes, the answer may no longer be the one we want! In particular, if tail has been called k times during the rotation, then the first k elements of the resulting list are invalid. There are two basic ways we can fix this problem. One is to keep a count of the number of invalid elements and extend RotationState with a third phase, Deleting, that deletes elements from the list a few at a time until there are no more invalid elements. This is the approach that corresponds most closely with the definition of global rebuilding. However, a better approach in this case is to avoid placing the invalid elements on the answer list to begin with. We keep track of the number of valid elements in f', and quit copying elements from f' to r' when this number reaches zero. Every call to tail during the rotation decrements the number of valid elements.

datatype α RotationState =
   REVERSING **of** int $\times$ α list $\times$ α list $\times$ α list $\times$ α list
   | APPENDING **of** int $\times$ α list $\times$ α list
   | DONE **of** α list

fun startRotation (f, r) = REVERSING $(0, f, [\,], r, [\,])$

fun exec (REVERSING $(ok, x :: f, f', y :: r, r')$) =
   REVERSING $(ok+1, f, x :: f', r, y :: r')$
   | exec (REVERSING $(ok, [\,], f', [y], r')$) = APPENDING $(ok, f', y :: r')$
   | exec (APPENDING $(0, f', r')$) = DONE r'
   | exec (APPENDING $(ok, x :: f', r')$) = APPENDING $(ok-1, f', x :: r')$

fun invalidate (REVERSING (ok, f, f', r, r')) = REVERSING $(ok-1, f, f', r, r')$
   | invalidate (APPENDING $(0, f', x :: r')$) = DONE r'
   | invalidate (APPENDING (ok, f', r')) = APPENDING $(ok-1, f', r')$

This process finishes after a total of $2m + 2$ calls to exec and invalidate, where m is the initial length of f.

There are three more tricky details to consider. The first is that, during a rotation, the first few elements of the queue lie at the back of the f' field within the rotation state. How then are we to answer a head query? The solution to this dilemma is to keep a working copy of the old front list. We just have to make sure that the new copy of the front list is ready by the time the working copy is exhausted. During a rotation, the $lenf$ field measures the length of the list that is under construction, rather than of the working copy f. In between rotations, the $lenf$ field contains the length of f.

The second detail is exactly how many calls to exec we must issue per snoc and tail to guarantee that the rotation completes before either the next rotation is ready to begin or the working copy of the front list is exhausted. Assume that f has length m and r has length $m + 1$ at the beginning of a rotation. Then, the next rotation will begin after any combination of $2m+2$ insertions or deletions, but the working copy of the front list will be exhausted after just m deletions. Altogether, the rotation requires at most $2m + 2$ steps to complete. If we call exec twice per operation, including the operation that begins the rotation, then the rotation will complete at most m operations after it begins.

The third detail is that, since each rotation finishes long before the next rotation begins, we add an IDLE state to RotationState, such that exec IDLE = IDLE. Then we can blindly call exec without worrying about whether we are in the middle of a rotation or not.

The remaining details are by now routine and the complete implementation is shown in Figure 8.1.

Exercise 8.2 Prove that calling exec twice at the beginning of each rotation, and once for every remaining insertion or deletion is enough to finish the rotation on time. Modify the code accordingly.

Exercise 8.3 Replace the $lenf$ and $lenr$ fields with a single diff field that maintains the difference between the lengths of f and r. diff may be inaccurate during rebuilding, but must be accurate by the time rebuilding is finished.

8.3 Lazy Rebuilding

The implementation of physicist's queues in Section 6.4.2 is closely related to global rebuilding, but there is an important difference. As in global rebuilding, this implementation keeps two copies of the front list, the working copy, w, and the secondary copy, f, with all queries being answered by the working

```
structure HoodMelvilleQueue : QUEUE =
struct
  datatype α RotationState =
    IDLE
  | REVERSING of int × α list × α list × α list × α list
  | APPENDING of int × α list × α list
  | DONE of α list

  type α Queue = int × α list × α RotationState × int × α list

  fun exec (REVERSING (ok, x :: f, f', y :: r, r')) =
        REVERSING (ok+1, f, x :: f', r, y :: r')
    | exec (REVERSING (ok, [], f', [y], r')) = APPENDING (ok, f', y :: r')
    | exec (APPENDING (0, f', r')) = DONE r'
    | exec (APPENDING (ok, x :: f', r')) = APPENDING (ok−1, f', x :: r')
    | exec state = state

  fun invalidate (REVERSING (ok, f, f', r, r')) = REVERSING (ok−1, f, f', r, r'))
    | invalidate (APPENDING (0, f', x :: r')) = DONE r'
    | invalidate (APPENDING (ok, f', r')) = APPENDING (ok−1, f', r')
    | invalidate state = state

  fun exec2 (lenf, f, state, lenr, r) =
        case exec (exec state) of
          DONE newf ⇒ (lenf, newf, IDLE, lenr, r)
        | newstate ⇒ (lenf, f, newstate, lenr, r)

  fun check (q as (lenf, f, state, lenr, r)) =
        if lenr ≤ lenf then exec2 q
        else let val newstate = REVERSING (0, f, [], r, [])
             in exec2 (lenf+lenr, f, newstate, 0, []) end

  val empty = (0, [], IDLE, 0, [])
  fun isEmpty (lenf, f, state, lenr, r) = (lenf = 0)

  fun snoc ((lenf, f, state, lenr, r), x) = check (lenf, f, state, lenr+1, x :: r)
  fun head (lenf, [], state, lenr, r) = raise EMPTY
    | head (lenf, x :: f, state, lenr, r) = x
  fun tail (lenf, [], state, lenr, r) = raise EMPTY
    | tail (lenf, x :: f, state, lenr, r) =
        check (lenf−1, f, invalidate state, lenr, r)
end
```

Figure 8.1. Real-time queues based on global rebuilding.

copy. Updates to f (i.e., tail operations) are buffered, to be executed at the end of the rotation, by writing

... $tl (force f) ...

In addition, this implementation takes care to start (or at least set up) the rotation long before its result is needed. However, unlike global rebuilding, this implementation does not *execute* the rebuilding transformation (i.e., the rotation) concurrently with the normal operations; rather, it *pays for* the rebuilding transformation concurrently with the normal operations, but then executes the transformation all at once at some point after it has been paid for. In essence, we have replaced the complications of explicitly or implicitly coroutining the rebuilding transformation with the simpler mechanism of lazy evaluation. We call this variant of global rebuilding *lazy rebuilding*.

The implementation of banker's queues in Section 6.3.2 reveals a further simplification possible under lazy rebuilding. By incorporating nested suspensions into the basic data structure — for instance, by using streams instead of lists — we can often eliminate the distinction between the working copy and the secondary copy and employ a single structure that combines aspects of both. The "working" portion of that structure is the part that has already been paid for, and the "secondary" portion is the part that has not yet been paid for.

Global rebuilding has two advantages over batched rebuilding: it is suitable for implementing persistent data structures and it yields worst-case bounds rather than amortized bounds. Lazy rebuilding shares the first advantage, but, at least in its simplest form, yields amortized bounds. However, if desired, worst-case bounds can often be recovered using the scheduling techniques of Chapter 7. For example, the real-time queues in Section 7.2 combine lazy rebuilding with scheduling to achieve worst-case bounds. In fact, the combination of lazy rebuilding and scheduling can be viewed as an instance of global rebuilding in which the coroutines are reified in a particularly simple way using lazy evaluation.

8.4 Double-Ended Queues

As further examples of lazy rebuilding, we next present several implementations of double-ended queues, also known as *deques*. Deques differ from FIFO queues in that elements can be both inserted and deleted from either end of the queue. A signature for deques appears in Figure 8.2. This signature extends the signature for queues with three new functions: cons (insert an element at the front), last (return the rearmost element), and init (remove the rearmost element).

Remark Notice that the signature for queues is a strict subset of the signature for deques — the same names have been chosen for the type and the overlapping functions. Because deques are thus a strict extension of queues, Standard ML will allow us to use a deque module wherever a queue module is expected.

```
signature DEQUE =
sig
    type α Queue

    val empty   : α Queue
    val isEmpty : α Queue → bool

    (* insert, inspect, and remove the front element *)
    val cons    : α × α Queue → α Queue
    val head    : α Queue → α        (* raises EMPTY if queue is empty *)
    val tail    : α Queue → α Queue  (* raises EMPTY if queue is empty *)

    (* insert, inspect, and remove the rear element *)
    val snoc    : α Queue × α → α Queue
    val last    : α Queue → α        (* raises EMPTY if queue is empty *)
    val init    : α Queue → α Queue  (* raises EMPTY if queue is empty *)
end
```

Figure 8.2. Signature for double-ended queues.

8.4.1 Output-Restricted Deques

First, note that extending the queue implementations from Chapters 6 and 7 to support cons, in addition to snoc, is trivial. A queue that supports insertions at both ends, but deletions from only one end, is called an *output-restricted deque*.

For example, we can implement a cons function for the banker's queues of Section 6.3.2 as follows:

```
fun cons (x, (lenf, f, lenr, r)) = (lenf+1, $CONS (x, f), lenr, r)
```

Note that there is no need to call the check helper function because adding an element to f cannot possibly make f shorter than r.

Similarly, we can easily implement a cons function for the real-time queues of Section 7.2.

```
fun cons (x, (f, r, s)) = ($CONS (x, f), r, $CONS (x, s))
```

We add x to s only to maintain the invariant that $|s| = |f| - |r|$.

Exercise 8.4 Unfortunately, we cannot extend Hood and Melville's real-time queues with a cons function quite so easily, because there is no easy way to insert the new element into the rotation state. Instead, write a functor that extends *any* implementation of queues with a constant-time cons function, using the type

```
type α Queue = α list × α Q.Queue
```

where Q is the parameter to the functor. cons should insert elements into the new list, and head and tail should remove elements from the new list whenever it is non-empty.

8.4.2 Banker's Deques

Deques can be represented in essentially the same way as queues, as two streams (or lists), f and r, plus some associated information to help maintain balance. For queues, the notion of perfect balance is for all the elements to be in the front stream. For deques, the notion of perfect balance is for the elements to be evenly divided between the front and rear streams. Since we cannot afford to restore perfect balance after every operation, we will settle for guaranteeing that neither stream is more than about c times longer than the other, for some constant $c > 1$. Specifically, we maintain the following balance invariant:

$$|f| \leq c|r| + 1 \ \wedge \ |r| \leq c|f| + 1$$

The "+1" in each term allows for the only element of a singleton deque to be stored in either stream. Note that both streams are non-empty whenever the deque contains at least two elements. Whenever the invariant would otherwise be violated, we restore the deque to perfect balance by transferring elements from the longer stream to the shorter stream until both streams have the same length.

Using these ideas, we can adapt either the banker's queues of Section 6.3.2 or the physicist's queues of Section 6.4.2 to obtain deques that support every operation in $O(1)$ amortized time. Because the banker's queues are slightly simpler, we choose to work with that implementation.

The type of banker's deques is precisely the same as for banker's queues.

type α Queue = int × α Stream × int × α Stream

The functions on the front element are defined as follows:

fun cons (x, (lenf, f, lenr, r)) = check (lenf+1, $CONS (x, f), lenr, r)
fun head (lenf, $NIL, lenr, $CONS (x, _)) = x
 | head (lenf, $CONS (x, f'), lenr, r) = x
fun tail (lenf, $NIL, lenr, $CONS (x, _)) = empty
 | tail (lenf, $CONS (x, f'), lenr, r) = check (lenf−1, f', lenr, r)

The first clauses of head and tail handle singleton deques where the single element is stored in the rear stream. The functions on the rear element — snoc, last, and init — are defined symmetrically.

The interesting portion of this implementation is the check helper function, which restores the deque to perfect balance when one stream becomes too long by first truncating the longer stream to half the combined length of both streams and then transferring the remaining elements of the longer stream onto the back of the shorter stream. For example, if $|f| > c|r| + 1$, then check replaces f with take (i, f) and r with r ++ reverse (drop (i, f)), where $i = \lfloor (|f| + |r|)/2 \rfloor$. The full definition of check is

```
fun check (q as (lenf, f, lenr, r)) =
    if lenf > c*lenr + 1 then
        let val i = (lenf + lenr) div 2      val j = lenf + lenr − i
            val f' = take (i, f)             val r' = r ++ reverse (drop (i, f))
        in (i, f', j, r') end
    else if lenr > c*lenf + 1 then
        let val j = (lenf + lenr) div 2      val i = lenf + lenr − j
            val r' = take (j, r)             val f' = f ++ reverse (drop (j, r))
        in (i, f', j, r') end
    else q
```

This implementation is summarized in Figure 8.3.

Remark Because of the symmetry of this implementation, we can reverse a deque in $O(1)$ time by simply swapping the roles of f and r.

```
fun reverse (lenf, f, lenr, r) = (lenr, r, lenf, f)
```

Many other implementations of deques share this property [Hoo92, CG93]. Rather than essentially duplicating the code for the functions on the front element and the functions on the rear element, we could define the functions on the rear element in terms of reverse and the corresponding functions on the front element. For example, we could implement init as

```
fun init q = reverse (tail (reverse q))
```

Of course, init will be slightly faster if implemented directly.   ◇

To analyze these deques, we again turn to the banker's method. For both the front and rear streams, let $d(i)$ be the number of debits on element i of the stream, and let $D(i) = \sum_{j=0}^{i} d(j)$. We maintain the debit invariants that, for both the front and rear streams,

$$D(i) \leq \min(ci + i, cs + 1 - t)$$

where $s = \min(|f|, |r|)$ and $t = \max(|f|, |r|)$. Since $d(0) = 0$, the heads of both streams are free of debits and so can be accessed at any time by head or last.

Theorem 8.1 cons *and* tail *(symmetrically,* snoc *and* init*) maintain the debit*

```
functor BankersDeque (val c : int) : DEQUE =       (* c > 1 *)
struct
  type α Queue = int × α Stream × int × α Stream

  val empty = (0, $NIL, 0, $NIL)
  fun isEmpty (lenf, f, lenr, r) = (lenf+lenr = 0)

  fun check (q as (lenf, f, lenr, r)) =
      if lenf > c*lenr + 1 then
        let val i = (lenf + lenr) div 2    val j = lenf + lenr − i
            val f' = take (i, f)           val r' = r ⧺ reverse (drop (i, f))
        in (i, f', j, r') end
      else if lenr > c*lenf + 1 then
        let val j = (lenf + lenr) div 2    val i = lenf + lenr − j
            val r' = take (j, r)           val f' = f ⧺ reverse (drop (j, r))
        in (i, f', j, r') end
      else q

  fun cons (x, (lenf, f, lenr, r)) = check (lenf+1, $CONS (x, f), lenr, r)
  fun head (lenf, $NIL, lenr, $NIL) = raise EMPTY
    | head (lenf, $NIL, lenr, $CONS (x, _)) = x
    | head (lenf, $CONS (x, f'), lenr, r) = x
  fun tail (lenf, $NIL, lenr, $NIL) = raise EMPTY
    | tail (lenf, $NIL, lenr, $CONS (x, _)) = empty
    | tail (lenf, $CONS (x, f'), lenr, r) = check (lenf−1, f', lenr, r)

  . . . snoc, last, and init defined symmetrically. . .
end
```

Figure 8.3. An implementation of deques based on lazy rebuilding and the banker's method.

invariants on both the front and rear streams by discharging at most 1 and $c + 1$ debits per stream, respectively.

Proof Similar to the proof of Theorem 6.1 on page 66.   □

By inspection, every operation has an $O(1)$ unshared cost, and by Theorem 8.1, every operation discharges no more than $O(1)$ debits. Therefore, every operation runs in $O(1)$ amortized time.

Exercise 8.5 Prove Theorem 8.1.

Exercise 8.6 Explore the tradeoffs in the choice of the balance constant c. Construct a sequence of operations for which the choice $c = 4$ would be significantly faster than $c = 2$. Now, construct a sequence of operations for which $c = 2$ would be significantly faster than $c = 4$.

8.4.3 Real-Time Deques

Real-time deques support every operation in $O(1)$ worst-case time. We obtain real-time deques from the deques of the previous section by scheduling both the front and rear streams.

As always, the first step in applying the scheduling technique is to convert all monolithic functions to incremental functions. In the previous implementation, the rebuilding transformation rebuilt f and r as f ++ reverse (drop (j, r)) and take (j, r) (or vice versa). take and ++ are already incremental, but reverse and drop are monolithic. We therefore rewrite f ++ reverse (drop (j, r)) as rotateDrop (f, j, r) where rotateDrop performs c steps of the drop for every step of the ++ and eventually calls rotateRev, which in turn performs c steps of the reverse for every remaining step of the ++. rotateDrop can be implemented as

```
fun rotateDrop (f, j, r) =
    if j < c then rotateRev (f, drop (j, r), $NIL)
    else let val ($CONS (x, f')) = f
        in $CONS (x, rotateDrop (f', j − c, drop (c, r))) end
```

Initially, $|r| = c|f| + 1 + k$ where $1 \leq k \leq c$. Every call to rotateDrop drops c elements of r and processes one element of f, except the last, which drops $j \bmod c$ elements of r and leaves f unchanged. Therefore, at the time of the first call to rotateRev, $|r| = c|f| + 1 + k - (j \bmod c)$. It will be convenient to insist that $|r| \geq c|f|$, so we require that $1 + k - (j \bmod c) \geq 0$. This is guaranteed only for $c < 4$. Since c must be greater than one, the only values of c that we allow are two and three. Then we can implement rotateRev as

```
fun rotateRev ($NIL, r, a) = reverse r ++ a
  | rotateRev ($CONS (x, f), r, a) =
      $CONS (x, rotateRev (f, drop (c, r), reverse (take (c, r)) ++ a))
```

Note that rotateDrop and rotateRev make frequent calls to drop and reverse, which were exactly the functions we were trying to eliminate. However, now drop and reverse are always called with arguments of bounded size, and therefore execute in $O(1)$ steps.

Once we have converted the monolithic functions to incremental functions, the next step is to schedule the execution of the suspensions in f and r. We maintain a separate schedule for each stream and execute a few suspensions per operation from each schedule. As with the real-time queues of Section 7.2, the goal is to ensure that both schedules are completely evaluated before the next rotation, so that the suspensions that are forced within rotateDrop and rotateRev are guaranteed to have already been memoized.

Exercise 8.7 Show that executing one suspension per stream per insertion and

```
functor RealTimeDeque (val c : int) : DEQUE =    (* c = 2 or c = 3 *)
struct
  type α Queue =
      int × α Stream × α Stream × int × α Stream × α Stream

  val empty = (0, $NIL, $NIL, 0, $NIL, $NIL)
  fun isEmpty (lenf, f, sf, lenr, r, sr) = (lenf+lenr = 0)

  fun exec1 ($CONS (x, s)) = s
    | exec1 s = s
  fun exec2 s = exec1 (exec1 s)

  fun rotateRev ($NIL, r, a) = reverse r ++ a
    | rotateRev ($CONS (x, f), r, a) =
        $CONS (x, rotateRev (f, drop (c, r), reverse (take (c, r)) ++ a))
  fun rotateDrop (f, j, r) =
      if j < c then rotateRev (f, drop (j, r), $NIL)
      else let val ($CONS (x, f')) = f
           in $CONS (x, rotateDrop (f', j − c, drop (c, r))) end

  fun check (q as (lenf, f, sf, lenr, r, sr)) =
      if lenf > c*lenr + 1 then
          let val i = (lenf + lenr) div 2    val j = lenf + lenr − i
              val f' = take (i, f)           val r' = rotateDrop (r, i, f)
          in (i, f', f', j, r', r') end
      else if lenr > c*lenf + 1 then
          let val j = (lenf + lenr) div 2    val i = lenf + lenr − j
              val r' = take (j, r)           val f' = rotateDrop (f, j, r)
          in (i, f', f', j, r', r') end
      else q

  fun cons (x, (lenf, f, sf, lenr, r, sr)) =
      check (lenf+1, $CONS (x, f), exec1 sf, lenr, r, exec1 sr)
  fun head (lenf, $NIL, sf, lenr, $NIL, sr) = raise EMPTY
    | head (lenf, $NIL, sf, lenr, $CONS (x, _), sr) = x
    | head (lenf, $CONS (x, f'), sf, lenr, r, sr) = x
  fun tail (lenf, $NIL, sf, lenr, $NIL, sr) = raise EMPTY
    | tail (lenf, $NIL, sf, lenr, $CONS (x, _), sr) = empty
    | tail (lenf, $CONS (x, f'), sf, lenr, r, sr) =
        check (lenf−1, f', exec2 sf, lenr, r, exec2 sr)

  ...snoc, last, and init defined symmetrically...
end
```

Figure 8.4. Real-time deques via lazy rebuilding and scheduling.

two suspensions per stream per deletion is enough to guarantee that both schedules are completely evaluated before the next rotation. ◇

This implementation is summarized in Figure 8.4.

8.5 Chapter Notes

Global Rebuilding Overmars introduced global rebuilding in [Ove83]. It has since been used in many situations, including real-time queues [HM81], real-time deques [Hoo82, GT86, Sar86, CG93], catenable deques [BT95], and the order maintenance problem [DS87].

Deques Hood [Hoo82] first modified the real-time queues of [HM81] to obtain real-time deques based on global rebuilding. Several other researchers later duplicated this work [GT86, Sar86, CG93]. These implementations are all similar to techniques used to simulate multihead Turing machines [Sto70, FMR72, LS81]. Hoogerwoord [Hoo92] proposed amortized deques based on batched rebuilding, but, as always with batched rebuilding, his implementation is not efficient when used persistently. The real-time deques in Figure 8.4 first appeared in [Oka95c].

Coroutines and Lazy Evaluation Streams (and other lazy data structures) have frequently been used to implement a form of coroutining between the producer of a stream and the consumer of a stream. Landin [Lan65] first pointed out this connection between streams and coroutines. See Hughes [Hug89] for some compelling applications of this feature.

9

Numerical Representations

Consider the usual representations of lists and natural numbers, along with several typical functions on each data type.

datatype α List =
  Nil
  | Cons **of** $\alpha \times \alpha$ List
fun tail (Cons (x, xs)) = xs
fun append (Nil, ys) = ys
  | append (Cons (x, xs), ys) =
    Cons $(x$, append $(xs, ys))$

datatype Nat =
  Zero
  | Succ **of** Nat
fun pred (Succ n) = n
fun plus (Zero, n) = n
  | plus (Succ m, n) =
    Succ (plus $(m, n))$

Other than the fact that lists contain elements and natural numbers do not, these implementations are virtually identical. Binomial heaps exhibit a similar relationship with binary numbers. These examples suggest a strong analogy between representations of the number n and representations of container objects of size n. Functions on the container strongly resemble arithmetic functions on the number. For example, inserting an element resembles incrementing a number, deleting an element resembles decrementing a number, and combining two containers resembles adding two numbers. This analogy can be exploited to design new implementations of container abstractions — simply choose a representation of natural numbers with certain desired properties and define the functions on the container objects accordingly. Call an implementation designed in this fashion a *numerical representation*.

In this chapter, we explore a host of numerical representations for two different abstractions: *heaps* and *random-access lists* (also known as *flexible arrays*). These abstractions stress different sets of arithmetic operations. Heaps require efficient increment and addition functions, whereas random-access lists require efficient increment and decrement functions.

9.1 Positional Number Systems

A *positional number system* [Knu73b] is a notation for writing a number as a sequence of digits $b_0 \ldots b_{m-1}$. The digit b_0 is called the *least significant digit* and the digit b_{m-1} is called the *most significant digit*. Except when writing ordinary, decimal numbers, we will always write sequences of digits from least significant to most significant.

Each digit b_i has weight w_i, so the value of the sequence $b_0 \ldots b_{m-1}$ is $\sum_{i=0}^{m-1} b_i w_i$. For any given positional number system, the sequence of weights is fixed, as is the set of digits D_i from which each b_i is chosen. For unary numbers, $w_i = 1$ and $D_i = \{1\}$ for all i, and for binary numbers $w_i = 2^i$ and $D_i = \{0, 1\}$. (By convention, we write all digits in typewriter font except for ordinary, decimal digits.) A number is said to be written in base B if $w_i = B^i$ and $D_i = \{0, \ldots, B - 1\}$. Usually, but not always, weights are increasing sequences of powers, and the set D_i is the same for every digit.

A number system is said to be *redundant* if there is more than one way to represent some numbers. For example, we can obtain a redundant system of binary numbers by taking $w_i = 2^i$ and $D_i = \{0, 1, 2\}$. Then the decimal number 13 can be written 1011, or 1201, or 122. By convention, we disallow trailing zeros, since otherwise almost all number systems are trivially redundant.

Computer representations of positional number systems can be *dense* or *sparse*. A dense representation is simply a list (or some other kind of sequence) of digits, including those digits that happen to be zero. A sparse representation, on the other hand, elides the zeros. It must then include information on either the rank (i.e., the index) or the weight of each non-zero digit. Figure 9.1 shows two different representations of binary numbers in Standard ML—one dense and one sparse—along with increment, decrement, and addition functions on each. Among the numerical representations that we have already seen, scheduled binomial heaps (Section 7.3) use a dense representation, while binomial heaps (Section 3.2) and lazy binomial heaps (Section 6.4.1) use sparse representations.

9.2 Binary Numbers

Given a positional number system, we can implement a numerical representation based on that number system as a sequence of trees. The number and sizes of the trees representing a collection of size n are governed by the representation of n in the positional number system. For each weight w_i, there are b_i trees of that size. For example, the binary representation of 73 is 1001001,

```
structure Dense =
struct
  datatype Digit = ZERO | ONE
  type Nat = Digit list    (* increasing order of significance *)

  fun inc [] = [ONE]
    | inc (ZERO :: ds) = ONE :: ds
    | inc (ONE :: ds) = ZERO :: inc ds        (* carry *)

  fun dec [ONE] = []
    | dec (ONE :: ds) = ZERO :: ds
    | dec (ZERO :: ds) = ONE :: dec ds        (* borrow *)

  fun add (ds, []) = ds
    | add ([], ds) = ds
    | add (d :: ds₁, ZERO :: ds₂) = d :: add (ds₁, ds₂)
    | add (ZERO :: ds₁, d :: ds₂) = d :: add (ds₁, ds₂)
    | add (ONE :: ds₁, ONE :: ds₂) =
        ZERO :: inc (add (ds₁, ds₂))          (* carry *)
end
```

```
structure SparseByWeight =
struct
  type Nat = int list    (* increasing list of weights, each a power of two *)

  fun carry (w, []) = [w]
    | carry (w, ws as w' :: ws') =
      if w < w' then w :: ws else carry (2*w, ws')

  fun borrow (w, ws as w' :: ws') =
      if w = w' then ws' else w :: borrow (2*w, ws)

  fun inc ws = carry (1, ws)
  fun dec ws = borrow (1, ws)

  fun add (ws, []) = ws
    | add ([], ws) = ws
    | add (m as w₁ :: ws₁, n as w₂ :: ws₂) =
      if w₁ < w₂ then w₁ :: add (ws₁, n)
      else if w₂ < w₁ then w₂ :: add (m, ws₂)
      else carry (2*w₁, add (ws₁, ws₂))
end
```

Figure 9.1. Two implementations of binary numbers.

so a collection of size 73 in a binary numerical representation would contain three trees, of sizes 1, 8, and 64, respectively.

Trees in numerical representations typically exhibit a very regular structure. For example, in binary numerical representations, all trees have sizes that are

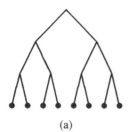  

(a)   (b)   (c)

Figure 9.2. Three trees of rank 3: (a) a complete binary leaf tree, (b) a binomial tree, and (c) a pennant.

powers of two. Three common kinds of trees that exhibit this structure are *complete binary leaf trees* [KD96], *binomial trees* [Vui78], and *pennants* [SS90].

Definition 9.1 (Complete binary leaf trees) A complete binary tree of rank 0 is a leaf and a complete binary tree of rank $r > 0$ is a node with two children, each of which is a complete binary tree of rank $r - 1$. A leaf tree is a tree that contains elements only at the leaves, unlike ordinary trees that contain elements at every node. A complete binary tree of rank r has $2^{r+1} - 1$ nodes, but only 2^r leaves. Hence, a complete binary leaf tree of rank r contains 2^r elements.

Definition 9.2 (Binomial trees) A binomial tree of rank r is a node with r children $c_1 \ldots c_r$, where c_i is a binomial tree of rank $r - i$. Alternatively, a binomial tree of rank $r > 0$ is a binomial tree of rank $r - 1$ to which another binomial tree of rank $r - 1$ has been added as the leftmost child. From the second definition, it is easy to see that a binomial tree of rank r contains 2^r nodes.

Definition 9.3 (Pennants) A pennant of rank 0 is a single node and a pennant of rank $r > 0$ is a node with a single child that is a complete binary tree of rank $r - 1$. The complete binary tree contains $2^r - 1$ elements, so the pennant contains 2^r elements.

Figure 9.2 illustrates the three kinds of trees. Which kind of tree is superior for a given data structure depends on the properties the data structure must maintain, such as the order in which elements should be stored in the trees. A key factor in the suitability of a particular kind of tree for a given data structure is how easily the tree supports functions analogous to carries and borrows in binary arithmetic. When simulating a carry, we *link* two trees of rank r to form a tree of rank $r + 1$. Symmetrically, when simulating a borrow, we *unlink* a

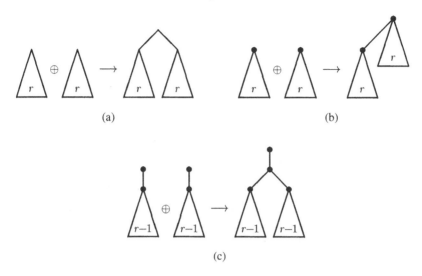

(a)   (b)

(c)

Figure 9.3. Linking two trees of rank r to obtain a tree of rank $r + 1$ for (a) complete binary leaf trees, (b) binomial trees, and (c) pennants.

tree of rank $r > 0$ to obtain two trees of rank $r - 1$. Figure 9.3 illustrates the link operation (denoted $\oplus$) on each of the three kinds of trees. Assuming that elements are not rearranged, each of the three kinds of trees can be linked or unlinked in $O(1)$ time.

We have already seen several variations of heaps based on binary arithmetic and binomial trees. We next explore a simple numerical representation for random-access lists. Then we discuss several variations of binary arithmetic that yield improved asymptotic bounds.

9.2.1 Binary Random-Access Lists

A *random-access list*, also called a one-sided flexible array, is a data structure that supports array-like lookup and update functions, as well as the usual cons, head, and tail functions on lists. A signature for random-access lists is shown in Figure 9.4.

We implement random-access lists using a binary numerical representation. A binary random-access list of size n contains a tree for each one in the binary representation of n. The rank of each tree corresponds to the rank of the corresponding digit; if the ith bit of n is one, then the random-access list contains a tree of size 2^i. We can use any of the three kinds of trees, and either a dense or

---

signature RANDOMACCESSLIST =
sig
  type α RList

  val empty   : α RList
  val isEmpty : α RList $\rightarrow$ bool

  val cons   : $\alpha \times \alpha$ RList $\rightarrow \alpha$ RList
  val head   : α RList $\rightarrow \alpha$
  val tail   : α RList $\rightarrow \alpha$ RList
     (∗ head *and* tail *raise* EMPTY *if list is empty* ∗)

  val lookup : int $\times \alpha$ RList $\rightarrow \alpha$
  val update : int $\times \alpha \times \alpha$ RList $\rightarrow \alpha$ RList
     (∗ lookup *and* update *raise* SUBSCRIPT *if index is out of bounds* ∗)
end

Figure 9.4. Signature for random-access lists.

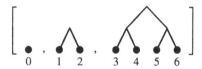

Figure 9.5. A binary random-access list containing the elements 0...6.

a sparse representation. For this example, we choose the simplest combination of features: complete binary leaf trees and a dense representation. The type α RList is thus

datatype α Tree = LEAF **of** α | NODE **of** int $\times \alpha$ Tree $\times \alpha$ Tree
datatype α Digit = ZERO | ONE **of** α Tree
type α RList = α Digit list

The integer in each node is the size of the tree. This number is redundant since the size of every tree is completely determined by the size of its parent or by its position in the list of digits, but we include it anyway for convenience. Trees are stored in increasing order of size, and the order of elements is left-to-right, both within and between trees. Thus, the head of the random-access list is the leftmost leaf of the smallest tree. Figure 9.5 shows a binary random-access list of size 7. Note that the maximum number of trees in a list of size n is $\lfloor \log(n + 1) \rfloor$ and the maximum depth of any tree is $\lfloor \log n \rfloor$.

Inserting an element into a binary random-access list (using cons) is analogous to incrementing a binary number. Recall the increment function on dense binary numbers:

```
fun inc [ ] = [ONE]
  | inc (ZERO :: ds) = ONE :: ds
  | inc (ONE :: ds) = ZERO :: inc ds
```

To add a new element to the front of the list, we first convert the element into a leaf, and then insert the leaf into the list of trees using a helper function consTree that follows the rules of inc.

```
fun cons (x, ts) = consTree (LEAF x, ts)
fun consTree (t, [ ]) = [ONE t]
  | consTree (t, ZERO :: ts) = ONE t :: ts
  | consTree (t₁, ONE t₂ :: ts) = ZERO :: consTree (link (t₁, t₂), ts)
```

The link helper function constructs a new tree from two equal-sized subtrees and automatically calculates the size of the new tree.

Deleting an element from a binary random-access list (using tail) is analogous to decrementing a binary number. Recall the decrement function on dense binary numbers:

```
fun dec [ONE] = [ ]
  | dec (ONE :: ds) = ZERO :: ds
  | dec (ZERO :: ds) = ONE :: dec ds
```

The corresponding function on lists of trees is unconsTree. When applied to a list whose first digit has rank r, unconsTree returns a pair containing a tree of rank r, and the new list without that tree.

```
fun unconsTree [ONE t] = (t, [ ])
  | unconsTree (ONE t :: ts) = (t, ZERO :: ts)
  | unconsTree (ZERO :: ts) =
      let val (NODE (_, t₁, t₂), ts') = unconsTree ts
      in (t₁, ONE t₂ :: ts') end
```

The head and tail functions remove the leftmost leaf using unconsTree and then either return its element or discard it, respectively.

```
fun head ts = let val (LEAF x, _) = unconsTree ts in x end
fun tail ts = let val (_, ts') = unconsTree ts in ts' end
```

The lookup and update functions do not have analogous arithmetic operations. Rather, they take advantage of the organization of binary random-access lists as logarithmic-length lists of logarithmic-depth trees. Looking up an element is a two-stage process. We first search the list for the correct tree, and then search the tree for the correct element. The helper function lookupTree uses the size field in each node to determine whether the ith element is in the left subtree or the right subtree.

```
fun lookup (i, ZERO :: ts) = lookup (i, ts)
  | lookup (i, ONE t :: ts) =
    if i < size t then lookupTree (i, t) else lookup (i − size t, ts)
fun lookupTree (0, LEAF x) = x
  | lookupTree (i, NODE (w, t₁, t₂)) =
    if i < w div 2 then lookupTree (i, t₁)
    else lookupTree (i − w div 2, t₂)
```

update works in same way but also copies the path from the root to the updated leaf.

```
fun update (i, y, ZERO :: ts) = ZERO :: update (i, y, ts)
  | update (i, y, ONE t :: ts) =
    if i < size t then ONE (updateTree (i, y, t)) :: ts
    else ONE t :: update (i − size t, y, ts)
fun updateTree (0, y, LEAF x) = LEAF y
  | updateTree (i, y, NODE (w, t₁, t₂)) =
    if i < w div 2 then NODE (w, updateTree (i, y, t₁), t₂)
    else NODE (w, t₁, updateTree (i − w div 2, y, t₂))
```

The complete code for this implementation is shown in Figure 9.6.

cons, head, and tail perform at most $O(1)$ work per digit and so run in $O(\log n)$ worst-case time. lookup and update take at most $O(\log n)$ time to find the right tree, and then at most $O(\log n)$ time to find the right element in that tree, for a total of $O(\log n)$ worst-case time.

Exercise 9.1 Write a function drop of type $int \times \alpha$ RList $\rightarrow \alpha$ RList that deletes the first k elements of a binary random-access list. Your function should run in $O(\log n)$ time.

Exercise 9.2 Write a function create of type $int \times \alpha \rightarrow \alpha$ RList that creates a binary random-access list containing n copies of some value x. This function should also run in $O(\log n)$ time. (You may find it helpful to review Exercise 2.5.)

Exercise 9.3 Reimplement BinaryRandomAccessList using a sparse representation such as

```
datatype α Tree = LEAF of α | NODE of int × α Tree × α Tree
type α RList = α Tree list
```

9.2.2 Zeroless Representations

One disappointing aspect of binary random-access lists is that the list functions cons, head, and tail run in $O(\log n)$ time instead of $O(1)$ time. Over the next three sections, we study variations of binary numbers that improve the running

```
structure BinaryRandomAccessList : RANDOMACCESSLIST =
struct
  datatype α Tree = LEAF of α | NODE of int × α Tree × α Tree
  datatype α Digit = ZERO | ONE of α Tree
  type α RList = α Digit list

  val empty = [ ]
  fun isEmpty ts = null ts

  fun size (LEAF x) = 1
    | size (NODE (w, t₁, t₂)) = w
  fun link (t₁, t₂) = NODE (size t₁+size t₂, t₁, t₂)
  fun consTree (t, [ ]) = [ONE t]
    | consTree (t, ZERO :: ts) = ONE t :: ts
    | consTree (t₁, ONE t₂ :: ts) = ZERO :: consTree (link (t₁, t₂), ts)
  fun unconsTree [ ] = raise EMPTY
    | unconsTree [ONE t] = (t, [ ])
    | unconsTree (ONE t :: ts) = (t, ZERO :: ts)
    | unconsTree (ZERO :: ts) =
        let val (NODE (_, t₁, t₂), ts') = unconsTree ts
        in (t₁, ONE t₂ :: ts') end

  fun cons (x, ts) = consTree (LEAF x, ts)
  fun head ts = let val (LEAF x, _) = unconsTree ts in x end
  fun tail ts = let val (_, ts') = unconsTree ts in ts' end

  fun lookupTree (0, LEAF x) = x
    | lookupTree (i, LEAF x) = raise SUBSCRIPT
    | lookupTree (i, NODE (w, t₁, t₂)) =
        if i < w div 2 then lookupTree (i, t₁)
        else lookupTree (i − w div 2, t₂)
  fun updateTree (0, y, LEAF x) = LEAF y
    | updateTree (i, y, LEAF x) = raise SUBSCRIPT
    | updateTree (i, y, NODE (w, t₁, t₂)) =
        if i < w div 2 then NODE (w, updateTree (i, y, t₁), t₂)
        else NODE (w, t₁, updateTree (i − w div 2, y, t₂))

  fun lookup (i, [ ]) = raise SUBSCRIPT
    | lookup (i, ZERO :: ts) = lookup (i, ts)
    | lookup (i, ONE t :: ts) =
        if i < size t then lookupTree (i, t) else lookup (i − size t, ts)
  fun update (i, y, [ ]) = raise SUBSCRIPT
    | update (i, y, ZERO :: ts) = ZERO :: update (i, y, ts)
    | update (i, y, ONE t :: ts) =
        if i < size t then ONE (updateTree (i, y, t)) :: ts
        else ONE t :: update (i − size t, y, ts)
end
```

Figure 9.6. Binary random-access lists.

times of all three functions to $O(1)$. We begin in this section with the head function.

Remark An obvious approach to making head run in $O(1)$ time is to store the first element separately from the rest of the list, à la the ExplicitMin functor of Exercise 3.7. Another solution is to use a sparse representation and either binomial trees or pennants, so that the head of the list is the root of the first tree. The solution we explore in this section has the advantage that it also improves the running times of lookup and update slightly. ◇

Currently, head is implemented via a call to unconsTree, which extracts the first element and rebuilds the list without that element. This approach yields compact code since unconsTree supports both head and tail, but wastes time building lists that are immediately discarded by head. For greater efficiency, we should implement head directly. As a special case, head can easily be made to run in $O(1)$ time whenever the first digit is non-zero.

```
fun head (ONE (LEAF x) :: _) = x
```

Inspired by this rule, we seek to arrange that the first digit is *always* non-zero. There are quite a few ad hoc solutions that satisfy this criterion, but a more principled solution is to use a *zeroless* representation, in which every digit is non-zero.

Zeroless binary numbers are constructed from ones and twos instead of zeros and ones. The weight of the ith digit is still 2^i. Thus, for example, the decimal number 16 can be written 2111 instead of 00001. We can implement the increment function on zeroless binary numbers as follows:

```
datatype Digit = ONE | TWO
type Nat = Digit list

fun inc [] = [ONE]
  | inc (ONE :: ds) = TWO :: ds
  | inc (TWO :: ds) = ONE :: inc ds
```

Exercise 9.4 Write decrement and addition functions for zeroless binary numbers. Note that carries during additions can involve either ones or twos. ◇

Now, if we replace the type of digits in binary random-access lists with

```
datatype α Digit = ONE of α Tree | TWO of α Tree × α Tree
```

then we can implement head as

```
fun head (ONE (LEAF x) :: _) = x
  | head (TWO(LEAF x, LEAF y) :: _) = x
```

which clearly runs in $O(1)$ worst-case time.

Exercise 9.5 Implement the remaining functions for this type.

Exercise 9.6 Show that lookup and update on element i now run in $O(\log i)$ time.

Exercise 9.7 Under certain conditions, red-black trees (Section 3.3) can be viewed as a numerical representation. Compare and contrast zeroless binary random-access lists to red-black trees in which insertions are restricted to the leftmost position. Focus on the cons and insert functions and on the shape invariants of the structures produced by these functions.

9.2.3 Lazy Representations

Suppose we represent binary numbers as digit streams rather than digit lists. Then, the increment function becomes

```
fun lazy inc ($NIL) = $CONS (ONE, $NIL)
    | inc ($CONS (ZERO, ds)) = $CONS (ONE, ds)
    | inc ($CONS (ONE, ds)) = $CONS (ZERO, inc ds)
```

Note that this function is incremental.

In Section 6.4.1, we saw how lazy evaluation could be used to make insertions into binomial heaps run in $O(1)$ amortized time, so it should be no surprise that this version of inc also runs in $O(1)$ amortized time. We can prove this using the banker's method.

Proof Allow one debit on each ZERO and zero debits on each ONE. Suppose ds begins with k ONEs followed by a ZERO. Then inc ds changes each of these ONEs to a ZERO and the ZERO to a ONE. Allocate a new debit for each of these steps. Now, each of the ZEROs has a single debit, but the ONE has two debits: the debit inherited from the original suspension at that location plus the newly created debit. Discharging both debits restores the invariant. Since the amortized cost of a function is its unshared cost (in this case $O(1)$) plus the number of debits it discharges (in this case two), inc runs in $O(1)$ amortized time. $\square$

Now, consider the decrement function.

```
fun lazy dec ($CONS (ONE, $NIL)) = $NIL
    | dec ($CONS (ONE, ds)) = $CONS (ZERO, ds)
    | dec ($CONS (ZERO, ds)) = $CONS (ONE, dec ds)
```

Since this function follows the same pattern as inc, but with the roles of the digits reversed, we would expect that a similar proof would yield a similar bound. And, in fact, it does provided we do not use *both* increments and decrements. However, if we use both functions, that at least one must be charged $O(\log n)$ amortized time. To see why, consider a sequence of increments and decrements that cycle between $2^k - 1$ and 2^k. In that case, every operation touches every digit, taking $O(n \log n)$ time altogether.

But didn't we prove that both functions run in $O(1)$ amortized time? What went wrong? The problem is that the two proofs require contradictory debit invariants. To prove that inc runs in $O(1)$ amortized time, we require that each ZERO has one debit and each ONE has zero debits. To prove that dec runs in $O(1)$ amortized time, we require that each ONE has one debit and each ZERO has zero debits.

The critical property that inc and dec both satisfy when used without the other is that at least half the operations that reach a given position in the stream terminate at that position. In particular, every inc or dec processes the first digit, but only every other operation processes the second digit. Similarly, every fourth operation processes the third digit, and so on. Intuitively, then, the amortized cost of a single operation is approximately

$$O(1 + 1/2 + 1/4 + 1/8 + \cdots) = O(1).$$

Classify the possible values of a digit as either *safe* or *dangerous* such that a function that reaches a safe digit always terminates there, but a function that reaches a dangerous digit might continue on to the next digit. To achieve the property that no two successive operations at a given index both proceed to the next index, we must guarantee that, whenever an operation processes a dangerous digit and continues on, it transforms the dangerous digit into a safe digit. Then, the next operation that reaches this digit is guaranteed not to continue. We can formally prove that every operation runs in $O(1)$ amortized time using a debit invariant in which a safe digit is allowed one debit, but a dangerous digit is allowed zero debits.

Now, the increment function requires that the largest digit be classified as dangerous, and the decrement function requires that the smallest digit be classified as dangerous. To support both functions simultaneously, we need a third digit to be the safe digit. Therefore, we switch to *redundant* binary numbers, in which each digit can be zero, one, or two. We can then implement inc and dec as follows:

```
datatype Digit = ZERO | ONE | TWO
type Nat = Digit Stream
```

fun lazy inc ($NIL) = $CONS (ONE, $NIL)
  | inc ($CONS (ZERO, *ds*)) = $CONS (ONE, *ds*)
  | inc ($CONS (ONE, *ds*)) = $CONS (TWO, *ds*)
  | inc ($CONS (TWO, *ds*)) = $CONS (ONE, inc *ds*)

fun lazy dec ($CONS (ONE, $NIL)) = $NIL
  | dec ($CONS (ONE, *ds*)) = $CONS (ZERO, *ds*)
  | dec ($CONS (TWO, *ds*)) = $CONS (ONE, *ds*)
  | dec ($CONS (ZERO, *ds*)) = $CONS (ONE, dec *ds*)

Note that the recursive cases of inc and dec—on TWO and ZERO, respectively—both produce ONEs. ONE is classified as safe, and ZERO and TWO are classified as dangerous. To see how redundancy helps us, consider incrementing the redundant binary number 222222 to get 1111111. This operation takes seven steps. However, decrementing this value does not return to 222222. Instead, it yields 0111111 in only one step. Thus, alternating increments and decrements no longer pose a problem.

Lazy binary numbers can serve as template for many other data structures. In Chapter 11, we will generalize this template into a design technique called *implicit recursive slowdown*.

Exercise 9.8 Prove that inc and dec both run in $O(1)$ amortized time using a debit invariant that allows one debit per ONE and zero debits per ZERO or TWO.

Exercise 9.9 Implement cons, head, and tail for random-access lists based on zeroless redundant binary numbers, using the type

datatype α Digit =
    ONE **of** α Tree
    | TWO **of** α Tree $\times$ α Tree
    | THREE **of** α Tree $\times$ α Tree $\times$ α Tree
  type α RList = Digit Stream

Show that all three functions run in $O(1)$ amortized time.

Exercise 9.10 As demonstrated by scheduled binomial heaps in Section 7.3, we can apply scheduling to lazy binary numbers to achieve $O(1)$ worst-case bounds. Reimplement cons, head, and tail from the preceding exercise so that each runs in $O(1)$ worst-case time. You may find it helpful to have two distinct TWO constructors (say, TWO and TWO') so that you can distinguish between recursive and non-recursive cases of cons and tail.

9.2.4 Segmented Representations

Another variation of binary numbers that yields $O(1)$ worst-case bounds is *segmented* binary numbers. The problem with ordinary binary numbers is that carries and borrows can cascade. For example, incrementing $2^k - 1$ causes k carries in binary arithmetic. Symmetrically, decrementing 2^k causes k borrows. Segmented binary numbers solve this problem by allowing multiple carries or borrows to be executed in a single step.

Notice that incrementing a binary number takes k steps whenever the number begins with a block of k ones. Similarly, decrementing a binary number takes k steps whenever the number begins with a block of k zeros. Segmented binary numbers group contiguous sequences of identical digits into blocks so that we can execute a carry or borrow on an entire block in a single step. We represent segmented binary numbers as alternating blocks of zeros and ones using the following datatype:

```
datatype DigitBlock = ZEROS of int | ONES of int
type Nat = DigitBlock list
```

The integer in each DigitBlock represents the block's length.

We use the helper functions zeros and ones to add new blocks to the front of a list of blocks. These functions merge adjacent blocks of the same digit and discard empty blocks. In addition, zeros discards any trailing zeros.

```
fun zeros (i, []) = []
  | zeros (0, blks) = blks
  | zeros (i, ZEROS j :: blks) = ZEROS (i+j) :: blks
  | zeros (i, blks) = ZEROS i :: blks

fun ones (0, blks) = blks
  | ones (i, ONES j :: blks) = ONES (i+j) :: blks
  | ones (i, blks) = ONES i :: blks
```

Now, to increment a segmented binary number, we inspect the first block of digits (if any). If the first block contains zeros, then we replace the first zero with a one, creating a new singleton block of ones and shrinking the block of zeros by one. If the first block contains i ones, then we perform i carries in a single step by changing the ones to zeros and incrementing the next digit.

```
fun inc [] = [ONES 1]
  | inc (ZEROS i :: blks) = ones (1, zeros (i−1, blks))
  | inc (ONES i :: blks) = ZEROS i :: inc blks
```

In the third line, we know the recursive call to inc cannot loop because the next block, if any, must contain zeros. In the second line, the helper functions deal gracefully with the special case that the leading block contains a single zero.

Decrementing a segmented binary number is almost exactly the same, but with the roles of zeros and ones reversed.

```
fun dec (ONES i :: blks) = zeros (1, ones (i−1, blks))
  | dec (ZEROS i :: blks) = ONES i :: dec blks
```

Again, we know that the recursive call cannot loop because the next block must contain ones.

Unfortunately, although segmented binary numbers support inc and dec in $O(1)$ worst-case time, numerical representations based on segmented binary numbers end up being too complicated to be practical. The problem is that the idea of changing an entire block of ones to zeros, or vice versa, does not translate well to the realm of trees. More practical solutions can be obtained by combining segmentation with redundant binary numbers. Then we can return to processing digits (and therefore trees) one at a time. What segmentation gives us is the ability to process a digit in the middle of a sequence, rather than only at the front.

For example, consider a redundant representation in which blocks of ones are represented as a segment.

datatype Digits = ZERO | ONES **of** int | TWO
type Nat = Digits list

We define a helper function ones to handle the details of merging adjacent blocks and deleting empty blocks.

```
fun ones (0, ds) = ds
  | ones (i, ONES j :: ds) = ONES (i+j) :: ds
  | ones (i, ds) = ONES i :: ds
```

Think of a TWO as representing a carry in progress. To prevent cascades of carries, we must guarantee that we never have more than one TWO in a row. We maintain the invariant that the last non-one digit before each TWO is a ZERO. This invariant can be characterized by either the regular expression $(0 \mid 1 \mid 01^*2)^*$ or, if we also take into account the lack of trailing zeros, the regular expression $(0^*1 \mid 0^+1^*2)^*$. Note that the first digit is never a TWO. Thus, we can increment a number in $O(1)$ worst-case time by blindly incrementing the first digit.

```
fun simpleInc [] = [ONES 1]
  | simpleInc (ZERO :: ds) = ones (1, ds)
  | simpleInc (ONES i :: ds) = TWO :: one (i−1,ds)
```

The third line obviously violates the invariant by producing a leading TWO, but the second line might also violate the invariant if the first non-one digit in ds is a TWO. We restore the invariant with a function fixup that checks whether the first non-one digit is a TWO. If so, fixup replaces the TWO with a ZERO and increments the following digit, which is guaranteed not to be TWO.

```
fun fixup (TWO :: ds) = ZERO :: simpleInc ds
  | fixup (ONES i :: TWO :: ds) = ONES i :: ZERO :: simpleInc ds
  | fixup ds = ds
```

The second line of fixup is where we take advantage of segmentation, by skipping over a block of ones to check whether the next digit is a TWO. Finally, inc calls simpleInc, followed by fixup.

fun inc *ds* = fixup (simpleInc *ds*)

This implementation can also serve as template for many other data structures. Such a data structure comprises a sequence of levels, where each level can be classified as *green, yellow,* or *red*. Each color corresponds to a digit in the above implementation. Green corresponds to ZERO, yellow to ONE, and red to TWO. An operation on any given object may degrade the color of the first level from green to yellow, or from yellow to red, but never from green to red. The invariant is that the last non-yellow level before a red level is always green. A fixup procedure maintains the invariant by checking if the first non-yellow level is red. If so, the fixup procedure changes the color of the level from red to green, possibly degrading the color of the following level from green to yellow, or from yellow to red. Consecutive yellow levels are grouped in a block to support efficient access to the first non-yellow level. Kaplan and Tarjan [KT95] call this general technique *recursive slowdown*.

Exercise 9.11 Extend binomial heaps with segmentation so that insert runs in $O(1)$ worst-case time. Use the type

datatype Tree = NODE **of** Elem.T × Tree list
datatype Digit = ZERO | ONES **of** Tree list | TWO **of** Tree × Tree
type Heap = Digit list

Restore the invariant after a merge by eliminating all TWOs.

Exercise 9.12 The example implementation of binary numbers based on recursive slowdown supports inc in $O(1)$ worst-case time, but might require up to $O(\log n)$ for dec. Reimplement segmented, redundant binary numbers to support both inc and dec in $O(1)$ worst-case time by allowing each digit to be 0, 1, 2, 3, or 4, where 0 and 4 are red, 1 and 3 are yellow, and 2 is green.

Exercise 9.13 Implement cons, head, tail, and lookup for a numerical representation of random-access lists based on the number system of the previous exercise. Your implementation should support cons, head, and tail in $O(1)$ worst-case time, and lookup in $O(\log i)$ worst-case time.

9.3 Skew Binary Numbers

In lazy binary numbers and segmented binary numbers, we have seen two methods for improving the asymptotic behavior of the increment and decrement functions from $O(\log n)$ to $O(1)$. In this section, we consider a third method, which is usually simpler and faster in practice, but which involves a more radical departure from ordinary binary numbers.

In *skew binary numbers* [Mye83, Oka95b], the weight w_i of the ith digit is $2^{i+1} - 1$, rather than 2^i as in ordinary binary numbers. Digits may be zero, one, or two (i.e., $D_i = \{0, 1, 2\}$). For example, the decimal number 92 could be written 002101 (least-significant digit first).

This number system is redundant, but, if we add the further constraint that only the lowest non-zero digit may be two, then we regain unique representations. Such a number is said to be in *canonical form*. Henceforth, we will assume that all skew binary numbers are in canonical form.

Theorem 9.1 (Myers [Mye83]) *Every natural number has a unique skew binary canonical form.*

Recall that the weight of digit i is $2^{i+1} - 1$ and note that $1 + 2(2^{i+1} - 1) = 2^{i+2} - 1$. This implies that we can increment a skew binary number whose lowest non-zero digit is two by resetting the two to zero and incrementing the next digit from zero to one or from one to two. (The next digit cannot already be two.) Incrementing a skew binary number that does not contain a two is even easier — simply increment the lowest digit from zero to one or from one to two. In both cases, the result is still in canonical form. And, assuming we can find the lowest non-zero digit in $O(1)$ time, both cases take only $O(1)$ time!

We cannot use a dense representation for skew binary numbers since scanning for the lowest non-zero digit would take more than $O(1)$ time. Instead, we choose a sparse representation, so that we always have immediate access to the lowest non-zero digit.

type Nat = int list

The integers represent either the rank or weight of each non-zero digit. For now, we use weights. The weights are stored in increasing order, except that the smallest two weights may be identical, indicating that the lowest non-zero digit is two. Given this representation, we implement inc as follows:

```
fun inc (ws as w₁ :: w₂ :: rest) =
    if w₁ = w₂ then (1+w₁+w₂) :: rest else 1 :: ws
  | inc ws = 1 :: ws
```

The first clause checks whether the first two weights are equal and then either combines the weights into the next larger weight (incrementing the next digit) or adds a new weight of 1 (incrementing the smallest digit). The second clause handles the case that *ws* is empty or contains only a single weight. Clearly, inc runs in only $O(1)$ worst-case time.

Decrementing a skew binary number is just as easy as incrementing a number. If the lowest digit is non-zero, then we simply decrement that digit from two to one or from one to zero. Otherwise, we decrement the lowest non-zero digit and reset the previous zero to two. This can be implemented as follows:

fun dec (1 :: *ws*) = *ws*
  | dec (*w* :: *ws*) = (*w* div 2) :: (*w* div 2) :: *ws*

In the second line, note that if $w = 2^{k+1} - 1$, then $\lfloor w/2 \rfloor = 2^k - 1$. Clearly, dec also runs in only $O(1)$ worst-case time.

9.3.1 Skew Binary Random-Access Lists

We next design a numerical representation for random-access lists, based on skew binary numbers. The basic representation is a list of trees, with one tree for each one digit and two trees for each two digit. The trees are maintained in increasing order of size, except that the smallest two trees are the same size when the lowest non-zero digit is two.

The sizes of the trees correspond to the weights in skew binary numbers, so a tree representing the *i*th digit has size $2^{i+1} - 1$. Up until now, we have mainly considered trees whose sizes are powers of two, but we have also encountered a kind of tree whose sizes have the desired form: complete binary trees. Therefore, we represent skew binary random-access lists as lists of complete binary trees.

To support head efficiently, the first element in the random-access list should be the root of the first tree, so we store the elements within each tree in left-to-right preorder and with the elements in each tree preceding the elements in the next tree.

In previous examples, we have stored a size or rank in every node, even when that information was redundant. For this example, we adopt the more realistic approach of maintaining size information only for the root of each tree in the list, and not for every subtree as well. The type of skew binary random-access lists is therefore

datatype α Tree = LEAF **of** α | NODE **of** $\alpha \times \alpha$ Tree $\times \alpha$ Tree
type α RList = (int $\times \alpha$ Tree) list

Now, we can define cons in analogy to inc.

fun cons (*x*, *ts* **as** (w_1, t_1) :: (w_2, t_2) :: *rest*) =
    if $w_1 = w_2$ **then** (1+w_1+w_2, NODE (*x*, t_1, t_2)) :: *rest*)
    else (1, LEAF *x*) :: *ts*
  | cons (*x*, *ts*) = (1, LEAF *x*) :: *ts*

head and tail inspect and remove the root of the first tree. tail returns the children of the root (if any) back to the front of the list, where they represent a new two digit.

fun head ((1, LEAF x) :: ts) = x
| head ((w, NODE (x, t_1, t_2)) :: ts) = x
fun tail ((1, LEAF x) :: ts) = ts
| tail ((w, NODE (x, t_1, t_2)) :: ts) = (w div 2, t_1) :: (w div 2, t_2) :: ts

To lookup an element, we first search the list for the right tree, and then search the tree for the right element. When searching a tree, we keep track of the size of the current tree.

fun lookup (i, (w, t) :: ts) =
  if $i < w$ **then** lookupTree (w, i, t)
  else lookup ($i-w$, ts)

fun lookupTree (1, 0, LEAF x) = x
| lookupTree (w, 0, NODE (x, t_1, t_2)) = x
| lookupTree (w, i, NODE (x, t_1, t_2)) =
  if $i < w$ div 2 **then** lookupTree (w div 2, $i-1$, t_1)
  else lookupTree (w div 2, $i - 1 - w$ div 2, t_2)

Note that in the penultimate line, we subtract one from i because we have skipped over x. In the last line, we subtract $1 + \lfloor w/2 \rfloor$ from i because we have skipped over x and all the elements in t_1. update and updateTree are defined similarly, and are shown in Figure 9.7, which contains the complete implementation.

It is easy to verify that cons, head, and tail run in $O(1)$ worst-case time. Like binary random-access lists, skew binary random-access lists are logarithmic-length lists of logarithmic-depth trees, so lookup and update run in $O(\log n)$ worst-case time. In fact, every unsuccessful step of lookup or update discards at least one element, so this bound can be reduced slightly to $O(\min(i, \log n))$.

Hint to Practitioners: Skew binary random-access lists are a good choice for applications that take advantage of both the list-like aspects and the array-like aspects of random-access lists. Although there are better implementations of lists, and better implementations of (persistent) arrays, none are better at both [Oka95b].

Exercise 9.14 Rewrite the HoodMelvilleQueue structure from Section 8.2.1 to use skew binary random-access lists instead of regular lists. Implement lookup and update functions on these queues.

```
structure SkewBinaryRandomAccessList : RANDOMACCESSLIST =
struct
  datatype α Tree = LEAF of α | NODE of α × α Tree × α Tree
  type α RList = (int × α Tree) list    (* integer is the weight of the tree *)

  val empty = [ ]
  fun isEmpty ts = null ts

  fun cons (x, ts as (w₁, t₁) :: (w₂, t₂) :: ts') =
        if w₁ = w₂ then (1+w₁+w₂, NODE (x, t₁, t₂)) :: ts'
        else (1, LEAF x) :: ts
    | cons (x, ts) = (1, LEAF x) :: ts
  fun head [ ] = raise EMPTY
    | head ((1, LEAF x) :: ts) = x
    | head ((w, NODE (x, t₁, t₂)) :: ts) = x
  fun tail [ ] = raise EMPTY
    | tail ((1, LEAF x) :: ts) = ts
    | tail ((w, NODE (x, t₁, t₂)) :: ts) = (w div 2, t₁) :: (w div 2, t₂) :: ts

  fun lookupTree (1, 0, LEAF x) = x
    | lookupTree (1, i, LEAF x) = raise SUBSCRIPT
    | lookupTree (w, 0, NODE (x, t₁, t₂)) = x
    | lookupTree (w, i, NODE (x, t₁, t₂)) =
        if i ≤ w div 2 then lookupTree (w div 2, i−1, t₁)
        else lookupTree (w div 2, i − 1 − w div 2, t₂)
  fun updateTree (1, 0, y, LEAF x) = LEAF y
    | updateTree (1, i, y, LEAF x) = raise SUBSCRIPT
    | updateTree (w, 0, y, NODE (x, t₁, t₂)) = NODE (y, t₁, t₂)
    | updateTree (w, i, y, NODE (x, t₁, t₂)) =
        if i ≤ w div 2 then NODE (x, updateTree (w div 2, i−1, y, t₁), t₂)
        else NODE (x, t₁, updateTree (w div 2, i − 1 − w div 2, y, t₂))

  fun lookup (i, [ ]) = raise SUBSCRIPT
    | lookup (i, (w, t) :: ts) =
        if i < w then lookupTree (w, i, t)
        else lookup (i−w, ts)
  fun update (i, y, [ ]) = raise SUBSCRIPT
    | update (i, y, (w, t) :: ts) =
        if i < w then (w, updateTree (w, i, y, t)) :: ts
        else (w, t) :: update (i−w, y, ts)
end
```

Figure 9.7. Skew binary random-access lists.

9.3.2 Skew Binomial Heaps

Finally, we consider a hybrid numerical representation for heaps based on both skew binary numbers and ordinary binary numbers. Incrementing a skew binary number is both quick and simple, and serves admirably as a template for the insert function. Unfortunately, addition of two arbitrary skew binary numbers is awkward. We therefore base the merge function on ordinary binary addition, rather than skew binary addition.

A *skew binomial tree* is a binomial tree in which every node is augmented with a list of up to r elements, where r is the rank of the node in question.

datatype Tree = NODE **of** int $\times$ Elem.T $\times$ Elem.T list $\times$ Tree list

Unlike ordinary binomial trees, the size of a skew binomial tree is not completely determined by its rank; rather the rank of a skew binomial tree determines a range of possible sizes.

Lemma 9.2 *If t is a skew binomial tree of rank r, then $2^r \leq |t| \leq 2^{r+1} - 1$.*

Exercise 9.15 Prove Lemma 9.2. $\diamondsuit$

Skew binomial trees may be *linked* or *skew linked*. The link function combines two trees of rank r to form a tree of rank $r + 1$ by making the tree with the larger root a child of the tree with the smaller root.

fun link (t_1 **as** NODE (r, x_1, xs_1, c_1), t_2 **as** NODE ($\_$, x_2, xs_2, c_2)) =
  if Elem.leq (x_1, x_2) **then** NODE (r+1, x_1, xs_1, $t_2 :: c_1$)
  else NODE (r+1, x_2, xs_2, $t_1 :: c_2$)

The skewLink function combines two trees of rank r with an additional element to form a tree of rank $r + 1$ by first linking the two trees, and then comparing the root of the resulting tree with the additional element. The smaller of the two elements remains as the root, and the larger is added to the auxiliary list of elements.

fun skewLink (x, t_1, t_2) =
  let val NODE (r, y, ys, c) = link (t_1, t_2)
  in
    if Elem.leq (x, y) **then** NODE (r, x, $y :: ys$, c)
    else NODE (r, y, $x :: ys$, c)
  end

A skew binomial heap is represented as a list of heap-ordered skew binomial trees of increasing rank, except that the first two trees may share the same rank. Since skew binomial trees of the same rank may have different sizes, there is no longer a direct correspondence between the trees in the heap and the digits in the skew binary number representing the size of the heap. For example, even though the skew binary representation of 4 is 11, a skew binomial heap of size 4 may contain one rank 2 tree of size 4; two rank 1 trees, each of size 2; a rank 1 tree of size 3 and a rank 0 tree; or a rank 1 tree of size 2 and two rank 0 trees. However, the maximum number of trees in a heap is still $O(\log n)$.

The big advantage of skew binomial heaps is that we can insert a new element in $O(1)$ time. We first compare the ranks of the two smallest trees. If they are the same, we skew link the new element with these two trees. Otherwise, we make a new singleton tree and add it to the front of the list.

```
fun insert (x, ts as t₁ :: t₂ :: rest) =
    if rank t₁ = rank t₂ then skewLink (x, t₁, t₂) :: rest
    else NODE (0, x, [ ], [ ]) :: ts
  | insert (x, ts) = NODE (0, x, [ ], [ ]) :: ts
```

The remaining functions are nearly identical to their counterparts from ordinary binomial heaps. We change the name of the old merge function to merge-Trees. It still walks through both lists of trees, performing a regular link (not a skew link!) whenever it finds two trees of equal rank. Since both mergeTrees and its helper function insTree expect lists of strictly increasing rank, merge normalizes its two arguments to remove any leading duplicates before calling mergeTrees.

```
fun normalize [ ] = [ ]
  | normalize (t :: ts) = insTree (t, ts)
fun merge (ts₁, ts₂) = mergeTrees (normalize ts₁, normalize ts₂)
```

findMin and removeMinTree are completely unaffected by the switch to skew binomial heaps since they both ignore ranks, being concerned only with the root of each tree. deleteMin is only slightly changed. It begins the same by removing the tree with the minimum root, reversing the list of children, and merging the reversed children with the remaining trees. But then it reinserts each of the elements from the auxiliary list attached to discarded root.

```
fun deleteMin ts =
    let val (NODE (_, x, xs, ts₁), ts₂) = removeMinTree ts
        fun insertAll ([ ], ts) = ts
          | insertAll (x :: xs, ts) = insertAll (xs, insert (x, ts))
    in insertAll (xs, merge (rev ts₁, ts₂)) end
```

Figure 9.8 presents the complete implementation of skew binomial heaps.

insert runs in $O(1)$ worst-case time, while merge, findMin, and deleteMin run in the same time as their counterparts for ordinary binomial queues, i.e., $O(\log n)$ worst-case time each. Note that the various phases of deleteMin — finding the tree with the minimum root, reversing the children, merging the children with the remaining trees, and reinserting the auxiliary elements — take $O(\log n)$ time each.

If desired, we can improve the running time of findMin to $O(1)$ using the ExplicitMin functor of Exercise 3.7. In Section 10.2.2, we will see how to improve the running time of merge to $O(1)$ as well.

```
functor SkewBinomialHeap (Element : ORDERED) : HEAP =
struct
  structure Elem = Element
  datatype Tree = NODE of int × Elem.T × Elem.T list × Tree list
  type Heap = Tree list
  val empty = [ ]
  fun isEmpty ts = null ts
  fun rank (NODE (r, x, xs, c)) = r
  fun root (NODE (r, x, xs, c)) = x
  fun link (t₁ as NODE (r, x₁, xs₁, c₁), t₂ as NODE (_, x₂, xs₂, c₂)) =
      if Elem.leq (x₁, x₂) then NODE (r+1, x₁, xs₁, t₂ :: c₁)
      else NODE (r+1, x₂, xs₂, t₁ :: c₂)
  fun skewLink (x, t₁, t₂) =
      let val NODE (r, y, ys, c) = link (t₁, t₂)
      in
          if Elem.leq (x, y) then NODE (r, x, y :: ys, c)
          else NODE (r, y, x :: ys, c)
      end
  fun insTree (t, [ ]) = [t]
    | insTree (t₁, t₂ :: ts) =
      if rank t₁ < rank t₂ then t₁ :: t₂ :: ts else insTree (link (t₁, t₂), ts)
  fun mergeTrees (ts₁, [ ]) = ts₁
    | mergeTrees ([ ], ts₂) = ts₂
    | mergeTrees (ts₁ as t₁ :: ts₁', ts₂ as t₂ :: ts₂') =
      if rank t₁ < rank t₂ then t₁ :: mergeTrees (ts₁', ts₂)
      else if rank t₂ < rank t₁ then t₂ :: mergeTrees (ts₁,ts₂')
      else insTree (link (t₁, t₂), mergeTrees (ts₁', ts₂'))
  fun normalize [ ] = [ ]
    | normalize (t :: ts) = insTree (t, ts)
  fun insert (x, ts as t₁ :: t₂ :: rest) =
      if rank t₁ = rank t₂ then skewLink (x, t₁, t₂) :: rest
      else NODE (0, x, [ ], [ ]) :: ts
    | insert (x, ts) = NODE (0, x, [ ], [ ]) :: ts
  fun merge (ts₁, ts₂) = mergeTrees (normalize ts₁, normalize ts₂)

  fun removeMinTree [ ] = raise EMPTY
    | removeMinTree [t] = (t, [ ])
    | removeMinTree (t :: ts) =
      let val (t', ts') = removeMinTree ts
      in if Elem.leq (root t, root t') then (t, ts) else (t', t :: ts') end

  fun findMin ts = let val (t, _) = removeMinTree ts in root t end
  fun deleteMin ts =
      let val (NODE (_, x, xs, ts₁), ts₂) = removeMinTree ts
          fun insertAll ([ ], ts) = ts
            | insertAll (x :: xs, ts) = insertAll (xs, insert (x, ts))
      in insertAll (xs, merge (rev ts₁, ts₂)) end
end
```

Figure 9.8. Skew binomial heaps.

Exercise 9.16 Suppose we want a delete function of type Elem.T × Heap → Heap. Write a functor that takes an implementation H of heaps and produces an implementation of heaps that supports delete as well as all the other usual heap functions. Use the type

type Heap = H.Heap × H.Heap

where one of the primitive heaps represents positive occurrences of elements and the other represents negative occurrences. A negative occurrence of an element means that that element has been deleted, but not yet physically removed from the heap. Positive and negative occurrences of the same element cancel each other out and are physically removed when both become the minimum elements of their respective heaps. Maintain the invariant that the minimum element of the positive heap is strictly smaller than the minimum element of the negative heap. (This implementation has the curious property that an element can be deleted before it has been inserted, but this is acceptable for many applications.)

9.4 Trinary and Quaternary Numbers

In computer science, we are so accustomed to thinking about binary numbers, that we sometimes forget that other bases are possible. In this section, we consider uses of base 3 and base 4 arithmetic in numerical representations.

The weight of each digit in base k is k^r, so we need families of trees with sizes of this form. We can generalize each of the families of trees used in binary numerical representations as follows.

Definition 9.4 (Complete k-ary leaf trees) A complete k-ary tree of rank 0 is a leaf and a complete k-ary tree of rank $r > 0$ is a node with k children, each of which is a complete k-ary tree of rank $r - 1$. A complete k-ary tree of rank r has $(k^{r+1} - 1)/(k - 1)$ nodes and k^r leaves. A complete k-ary leaf tree is a complete k-ary tree that contains elements only at the leaves.

Definition 9.5 (k-nomial trees) A k-nomial tree of rank r is a node with $k - 1$ children of each rank from $r - 1$ to 0. Alternatively, a k-nomial tree of rank $r > 0$ is a k-nomial tree of rank $r-1$ to which $k-1$ other k-nomial trees of rank $r - 1$ have been added as the leftmost children. From the second definition, it is easy to see that a k-nomial tree of rank r contains k^r nodes.

Definition 9.6 (k-ary pennants) A k-ary pennant of rank 0 is a single node and a k-ary pennant of rank $r > 0$ is a node with $k - 1$ children, each of which is a complete k-ary tree of rank $r - 1$. Each of the subtrees contains $(k^r - 1)/(k - 1)$ nodes, so the entire tree contains k^r nodes.

The advantage of choosing bases larger than 2 is that fewer digits are needed to represent each number. Whereas a number in base 2 contains approximately $\log_2 n$ digits, a number in base k contains approximately $\log_k n = \log_2 n / \log_2 k$ digits. For example, base 4 uses approximately half as many digits as base 2. On the other hand, there are now more possible values for each digit, so processing each digit might take longer. In numerical representations, processing a digit in base k often takes about $k + 1$ steps, so an operation that processes every digit should take about $(k + 1)\log_k n = \frac{k+1}{\log_2 k}\log n$ steps altogether. The following table displays values of $(k + 1)/\log_2 k$ for $k = 2, \ldots, 8$.

k	2	3	4	5	6	7	8
$(k + 1)/\log_2 k$	3.00	2.52	2.50	2.58	2.71	2.85	3.0

This table suggests that numerical representations based on trinary or quaternary numbers might be as much as 16% faster than numerical representations based on binary numbers. Other factors, such as increased code size, tend to make larger bases less effective as k increases, so one rarely observes speedups that large in practice. In fact, trinary and quaternary representations often run slower than binary representations on small data sets. However, for large data sets, trinary and quaternary representations often yield speedups of 5 to 10%.

Exercise 9.17 Implement trinomial heaps using the type

```
datatype Tree = NODE of Elem.T × (Tree × Tree) list
datatype Digit = ZERO | ONE of Tree | TWO of Tree × Tree
type Heap = Digit list
```

Exercise 9.18 Implement zeroless quaternary random-access lists using the type

```
datatype α Tree = LEAF of α | NODE of α Tree vector
datatype α RList = α Tree vector list
```

where each vector in a NODE contains four trees, and each vector in a list contains one to four trees.

Exercise 9.19 We can also adapt the notion of skew binary numbers to arbitrary bases. In skew k-ary numbers, the ith digit has weight $(k^{i+1} - 1)/(k-1)$. Each digit is chosen from $\{0, \ldots, k - 1\}$ except that the lowest non-zero digit may be k. Implement skew trinary random-access lists using the type

datatype α Tree = LEAF **of** α | NODE **of** $\alpha \times \alpha$ Tree $\times \alpha$ Tree $\times \alpha$ Tree
type α RList = (int $\times \alpha$ Tree) list

9.5 Chapter Notes

Data structures that can be cast as numerical representations are surprisingly common, but only rarely is the connection to a variant number system noted explicitly [GMPR77, Mye83, CMP88, KT96b]. Skew binary random-access lists originally appeared in [Oka95b]. Skew binomial heaps originally appeared in [BO96].

10
Data-Structural Bootstrapping

The term *bootstrapping* refers to "pulling yourself up by your bootstraps". This seemingly nonsensical image is representative of a common situation in computer science: problems whose solutions require solutions to (simpler) instances of the same problem.

For example, consider loading an operating system from disk or tape onto a bare computer. Without an operating system, the computer cannot even read from the disk or tape! One solution is a *bootstrap loader*, a very tiny, incomplete operating system whose only purpose is to read in and pass control to a somewhat larger, more capable operating system that in turn reads in and passes control to the actual, desired operating system. This can be viewed as an instance of bootstrapping a complete solution from an incomplete solution.

Another example is bootstrapping a compiler. A common activity is to write the compiler for a new language in the language itself. But then how do you compile that compiler? One solution is to write a very simple, inefficient interpreter for the language in some other, existing language. Then, using the interpreter, you can execute the compiler on itself, thereby obtaining an efficient, compiled executable for the compiler. This can be viewed as an instance of bootstrapping an efficient solution from an inefficient solution.

In his thesis [Buc93], Adam Buchsbaum describes two algorithmic design techniques he collectively calls *data-structural bootstrapping*. The first technique, *structural decomposition*, involves bootstrapping complete data structures from incomplete data structures. The second technique, *structural abstraction*, involves bootstrapping efficient data structures from inefficient data structures. In this chapter, we reexamine these two techniques, along with a third technique for bootstrapping data structures with aggregate elements from data structures with atomic elements.

10.1 Structural Decomposition

Structural decomposition is a technique for bootstrapping complete data structures from incomplete data structures. Typically, this involves taking an implementation that can handle objects only up to some bounded size (perhaps even zero), and extending it to handle objects of unbounded size.

Consider typical recursive datatypes such as lists and binary leaf trees:

datatype α List = NIL | CONS **of** α × α List
datatype α Tree = LEAF **of** α | NODE **of** α Tree × α Tree

In some ways, these can be regarded as instances of structural decomposition. Both consist of a simple implementation of objects of some bounded size (zero for lists and one for trees) and a rule for recursively decomposing larger objects into smaller objects until eventually each object is small enough to be handled by the bounded case.

However, both of these definitions are particularly simple in that the recursive component in each definition is identical to the type being defined. For instance, the recursive component in the definition of α List is also α List. Such a datatype is called *uniformly recursive*.

In general, we reserve the term *structural decomposition* to describe recursive data structures that are *non-uniform*. For example, consider the following definition of sequences:

datatype α Seq = NIL' | CONS' **of** α × (α × α) Seq

Here, a sequence is either empty or a single element together with a sequence of pairs of elements. The recursive component (α × α) Seq is different from α Seq so this datatype is non-uniform.

Why might such a non-uniform definition be preferable to a uniform definition? The more sophisticated structure of non-uniform types often supports more efficient algorithms than their uniform cousins. For example, compare the following size functions on lists and sequences.

fun sizeL NIL = 0
 | sizeL (CONS (*x*, *xs*)) = 1 + sizeL *xs*

fun sizeS NIL' = 0
 | sizeS (CONS' (*x*, *ps*)) = 1 + 2 * sizeS *ps*

The function on lists runs in $O(n)$ time whereas the function on sequences runs in $O(\log n)$ time.

10.1.1 Non-Uniform Recursion and Standard ML

Unfortunately, we usually cannot implement structural decomposition directly in Standard ML. Although Standard ML allows the definition of non-uniform recursive datatypes. the type system disallows most of the interesting functions on such types. For instance, consider the sizeS function on sequences. This function would be rejected by Standard ML because the type system requires that all recursive calls in the body of a recursive function have the same type as the enclosing function (i.e., recursive function definitions must be uniform). The sizeS function violates this restriction because the outer sizeS has type α Seq $\rightarrow$ int but the inner sizeS has type $(\alpha \times \alpha)$ Seq $\rightarrow$ int.

It is always possible to convert a non-uniform type into a uniform type by introducing a new datatype to collapse the different instances into a single type. For example, by collapsing elements and pairs, the Seq type could be rewritten

datatype α EP = ELEM **of** α | PAIR **of** α EP $\times$ α EP
datatype α Seq = NIL' | CONS' **of** α EP $\times$ α Seq

Then the sizeS function would be perfectly legal as written; both the outer sizeS and the inner sizeS would have type α Seq $\rightarrow$ int.

Since it is always possible to convert non-uniform types to uniform types, structural decomposition really refers more to how we think about a datatype than to how it is implemented. For example, consider the revised definition of α Seq above. The α EP type is isomorphic to binary leaf trees, so the revised version of α Seq is equivalent to α Tree list. However, we would tend to think of a list of trees differently than we would think of a sequence of pairs — some algorithms will seem simpler or more natural for one of the representations, and some for the other. We will see some examples of this in the next section.

There are also several pragmatic reasons to prefer the non-uniform definition of α Seq over the uniform one. First, it is more concise; there is one type instead of two, and there is no need to manually insert ELEM and PAIR constructors everywhere. Second, depending on the language implementation, it may be more efficient; there is no need to pattern match against ELEM and PAIR constructors, nor to build run-time representations of these constructors in memory. Third, and most importantly, it allows the type system to catch many more programmer errors. The type in the non-uniform definition ensures that the outermost CONS' constructor contains a single element, the second a pair of elements, the third a pair of pairs of elements, and so on. The type in the uniform definition ensures neither that pairs are balanced nor that the nesting depth of pairs increases by one per level. Instead, these restrictions must be established by the programmer as system invariants. But if the programmer accidentally violates these invariants — say, by using an element where a pair is expected — the type system will be of no help in catching the error.

For these reasons, we will often present code as if Standard ML supported non-uniform recursive function definitions, also known as *polymorphic recursion* [Myc84]. This code will not be executable but will be easier to read. It can always be converted back into legal Standard ML using the kinds of coercions described on the previous page.

10.1.2 Binary Random-Access Lists Revisited

For all of its virtues, the α Seq type that we have been discussing is useless for representing sequences. The problem is that it can only represent sequences with $2^k - 1$ elements. Thinking in terms of numerical representations, the CONS' constructor gives us a way to write one bits, but there is no way to write zero bits. This is easily corrected by adding another constructor to the type. We also rename the CONS' constructor to emphasize the analogy to binary numbers.

datatype α Seq = NIL | ZERO **of** $(\alpha \times \alpha)$ Seq | ONE **of** $\alpha \times (\alpha \times \alpha)$ Seq

Now, we can represent the sequence $0\ldots 10$ as

ONE (0, ONE ((1,2), ZERO (ONE ((((3,4),(5,6)),((7,8),(9,10))), NIL))))

The size of this sequence is eleven, written 1101 in binary.

The pairs in this type are always balanced. In fact, another way to think of pairs of elements or pairs of pairs of elements, etc., is as complete binary leaf trees. Thus, this type is essentially equivalent to the type of binary random-access lists from Section 9.2.1, but with the invariants of that structure made manifest.

Let's reimplement the functions on binary random-access lists, this time thinking in terms of elements and sequences of pairs rather than lists of complete binary leaf trees. The functions all still run in $O(\log n)$ time, but, as we will see, this new way of thinking yields algorithms that are usually both shorter and easier to understand.

We begin with the cons function. The first two clauses are easy.

```
fun cons (x, NIL) = ONE (x, NIL)
  | cons (x, ZERO ps) = ONE (x, ps)
```

To add a new element to a sequence of the form ONE (y, ps), we pair the new element with the existing element and add the pair to the sequence of pairs.

```
fun cons (x, ONE (y, ps)) = ZERO (cons ((x, y), ps))
```

This is where we need polymorphic recursion—the outer cons has type

$$\alpha \times \alpha \ \mathsf{Seq} \to \alpha \ \mathsf{Seq}$$

while the inner cons has type

$$(\alpha \times \alpha) \times (\alpha \times \alpha) \ \mathsf{Seq} \to (\alpha \times \alpha) \ \mathsf{Seq}.$$

We implement the head and tail functions in terms of an auxiliary function uncons that deconstructs a sequence into its first element and the remaining sequence.

```
fun head xs = let val (x, _) = uncons xs in x end
fun tail xs = let val (_, xs') = uncons xs in xs' end
```

We obtain the uncons function by reading each of the clauses for cons backwards.

```
fun uncons (ONE (x, NIL)) = (x, NIL)
  | uncons (ONE (x, ps)) = (x, ZERO ps)
  | uncons (ZERO ps) = let val ((x, y), ps') = uncons ps
                       in (x, ONE (y, ps')) end
```

Next, consider the lookup function. Given a sequence ONE (x, ps), we either return x or repeat the query on ZERO ps.

```
fun lookup (0, ONE (x, ps)) = x
  | lookup (i, ONE (x, ps)) = lookup (i−1, ZERO ps)
```

To lookup the element at index i in a sequence of pairs, we lookup the pair at index $\lfloor i/2 \rfloor$ and then extract the appropriate element from that pair.

```
fun lookup (i, ZERO ps) = let val (x, y) = lookup (i div 2, ps)
                          in if i mod 2 = 0 then x else y end
```

Finally, we turn to the update function. The clauses for the ONE constructor are simply

```
fun update (0, e, ONE (x, ps)) = ONE (e, ps)
  | update (i, e, ONE (x, ps)) = cons (x, update (i−1, e, ZERO ps))
```

However, in trying to update an element in a sequence of pairs, we run into a slight problem. We need to update the pair at index $\lfloor i/2 \rfloor$, but to construct the new pair, we need the other element from the old pair. Thus, we precede the update with a lookup.

```
fun update (i, e, ZERO ps) =
    let val (x, y) = lookup (i div 2, ps)
        val p = if i mod 2 = 0 then (e, y) else (x, e)
    in ZERO (update (i−1, p, ps)) end
```

Exercise 10.1 Prove that this version of update runs in $O(\log^2 n)$ time. ◇

To restore the $O(\log n)$ bound on the update function, we must eliminate the call to lookup. But then how do we get the other element from which to construct the new pair? Well, if we cannot bring Mohammed to the mountain, then we must send the mountain to Mohammed. That is, instead of fetching the old pair and constructing the new pair locally, we send a function to construct the new pair from the old pair wherever the old pair is found. We use a helper function fupdate that takes a function to apply to the ith element of a sequence. Then update is simply

fun update (*i, y, xs*) = fupdate (**fn** *x* ⇒ *y, i, xs*)

The key step in fupdate is promoting a function f on elements to a function f' that takes a pair and applies f to either the first or second element of the pair, depending on the parity of i.

fun f' (*x, y*) = **if** *i* mod 2 = 0 **then** (*f x, y*) **else** (*x, f y*)

Given this definition, the rest of fupdate is straightforward.

fun fupdate (*f*, 0, ONE (*x, ps*)) = ONE (*f x, ps*)
  | fupdate (*f, i*, ONE (*x, ps*)) = cons (*x*, fupdate (*f, i*−1, ZERO *ps*))
  | fupdate (*f, i*, ZERO *ps*) =
    let fun f' (*x, y*) = **if** *i* mod 2 = 0 **then** (*f x, y*) **else** (*x, f y*)
    in ZERO (fupdate (*f', i* div 2, *ps*)) **end**

The complete implementation is shown in Figure 10.1.

Comparing Figures 10.1 and 9.6, we see that this implementation is significantly more concise and that the individual functions are significantly simpler, with the possible exception of update. (And even update is simpler if you are comfortable with higher-order functions.) These benefits arise from recasting the data structure as a non-uniform type that directly reflects the desired invariants.

Exercise 10.2 Reimplement AltBinaryRandomAccessList so that cons, head, and tail all run in $O(1)$ amortized time, using the type

datatype α RList =
  NIL
  | ONE **of** $\alpha \times (\alpha \times \alpha)$ RList susp
  | TWO **of** $\alpha \times \alpha \times (\alpha \times \alpha)$ RList susp
  | THREE **of** $\alpha \times \alpha \times \alpha \times (\alpha \times \alpha)$ RList susp

10.1.3 Bootstrapped Queues

Consider the use of ++ in the banker's queues of Section 6.3.2. During a rotation, the front stream *f* is replaced by *f* ++ reverse *r*. After a series of rotations,

```
structure AltBinaryRandomAccessList : RANDOMACCESSLIST =
(* assumes polymorphic recursion! *)
struct
  datatype α RList =
      NIL | ZERO of (α × α) RList | ONE of α × (α × α) RList

  val empty = NIL
  fun isEmpty NIL = true | isEmpty _ = false

  fun cons (x, NIL) = ONE (x, NIL)
    | cons (x, ZERO ps) = ONE (x, ps)
    | cons (x, ONE (y, ps)) = ZERO (cons ((x, y), ps))

  fun uncons NIL = raise EMPTY
    | uncons (ONE (x, NIL)) = (x, NIL)
    | uncons (ONE (x, ps)) = (x, ZERO ps)
    | uncons (ZERO ps) = let val ((x, y), ps') = uncons ps
                         in (x, ONE (y, ps')) end

  fun head xs = let val (x, _) = uncons xs in x end
  fun tail xs = let val (_, xs') = uncons xs in xs' end

  fun lookup (i, NIL) = raise SUBSCRIPT
    | lookup (0, ONE (x, ps)) = x
    | lookup (i, ONE (x, ps)) = lookup (i−1, ZERO ps)
    | lookup (i, ZERO ps) = let val (x, y) = lookup (i div 2, ps)
                            in if i mod 2 = 0 then x else y end

  fun fupdate (f, i, NIL) = raise SUBSCRIPT
    | fupdate (f, 0, ONE (x, ps)) = ONE (f x, ps)
    | fupdate (f, i, ONE (x, ps)) = cons (x, fupdate (f, i−1, ZERO ps))
    | fupdate (f, i, ZERO ps) =
        let fun f' (x, y) = if i mod 2 = 0 then (f x, y) else (x, f y)
        in ZERO (fupdate (f', i div 2, ps)) end

  fun update (i, y, xs) = fupdate (fn x ⇒ y, i, xs)
end
```

Figure 10.1. An alternative implementation of binary random-access lists.

the front stream has the form

$$((f \mathbin{+\!\!+} \text{reverse } r_1) \mathbin{+\!\!+} \text{reverse } r_2) \mathbin{+\!\!+} \cdots \mathbin{+\!\!+} \text{reverse } r_k$$

Append is well-known to be inefficient in left-associative contexts like this because it repeatedly processes the elements of the leftmost streams. For example, in this case, the elements of f will be processed k times (once by each $\mathbin{+\!\!+}$), and the elements of r_i will be processed $k - i + 1$ times (once by reverse and once for each following $\mathbin{+\!\!+}$). In general, left-associative appends can easily lead to quadratic behavior. In this case, fortunately, the total cost of the appends is still linear because each r_i is at least twice as long as the one before. Still, this repeated processing does sometimes make these queues slow in practice. In this section, we use structural decomposition to eliminate this inefficiency.

Given that the front stream has the described form, we decompose it into two parts: f and the collection $m = \{\text{reverse } r_1, \ldots, \text{reverse } r_k\}$. Then we can represent f as a list and each reverse r_i as a suspended list. We also change the rear stream r to a list. These changes eliminate the vast majority of suspensions and avoid almost all of the overheads associated with lazy evaluation. But how should we represent the collection m? As we will see, this collection is accessed in FIFO order, so using structural decomposition we can represent it as a queue of suspended lists. As with any recursive type, we need a base case, so we represent empty queues with a special constructor.† The new representation is therefore

datatype α Queue =
    E | Q **of** int × α list × α list susp Queue × int × α list

The first integer, *lenfm*, is the combined length of f and all the suspended lists in m (i.e., what used to be simply *lenf* in the old representation). The second integer, *lenr*, is as usual the length of r. The usual balance invariant becomes *lenr* ≤ *lenfm*. In addition, we require that f be non-empty. (In the old representation, f could be empty if the entire queue was empty, but now we represent that case separately.)

As always, the queue functions are simple to describe.

fun snoc (E, *x*) = Q (1, [*x*], E, 0, [])
  | snoc (Q (*lenfm*, *f*, *m*, *lenr*, *r*), *x*) = checkQ (*lenfm*, *f*, *m*, *lenr*+1, *x* :: *r*)
fun head (Q (*lenfm*, *x* :: *f*', *m*, *lenr*, *r*)) = *x*
fun tail (Q (*lenfm*, *x* :: *f*', *m*, *lenr*, *r*)) = checkQ (*lenfm*−1, *f*', *m*, *lenr*, *r*)

The interesting cases are in the helper function checkQ. If r is too long, checkQ creates a suspension to reverse r and adds the suspension to m. After checking the length of r, checkQ invokes a second helper function checkF that guarantees that f is non-empty. If both f and m are empty, then the entire queue is empty. Otherwise, if f is empty we remove the first suspension from m, force it, and install the resulting list as the new f.

fun checkF (*lenfm*, [], E, *lenr*, *r*) = E
  | checkF (*lenfm*, [], *m*, *lenr*, *r*) =
      Q (*lenfm*, force (head *m*), tail *m*, *lenr*, *r*)
  | checkF *q* = Q *q*
fun checkQ (*q* **as** (*lenfm*, *f*, *m*, *lenr*, *r*)) =
      if *lenr* ≤ *lenfm* **then** checkF *q*
      else checkF (*lenfm*+*lenr*, *f*, snoc (*m*, $rev *r*), 0, [])

---

† A slightly more efficient alternative is to represent queues up to some fixed size simply as lists.

```
structure BootstrappedQueue : QUEUE =
(* assumes polymorphic recursion! *)
struct
  datatype α Queue =
      E | Q of int × α list × α list susp Queue × int × α list

  val empty = E
  fun isEmpty E = true | isEmpty _ = false

  fun checkQ (q as (lenfm, f, m, lenr, r)) =
      if lenr ≤ lenfm then checkF q
      else checkF (lenfm+lenr, f, snoc (m, $rev r), 0, [ ])
  and checkF (lenfm, [ ], E, lenr, r) = E
    | checkF (lenfm, [ ], m, lenr, r) =
        Q (lenfm, force (head m), tail m, lenr, r)
    | checkF q = Q q

  and snoc (E, x) = Q (1, [x], E, 0, [ ])
    | snoc (Q (lenfm, f, m, lenr, r), x) = checkQ (lenfm, f, m, lenr+1, x :: r)
  and head E = raise EMPTY
    | head (Q (lenfm, x :: f', m, lenr, r)) = x
  and tail E = raise EMPTY
    | tail (Q (lenfm, x :: f', m, lenr, r)) = checkQ (lenfm−1, f', m, lenr, r)
end
```

Figure 10.2. Bootstrapped queues based on structural decomposition.

Note that checkQ and checkF call snoc and tail, which in turn call checkQ. These functions must therefore all be defined mutually recursively. The complete implementation appears in Figure 10.2.

These queues create a suspension to reverse the rear list at exactly the same time as banker's queues, and force the suspension one operation earlier than banker's queues. Thus, since the reverse computation contributes only $O(1)$ amortized time to each operation on banker's queues, it also contributes only $O(1)$ amortized time to each operation on bootstrapped queues. However, the running times of snoc and tail are not constant! Note that snoc calls checkQ, which in turn might call snoc on m. In this way we might get a cascade of calls to snoc, one at each level of the queue. However, successive lists in m at least double in size so the length of m is $O(\log n)$. Since the size of the middle queue decreases by at least a logarithmic factor at each level, the depth of the entire queue is at most $O(\log^* n)$. snoc performs $O(1)$ amortized work at each level, so in total snoc requires $O(\log^* n)$ amortized time.

Similarly, tail might result in recursive calls to both snoc (from checkQ) and tail (from checkF). Note that, when this happens, tail is called on the result of the snoc. Now, the snoc might recursively call itself and the tail might again recursively call both snoc and tail. However, from Exercise 10.3, we know that the snoc and tail never both recursively call snoc. Therefore, both snoc and tail are called at most once per level. Since both snoc and tail do $O(1)$ amortized work at each level, the total amortized cost of tail is also $O(\log^* n)$.

Remark $O(\log^* n)$ is constant in practice. To have a depth of more than five, a queue would need to contain at least 2^{65536} elements. In fact, if one represents queues of up to size four simply as lists, then queues with fewer than about four billion elements have at most three levels.

Hint to Practitioners: In practice, variations on these queues are the fastest known implementations for applications that use persistence sparingly, but that require good behavior even in pathological cases.

Exercise 10.3 Consider the expression tail (snoc (q, x)). Show that the calls to tail and snoc will never both recursively call snoc.

Exercise 10.4 Implement these queues without polymorphic recursion using the types

> **datatype** α EL = ELEM **of** α | LIST **of** α EL list susp
> **datatype** α Queue = E | Q **of** int $\times$ α EL list $\times$ α Queue $\times$ int $\times$ α EL list

Exercise 10.5 Another way to eliminate the need for polymorphic recursion is to represent the middle using some other implementation of queues. Then the type of bootstrapped queues is

> **datatype** α Queue =
>   E | Q **of** int $\times$ α list $\times$ α list susp PrimQ.Queue $\times$ int $\times$ α list

where PrimQ is the other implementation of queues.

(a) Implement this variation of bootstrapped queues as a functor of the form

> **functor** BootstrapQueue (PrimQ : QUEUE) : QUEUE = . . .

(b) Prove that if PrimQ is instantiated to some implementation of real-time queues, then all operations on the resulting bootstrapped queues take $O(1)$ amortized time.

10.2 Structural Abstraction

The second class of data-structural bootstrapping is *structural abstraction*, which is typically used to extend an implementation of collections, such as lists or heaps, with an efficient join function for combining two collections. For many implementations, designing an efficient insert function, which adds a single element to a collection, is easy, but designing an efficient join function is difficult. Structural abstraction creates collections that contain other collections as elements. Then two collections can be joined by simply inserting one collection into the other.

The ideas of structural abstraction can largely be described at the level of types. Suppose α C is a collection type with elements of type α, and that this type supports an efficient insert function, with signature

val insert : $\alpha \times \alpha$ C $\to \alpha$ C

Call α C the *primitive* type. From this type, we wish to derive a new datatype, α B, called the *bootstrapped* type, such that α B supports both insert and join efficiently, with signatures

val insert$_B$: $\alpha \times \alpha$ B $\to \alpha$ B
val join$_B$: α B $\times \alpha$ B $\to \alpha$ B

(We use the subscript to distinguish functions on the bootstrapped type from functions on the primitive type.) The bootstrapped type should also support an efficient unit function for creating a new singleton collection.

val unit$_B$: $\alpha \to \alpha$ B

Then, insert$_B$ can be implemented simply as

fun insert$_B$ (*x*, *b*) = join$_B$ (unit$_B$ *x*, *b*)

The basic idea of structural abstraction is to represent bootstrapped collections as primitive collections of other bootstrapped collections. Then join$_B$ can be implemented in terms of insert (not insert$_B$!) roughly as

fun join$_B$ (*b*$_1$, *b*$_2$) = insert (*b*$_1$, *b*$_2$)

This inserts *b*$_1$ as an element of *b*$_2$. Alternatively, one could insert *b*$_2$ as an element of *b*$_1$, but the point is that join has been reduced to simple insertion.

Of course, things are not quite that simple. Based on the above description, we might attempt to define α B as

datatype α B = B **of** (α B) C

This definition can be viewed as specifying an isomorphism

$$\alpha\ B \cong (\alpha\ B)\ C$$

By unrolling this isomorphism a few times, we can quickly spot the flaw in this definition.

$$\alpha\ B \cong (\alpha\ B)\ C \cong ((\alpha\ B)\ C)\ C \cong \cdots \cong ((\cdots C)\ C)\ C$$

The type α has disappeared, so there is no way to actually store an element in this collection! We can solve this problem by making each bootstrapped collection a pair of a single element with a primitive collection.

datatype α B = B **of** $\alpha \times (\alpha\ B)$ C

Then, for instance, unit_B can be defined as

fun $\text{unit}_B\ x$ = B (x, empty)

where empty is the empty primitive collection.

But now we have another problem. If every bootstrapped collection contains at least a single element, how do we represent the empty bootstrapped collection? We therefore refine the type one more time.

datatype α B = E | B **of** $\alpha \times (\alpha\ B)$ C

Remark Actually, we always arrange that the primitive collection C contains only non-empty bootstrapped collections. This situation can be described more precisely by the types

datatype $\alpha\ B^+$ = B^+ **of** $\alpha \times (\alpha\ B^+)$ C
datatype α B = E | NE **of** B^+

Unfortunately, definitions of this form lead to more verbose code, so we stick with the earlier less precise, but more concise, definition. $\diamond$

Now, we can refine the above templates for insert_B and join_B as

fun $\text{insert}_B\ (x, E)$ = B (x, empty)
  | $\text{insert}_B\ (x, B\ (y, c))$ = B $(x, \text{insert}\ (\text{unit}_B\ y, c))$
fun $\text{join}_B\ (b, E)$ = b
  | $\text{join}_B\ (E, b)$ = b
  | $\text{join}_B\ (B\ (x, c), b)$ = B $(x, \text{insert}\ (b, c))$

These templates can easily be varied in several ways. For instance, in the second clause of insert_B, we could reverse the roles of x and y. Similarly, in the third clause of join_B, we could reverse the roles of the first argument and the second argument.

```
signature CATENABLELIST =
sig
  type α Cat

  val empty   : α Cat
  val isEmpty : α Cat → bool

  val cons : α × α Cat → α Cat
  val snoc : α Cat × α → α Cat
  val ++   : α Cat × α Cat → α Cat

  val head : α Cat → α        (* raises EMPTY if list is empty *)
  val tail : α Cat → α Cat    (* raises EMPTY if list is empty *)
end
```

Figure 10.3. Signature for catenable lists.

For any given collection, there is typically some distinguished element that can be inspected or deleted, such as the first element or the smallest element. The insert$_B$ and join$_B$ templates should be instantiated in such a way that the distinguished element in the bootstrapped collection B (*x, c*) is *x* itself. The creative part of designing a bootstrapped data structure using structural abstraction is implementing the delete$_B$ routine that discards the distinguished element *x*. After discarding *x*, we are left with a primitive collection of type (α B) C, which must then be converted into a bootstrapped collection of type α B. The details of how this is accomplished vary from data structure to data structure.

We next instantiate these templates in two ways. First, we bootstrap queues to support catenation (i.e., append) efficiently. Second, we bootstrap heaps to support merge efficiently.

10.2.1 Lists With Efficient Catenation

The first data structure we will implement using structural abstraction is catenable lists, as specified by the signature in Figure 10.3. Catenable lists extend the usual list signature with an efficient append function (++). As a convenience, catenable lists also support snoc, even though we could easily simulate snoc (*xs, x*) by *xs* ++ cons (*x*, empty). Because of this ability to add elements to the rear of a list, a more accurate name for this data structure would be catenable output-restricted deques.

We obtain an efficient implementation of catenable lists that supports all operations in $O(1)$ amortized time by bootstrapping an efficient implementation of FIFO queues. The exact choice of implementation for the primitive queues

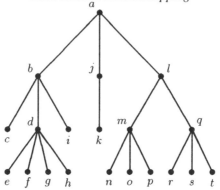

Figure 10.4. A tree representing the list $a \ldots t$.

is largely irrelevant; any of the persistent, constant-time queue implementations will do, whether amortized or worst-case.

Given an implementation Q of primitive queues matching the QUEUE signature, structural abstraction suggests that we can represent catenable lists as

datatype α Cat = E | C **of** $\alpha \times \alpha$ Cat Q.Queue

One way to interpret this type is as a tree where each node contains an element, and the children of each node are stored in a queue from left to right. Since we wish for the first element of the list to be easily accessible, we store it at the root of the tree. This suggests ordering the elements in a preorder, left-to-right traversal of the tree. A sample list containing the elements $a \ldots t$ is shown in Figure 10.4.

Now, head is simply

fun head (C (*x*, _)) = *x*

To catenate two non-empty lists, we link the two trees by making the second tree the last child of the first tree.

fun *xs* ++ E = *xs*
  | E ++ *ys* = *ys*
  | *xs* ++ *ys* = link (*xs*, *ys*)

The helper function link adds its second argument to the child queue of its first argument.

fun link (C (*x*, *q*), *ys*) = C (*x*, Q.snoc (*q*, *ys*))

cons and snoc simply call ++.

fun cons (*x*, *xs*) = C (*x*, Q.empty) ++ *xs*
fun snoc (*xs*, *x*) = *xs* ++ C (*x*, Q.empty)

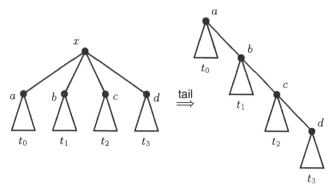

Figure 10.5. Illustration of the tail operation.

Finally, given a non-empty tree, tail should discard the root and somehow combine the queue of children into a single tree. If the queue is empty, then tail should return E. Otherwise we link all the children together.

fun tail (C (*x*, *q*)) = **if** Q.isEmpty *q* **then** E **else** linkAll *q*

Since catenation is associative, we can link the children in any order we desire. However, a little thought reveals that linking the children from right to left, as illustrated in Figure 10.5, will duplicate the least work on subsequent calls to tail. Therefore, we implement linkAll as

fun linkAll *q* = **let val** *t* = Q.head *q*
                     val *q'* = Q.tail *q*
              in if Q.isEmpty *q'* **then** *t* **else** link (*t*, linkAll *q'*) **end**

Remark linkAll is an instance of the foldr1 program schema.   ◇

In this implementation, tail may take as much as $O(n)$ time. We hope to reduce this to $O(1)$ amortized time, but to achieve this in the face of persistence, we must somehow incorporate lazy evaluation into the design. Since linkAll is the only routine that takes more than $O(1)$ time, it is the obvious candidate. We rewrite linkAll to suspend every recursive call. This suspension is forced when a tree is removed from a queue.

fun linkAll *q* = **let val** \$*t* = Q.head *q*
                     val *q'* = Q.tail *q*
              in if Q.isEmpty *q'* **then** *t* **else** link (*t*, \$linkAll *q'*) **end**

For this definition to make sense, the queues must contain tree suspensions rather than trees, so we redefine the type as

datatype α Cat = E | C **of** $\alpha \times \alpha$ Cat susp Q.Queue

```
functor CatenableList (Q : QUEUE) : CATENABLELIST =
struct
  datatype α Cat = E | C of α × α Cat susp Q.Queue

  val empty = E
  fun isEmpty E = true | isEmpty _ = false

  fun link (C (x, q), s) = C (x, Q.snoc (q, s))
  fun linkAll q = let val $t = Q.head q
                      val q' = Q.tail q
                  in if Q.isEmpty q' then t else link (t, $linkAll q') end

  fun xs ++ E = xs
    | E ++ xs = xs
    | xs ++ ys = link (xs, $ys)
  fun cons (x, xs) = C (x, Q.empty) ++ xs
  fun snoc (xs, x) = xs ++ C (x, Q.empty)

  fun head E = raise EMPTY
    | head (C (x, _)) = x
  fun tail E = raise EMPTY
    | tail (C (x, q)) = if Q.isEmpty q then E else linkAll q
end
```

Figure 10.6. Catenable lists.

To conform to this new type, ++ must spuriously suspend its second argument.

```
fun xs ++ E = xs
  | E ++ xs = xs
  | xs ++ ys = link (xs, $ys)
```

The complete implementation is shown in Figure 10.6.

head clearly runs in $O(1)$ worst-case time, while cons and snoc have the same time requirements as ++. We now prove that ++ and tail run in $O(1)$ amortized time using the banker's method. The unshared cost of each is $O(1)$, so we must merely show that each discharges only $O(1)$ debits.

Let $d_t(i)$ be the number of debits on the ith node of tree t and let $D_t(i) = \sum_{j=0}^{i} d_t(j)$ be the cumulative number of debits on all nodes of t up to and including node i. Finally, let D_t be the total number debits on all nodes in t (i.e., $D_t = D_t(|t| - 1)$). We maintain two invariants on debits.

First, we require that the number of debits on any node be bounded by the degree of the node (i.e., $d_t(i) \leq degree_t(i)$). Since the sum of degrees of all nodes in a non-empty tree is one less than the size of the tree, this implies that the total number of debits in a tree is bounded by the size of the tree (i.e., $D_t < |t|$). We maintain this invariant by incrementing the number of debits on a node only when we also increment its degree.

Second, we insist that $D_t(i)$ be bounded by some linear function on i. The particular linear function we choose is

$$D_t(i) \leq i + depth_t(i)$$

where $depth_t(i)$ is the length of the path from the root of t to node i. This invariant is called the *left-linear debit invariant*. Notice that the left-linear debit invariant guarantees that $d_t(0) = D_t(0) \leq 0 + 0 = 0$, so all debits on a node have been discharged by the time it reaches the root. (In fact, the root is not even suspended!) The only time we actually force a suspension is when the suspended node is about to become the new root.

Theorem 10.1 ++ *and* tail *maintain both debit invariants by discharging one and three debits, respectively.*

Proof (++) The only debit created by ++ is for the trivial suspension of its second argument. Since we are not increasing the degree of this node, we immediately discharge the new debit. Now, assume that t_1 and t_2 are non-empty and let $t = t_1 + t_2$. Let $n = |t_1|$. Note that the index, depth, and cumulative debits of each node in t_1 are unaffected by the catenation, so for $i < n$

$$\begin{aligned} D_t(i) &= D_{t_1}(i) \\ &\leq i + depth_{t_1}(i) \\ &= i + depth_t(i) \end{aligned}$$

The nodes in t_2 increase in index by n, increase in depth by one, and accumulate the total debits of t_1, so

$$\begin{aligned} D_t(n + i) &= D_{t_1} + D_{t_2}(i) \\ &< n + D_{t_2}(i) \\ &\leq n + i + depth_{t_2}(i) \\ &= n + i + depth_t(n + i) - 1 \\ &< (n + i) + depth_t(n + i) \end{aligned}$$

Thus, we do not need to discharge any further debits to maintain the left-linear debit invariant.

(tail) Let $t' = $ tail t. After discarding the root of t, we link the children $t_0 \ldots t_{m-1}$ from right to left. Let t'_j be the partial result of linking $t_j \ldots t_{m-1}$. Then $t' = t'_0$. Since every link except the outermost is suspended, we assign a single debit to the root of each t_j, $0 < j < m - 1$. Note that the degree of each of these nodes increases by one. We also assign a debit to the root of t'_{m-1} because the last call to linkAll is suspended even though it does not call link. Since the degree of this node does not change, we immediately discharge this final debit.

Now, suppose the ith node of t appears in t_j. By the left-linear debit invariant, we know that $D_t(i) < i + \mathit{depth}_t(i)$, but consider how each of these quantities changes with the tail. i decreases by one because the first element is discarded. The depth of each node in t_j increases by $j - 1$ (see Figure 10.5) while the cumulative debits of each node in t_j increase by j. Thus,

$$
\begin{aligned}
D_{t'}(i - 1) &= D_t(i) + j \\
&\leq i + \mathit{depth}_t(i) + j \\
&= i + (\mathit{depth}_{t'}(i - 1) - (j - 1)) + j \\
&= (i - 1) + \mathit{depth}_{t'}(i - 1) + 2
\end{aligned}
$$

Discharging the first two debits restores the invariant, bringing the total to three debits.   □

Hint to Practitioners: Given a good implementation of queues, this is the fastest known implementation of persistent catenable lists, especially for applications that use persistence heavily.

Exercise 10.6 Write a function flatten of type α Cat list $\rightarrow$ α Cat that catenates all the elements in a list of catenable lists. Show that your function runs in $O(1 + e)$ amortized time, where e is the number of empty catenable lists in the list.

10.2.2 Heaps With Efficient Merging

Next, we use structural abstraction on heaps to obtain an efficient merge operation.

Assume that we have an implementation of heaps that supports insert in $O(1)$ worst-case time and merge, findMin, and deleteMin in $O(\log n)$ worst-case time. The skew binomial heaps of Section 9.3.2 are one such implementation; the scheduled binomial heaps of Section 7.3 are another. Using structural abstraction, we improve the running time of both findMin and merge to $O(1)$ worst-case time.

For now, assume that the type of heaps is polymorphic in the type of elements, and that, for any type of elements, we magically know the right comparison function to use. Later we will account for the fact that both the type of elements and the comparison function on those elements are fixed at functor-application time.

Under the above assumption, the type of bootstrapped heaps can be given as

datatype α Heap = E | H **of** $\alpha \times (\alpha$ Heap) PrimH.Heap

where PrimH is the implementation of primitive heaps. The element stored at any given H node will be the minimum element in the subtree rooted at that node. The elements of the primitive heaps are themselves bootstrapped heaps. Within the primitive heaps, bootstrapped heaps are ordered with respect to their minimum elements (i.e., their roots). We can think of this type as a multiary tree in which the children of each node are stored in primitive heaps.

Since the minimum element is stored at the root, findMin is simply

fun findMin (H $(x, \_)$) = x

To merge two bootstrapped heaps, we insert the heap with the larger root into the heap with the smaller root.

```
fun merge (E, h) = h
  | merge (h, E) = h
  | merge (h₁ as H (x, p₁), h₂ as H (y, p₂)) =
    if x < y then H (x, PrimH.insert (h₂, p₁))
    else H (y, PrimH.insert (h₁, p₂))
```

(In the comparison $x < y$, we assume that $<$ is the right comparison function for these elements.) Now, insert is defined in terms of merge.

fun insert (x, h) = merge (H $(x,$ PrimH.empty), h)

Finally, we consider deleteMin, defined as

```
fun deleteMin (H (x, p)) =
    if PrimH.isEmpty p then E
    else let val (H (y, p₁)) = PrimH.findMin p
             val p₂ = PrimH.deleteMin p
         in H (y, PrimH.merge (p₁, p₂)) end
```

After discarding the root, we first check if the primitive heap p is empty. If it is, then the new heap is empty. Otherwise, we find and remove the minimum element in p, which is the bootstrapped heap with the overall minimum element; this element becomes the new root. Finally, we merge p_1 and p_2 to obtain the new primitive heap.

The analysis of these heaps is simple. Clearly, findMin runs in $O(1)$ worst-case time regardless of the underlying implementation of primitive heaps. insert and merge depend only on PrimH.insert. Since we have assumed that PrimH.insert runs in $O(1)$ worst-case time, so do insert and merge. Finally, deleteMin calls PrimH.findMin, PrimH.deleteMin, and PrimH.merge. Since each of these runs in $O(\log n)$ worst-case time, so does deleteMin.

Remark We can also bootstrap heaps with amortized bounds. For example, bootstrapping the lazy binomial heaps of Section 6.4.1 produces an implementation that supports findMin in $O(1)$ worst-case time, insert and merge in $O(1)$ amortized time, and deleteMin in $O(\log n)$ amortized time. ◇

Until now, we have assumed that heaps are polymorphic, but in fact the HEAP signature specifies that heaps are monomorphic — both the type of elements and the comparison function on those elements are fixed at functor-application time. The implementation of a heap is a functor that is parameterized by the element type and the comparison function. The functor that we use to bootstrap heaps maps heap functors to heap functors, rather than heap structures to heap structures. Using higher-order functors [MT94], this can be expressed as

```
functor Bootstrap (functor MakeH (Element : ORDERED)
                                 : HEAP where type Elem.T = Element.T)
                   (Element : ORDERED) : HEAP = ...
```

The Bootstrap functor takes the MakeH functor as an argument. The MakeH functor takes the ORDERED structure Element, which defines the element type and the comparison function, and returns a HEAP structure. Given MakeH, Bootstrap returns a functor that takes an ORDERED structure Element and returns a HEAP structure.

Remark The **where type** constraint in the signature for the MakeH functor is necessary to ensure that the functor returns a heap structure with the desired element type. This kind of constraint is extremely common with higher-order functors. ◇

Now, to create a structure of primitive heaps with bootstrapped heaps as elements, we apply MakeH to the ORDERED structure BootstrappedElem that defines the type of bootstrapped heaps and a comparison function that orders two bootstrapped heaps by their minimum elements. (The ordering relation is undefined on empty bootstrapped heaps.) This is expressed by the following mutually recursive structure declarations.

```
structure rec BootstrappedElem =
  struct
    datatype T = E | H of Elem.T × PrimH.Heap
    fun leq (H (x, _), H (y, _)) = Elem.leq (x, y)
      ... similar definitions for eq and lt ...
  end
and PrimH = MakeH (BootstrappedElem)
```

```
functor Bootstrap (functor MakeH (Element : ORDERED)
                                  : HEAP where type Elem.T = Element.T)
                  (Element : ORDERED) : HEAP =
struct
  structure Elem = Element

  (* recursive structures not supported in Standard ML! *)
  structure rec BootstrappedElem =
    struct
      datatype T = E | H of Elem.T × PrimH.Heap
      fun leq (H (x, _), H (y, _)) = Elem.leq (x, y)
      ... similar definitions for eq and lt...
    end
  and PrimH = MakeH (BootstrappedElem)

  open BootstrappedElem  (* expose E and H constructors *)

  type Heap = BootstrappedElem.T

  val empty = E
  fun isEmpty E = true | isEmpty _ = false

  fun merge (E, h) = h
    | merge (h, E) = h
    | merge (h₁ as H (x, p₁), h₂ as H (y, p₂)) =
        if Elem.leq (x, y) then H (x, PrimH.insert (h₂, p₁))
        else H (y, PrimH.insert (h₁, p₂))
  fun insert (x, h) = merge (H (x, PrimH.empty), h)

  fun findMin E = raise EMPTY
    | findMin (H (x, _)) = x
  fun deleteMin E = raise EMPTY
    | deleteMin (H (x, p)) =
        if PrimH.isEmpty p then E
        else let val (H (y, p₁)) = PrimH.findMin p
                 val p₂ = PrimH.deleteMin p
             in H (y, PrimH.merge (p₁, p₂)) end
end
```

Figure 10.7. Bootstrapped heaps.

where Elem is the ORDERED structure specifying the true elements of the bootstrapped heap. The complete implementation of the Bootstrap functor is shown in Figure 10.7.

Remark Standard ML does not support recursive structure declarations, and for good reason — this declaration does not make sense for MakeH functors that have effects. However, the MakeH functors to which we might consider applying Bootstrap, such as SkewBinomialHeap from Section 9.3.2, are well-behaved in this respect, and the recursive pattern embodied by the Bootstrap

```
signature HEAPWITHINFO =
sig
   structure Priority : ORDERED

   type α Heap

   val empty    : α Heap
   val isEmpty  : α Heap → bool

   val insert   : Priority.T × α × α Heap → α Heap
   val merge    : α Heap × α Heap → α Heap

   val findMin  : α Heap → Priority.T × α
   val deleteMin : α Heap → α Heap
            (∗ findMin and deleteMin raise EMPTY if heap is empty ∗)
end
```

Figure 10.8. Alternate signature for heaps.

functor does make sense for these functors. It is unfortunate that Standard ML
does not allow us to express bootstrapping in this fashion.

We can still implement bootstrapped heaps in Standard ML by inlining a particular choice for MakeH, such as SkewBinomialHeap or LazyBinomialHeap,
and then eliminating BootstrappedElem and PrimH as separate structures. The
recursion on structures then reduces to recursion on datatypes, which is supported by Standard ML.

Exercise 10.7 Inlining the LazyBinomialHeap functor of Section 6.4.1 as described above yields the types

```
datatype Tree = Node of int × Heap × Tree list
datatype Heap = E | NE of Elem.T × Tree list susp
```

Complete this implementation of bootstrapped heaps.

Exercise 10.8 Elements in a heap frequently contain other information besides the priority. For these kinds of elements, it is often more convenient to
use heaps that separate the priority from the rest of the element. Figure 10.8
gives an alternate signature for this kind of heap.

(a) Adapt either LazyBinomialHeap or SkewBinomialHeap to this new signature.

(b) Rewrite the Bootstrap functor as

    functor Bootstrap (PrimH : HEAPWITHINFO) : HEAPWITHINFO = ...

You will need neither higher-order functors nor recursive structures.

```
signature FINITEMAP =
sig
   type Key
   type α Map

   val empty  : α Map
   val bind   : Key × α × α Map → α Map
   val lookup : Key × α Map → α  (* raise NOTFOUND if key is not found *)
end
```

Figure 10.9. Signature for finite maps.

10.3 Bootstrapping To Aggregate Types

We have now seen several examples where collections of aggregate data (e.g., heaps of heaps) were useful in implementing collections of non-aggregate data (e.g., heaps of elements). However, collections of aggregate data are often useful in their own right. As a simple example, strings (i.e., sequences of characters) are frequently used as the element type of sets or the key type of finite maps. In this section, we illustrate bootstrapping finite maps defined over some simple type to finite maps defined over lists or even trees of that type.

10.3.1 Tries

Binary search trees work well when comparisons on the key or element type are cheap. This is true for simple types like integers or characters, but may not be true for aggregate types like strings. For example, consider representing a phone book using a binary search tree. A query for "Smith, Joan" might involve multiple comparisons against entries for "Smith, John", each of which inspects the first ten characters of both strings before returning.

A better solution for aggregate types such as strings is to choose a representation that takes advantage of the structure of that type. One such representation is *tries*, also known as a *digital search trees*. In this section, we will use tries to implement the FINITEMAP abstraction, shown in Figure 10.9.

In the following discussion, we assume that keys are strings, represented as lists of characters. We will often refer to characters as the *base type*. The ideas can easily be adapted to other sequence representations and other base types.

Now, a trie is a multiway tree where each edge is labelled with a character. Edges leaving the root of a trie represent the first character of a string, edges leaving children of the root represent the second character, and so on. To find the node associated with a given string, start at the root and follow the edges labelled by the characters of the string, in order. For example, the trie representing the strings `"cat"`, `"dog"`, `"car"`, and `"cart"` might be drawn

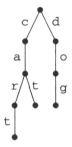

Note that entering a string into a trie also enters all the prefixes of that string into the trie. Only some of these prefixes constitute valid entries. In this example, `"c"`, `"ca"`, and `"car"` are all prefixes of `"cart"` but only `"car"` is valid. We therefore mark each node as either valid or invalid. For finite maps, we accomplish this with the built-in option datatype

datatype α option = NONE | SOME **of** α

If a given node is invalid, we mark it with NONE. If the node is valid, and the corresponding string is mapped to the value *x*, then we mark it with SOME *x*.

The critical remaining question is how to represent the edges leaving a node. Ordinarily, we would represent the children of a multiway node as a list of trees, but here we also need to represent the edge labels. Depending on the choice of base type and the expected density of the trie, we might represent the edges leaving a node as a vector, an association list, a binary search tree, or even, if the base type is itself a list or a string, another trie! But all of these are just finite maps from edges labels to tries. We abstract away from the particular representation of these edge maps by assuming that we are given a structure M implementing finite maps over the base type. Then the representation of a trie is simply

datatype α Map = TRIE **of** α option × α Map M.Map

The empty trie is represented by a single invalid node with no children.

val empty = TRIE (NONE, M.empty)

To lookup a string, we lookup each character in the appropriate edge map. When we reach the final node, we check whether it is valid or invalid.

```
fun lookup ([ ], TRIE (NONE, m)) = raise NOTFOUND
  | lookup ([ ], TRIE (SOME x, m)) = x
  | lookup (k :: ks, TRIE (v, m)) = lookup (ks, M.lookup (k, m))
```

```
functor Trie (M : FINITEMAP) : FINITEMAP =
struct
    type Key = M.Key list

    datatype α Map = TRIE of α option × α Map M.Map

    val empty = TRIE (NONE, M.empty)

    fun lookup ([ ], TRIE (NONE, m)) = raise NOTFOUND
      | lookup ([ ], TRIE (SOME x, m)) = x
      | lookup (k :: ks, TRIE (v, m)) = lookup (ks, M.lookup (k, m))

    fun bind ([ ], x, TRIE (_, m)) = TRIE (SOME x, m)
      | bind (k :: ks, x, TRIE (v, m)) =
            let val t = M.lookup (k, m) handle NOTFOUND ⇒ empty
                val t' = bind (ks, x, t)
            in TRIE (v, M.bind (k, t', m)) end
end
```

Figure 10.10. A simple implementation of tries.

Note that if a given string is not in the trie, then we may not even reach the final node. For example, if we were to lookup `"dark"` in our example trie, then the lookup of d would succeed but the lookup of a would fail. In that case, M.lookup would raise the NOTFOUND exception. This is also the appropriate response for lookup so we simply propagate the exception.

Remark This property of unsuccessful searches explains why tries can be even faster than hashing. An unsuccessful search in a trie might exit after examining only a few characters, whereas an unsuccessful search in a hash table must examine the entire string just to compute the hash function! ◇

The bind function is similar to the lookup function, except that we do not allow the call to M.lookup to fail. We force it to succeed by substituting the empty node whenever it raises the NOTFOUND exception.

```
fun bind ([ ], x, TRIE (_, m)) = TRIE (SOME x, m)
  | bind (k :: ks, x, TRIE (v, m)) =
        let val t = M.lookup (k, m) handle NOTFOUND ⇒ empty
            val t' = bind (ks, x, t)
        in TRIE (v, M.bind (k, t', m)) end
```

The complete implementation is shown in Figure 10.10.

Exercise 10.9 Very often, the set of keys to be stored in a trie has the property that no key is a proper prefix of another. For example, the keys might all be the same length, or the keys might all end in a unique character that occurs in no other position. Reimplement tries under this assumption, using the type

datatype α Map = Entry **of** α | TRIE **of** α Map M.Map

Exercise 10.10 Tries frequently contain long paths of nodes that each have only a single child. A common optimization is to collapse such paths into a single node. We accomplish this by storing with every node a substring that is the longest common prefix of every key in that subtrie. The type of tries is then

datatype α Map = TRIE **of** M.Key list $\times$ α option $\times$ α Map M.Map

Reimplement tries using this type. You should maintain the invariant that no node is both invalid and an only child. You may assume that the structure M provides an isEmpty function.

Exercise 10.11 (Schwenke [Sch97]) Another common data structure that involves multiple layers of finite maps is the *hash table*. Complete the following implementation of abstract hash tables.

```
functor HashTable (structure Approx : FINITEMAP
                   structure Exact  : FINITEMAP
                   val hash : Exact.Key → Approx.Key) : FINITEMAP =
struct
   type Key = Exact.Key
   type α Map = α Exact.Map Approx.Map
   ...
   fun lookup (k, m) = Exact.lookup (k, Approx.lookup (hash k, m))
   ...
end
```

The advantage of this representation is that Approx can use an efficient key type (such as integers) and Exact can use a trivial implementation (such as association lists).

10.3.2 Generalized Tries

The idea of tries can also be generalized to other aggregate types, such as trees [CM95]. First, consider how the edge maps of the previous section reflect the type of the cons constructor. The edge maps are represented by the type α Map M.Map. The outer map indexes the first field of the cons constructor and the inner map indexes the second field of the cons constructor. Looking up the head of a cons cell in the outer map returns the inner map in which to lookup the tail of the cons cell.

We can generalize this scheme to binary trees, which have three fields, by adding a third map layer. For example, given binary trees of type

datatype α Tree = E | T **of** $\alpha \times \alpha$ Tree $\times \alpha$ Tree

we can represent the edge maps in tries over these trees as α Map Map M.Map. The outer map indexes the first field of the T constructor, the middle map indexes the second field, and the inner map indexes the third field. Looking up the element at a given node in the outer map returns the middle map in which to lookup the left subtree. That lookup, in turn, returns the inner map in which to lookup the right subtree.

More formally, we represent tries over binary trees as

datatype α Map = TRIE **of** α option $\times \alpha$ Map Map M.Map

Notice that this is a non-uniform recursive type, so we will need polymorphic recursion in the functions over this type.

Now, the lookup function performs three lookups for each T constructor, corresponding to the three fields of the constructor. When it reaches the final node, it checks whether the node is valid.

fun lookup (E, TRIE (NONE, *m*)) = **raise** NOTFOUND
  | lookup (E, TRIE (SOME *x*, *m*)) = *x*
  | lookup (T (*k*, *a*, *b*), TRIE (*v*, *m*)) =
    lookup (*b*, lookup (*a*, M.lookup (*k*, *m*)))

The bind function is similar. It is shown in Figure 10.11, which summarizes the entire implementation of tries over trees.

Exercise 10.12 Reimplement the TrieOfTrees functor without polymorphic recursion using the types

datatype α Map = TRIE **of** α EM option $\times \alpha$ Map M.Map
and α EM = ELEM **of** α | MAP **of** α Map

Exercise 10.13 Implement tries whose keys are multiway trees of type

datatype α Tree = T **of** $\alpha \times \alpha$ Tree list

With these examples, we can generalize the notion of tries to any recursive type involving products and sums. We need only a few simple rules about how to construct a finite map for a structured type given finite maps for its component parts. Let α Map$_\tau$ be the type of finite maps over type τ.

For products, we already know what to do; to lookup a pair in a trie, we first lookup the first element of the pair and get back a map in which to lookup the second element. Thus,

$$\tau = \tau_1 \times \tau_2 \Rightarrow \alpha \, \mathsf{Map}_\tau = \alpha \, \mathsf{Map}_{\tau_2} \, \mathsf{Map}_{\tau_1}$$

---

datatype α Tree = E | T **of** $\alpha \times \alpha$ Tree $\times$ α Tree

functor TrieOfTrees (M : FINITEMAP) : FINITEMAP =
(* *assumes polymorphic recursion!* *)
struct
  type Key = M.Key Tree

  datatype α Map = TRIE **of** α option $\times$ α Map Map M.Map

  val empty = TRIE (NONE, M.empty)

  fun lookup (E, TRIE (NONE, *m*)) = **raise** NOTFOUND
   | lookup (E, TRIE (SOME *x*, *m*)) = *x*
   | lookup (T (*k*, *a*, *b*), TRIE (*v*, *m*)) =
     lookup (*b*, lookup (*a*, M.lookup (*k*, *m*)))

  fun bind (E, *x*, TRIE (_, *m*)) = TRIE (SOME *x*, *m*)
   | bind (T (*k*, *a*, *b*), *x*, TRIE (*v*, *m*)) =
     let val *tt* = M.lookup (*k*, *m*) **handle** NOTFOUND $\Rightarrow$ empty
       val *t* = lookup (*a*, *tt*) **handle** NOTFOUND $\Rightarrow$ empty
       val *t'* = bind (*b*, *x*, *t*)
       val *tt'* = bind (*a*, *t'*, *tt*)
     in TRIE (*v*, M.bind (*k*, *tt'*, *m*)) **end**
end

Figure 10.11. Generalized Tries.

Now, what about sums? Recall the types of trees and tries over trees:

datatype α Tree = E | T **of** $\alpha \times \alpha$ Tree $\times$ α Tree
datatype α Map = TRIE **of** α option $\times$ α Map Map M.Map

Obviously the type α Map Map M.Map corresponds to the T constructor, but what corresponds to the E constructor? Well, the α option type is really nothing more or less than a very efficient implementation of finite maps over the unit type, which is essentially equivalent to the missing body of the E constructor. From this, we infer the general rule for sums:

$$\tau = \tau_1 + \tau_2 \Rightarrow \alpha \text{ Map}_\tau = \alpha \text{ Map}_{\tau_1} \times \alpha \text{ Map}_{\tau_2}$$

Exercise 10.14 Complete the following functors that implement the above rules for products and sums.

  functor ProductMap (M$_1$: FINITEMAP) (M$_2$: FINITEMAP) : FINITEMAP =
  struct
    type Key = M$_1$.Key $\times$ M$_2$.Key
    . . .
  end

datatype (α, β) Sum = LEFT **of** α | RIGHT **of** β
functor SumMap (M_1 : FINITEMAP) (M_2 : FINITEMAP) : FINITEMAP =
struct
    type Key = (M_1.Key, M_2.Key) Sum
    ...
end

Exercise 10.15 Given a structure M that implements finite maps over the type
Id of identifiers, implement tries over the type Exp of lambda expressions,
where

datatype Exp = VAR **of** Id | LAM **of** Id $\times$ Exp | APP **of** Exp $\times$ Exp

You may find it helpful to extend the type of tries with a separate constructor
for the empty map.

10.4 Chapter Notes

Data-Structural Bootstrapping Buchsbaum and colleagues identified data-
structural bootstrapping as a general data structure design technique in [Buc93,
BT95, BST95]. Structural decomposition and structural abstraction had previously been used in [Die82] and [DST94], respectively.

Catenable Lists Although it is relatively easy to design alternative representations of persistent lists that support efficient catenation (see, for example,
[Hug86]), such alternative representations seem almost inevitably to sacrifice
efficiency of the head or tail functions.

Myers [Mye84] described a representation based on AVL trees that supports
all relevant list functions in $O(\log n)$ time. Tarjan and colleagues [DST94,
BT95, KT95] investigated a series of sub-logarithmic implementations, cul-
minating in a implementation that supports catenation and all other usual list
functions in $O(1)$ worst-case time. The implementation of catenable lists in
Section 10.2.1 first appeared in [Oka95a]. It is much simpler than Kaplan and
Tarjan's, but yields amortized bounds rather than worst-case bounds.

Mergeable Heaps Many imperative implementations support insert, merge,
and findMin in $O(1)$ amortized time, and deleteMin in $O(\log n)$ amortized
time, including binomial queues [KL93], Fibonacci heaps [FT87], relaxed
heaps [DGST88], V-heaps [Pet87], bottom-up skew heaps [ST86b], and pairing heaps [FSST86]. However, of these, only pairing heaps appear to retain
their amortized efficiency when combined with lazy evaluation in a persistent
setting (see Section 6.5), and, unfortunately, the bounds for pairing heaps have
only been conjectured, not proved.

Brodal [Bro95, Bro96] achieves equivalent worst-case bounds. His original data structure [Bro95] can be implemented purely functionally (and thus made persistent) by combining the recursive-slowdown technique of Kaplan and Tarjan [KT95] with a purely functional implementation of real-time deques, such as the real-time deques of Section 8.4.3. However, such an implementation would be both complicated and slow. Brodal and Okasaki simplify this implementation in [BO96], using skew binomial heaps (Section 9.3.2) and structural abstraction (Section 10.2.2).

Polymorphic Recursion   Several attempts have been made to extend Standard ML with polymorphic recursion, such as [Myc84, Hen93, KTU93]. One complication is that type inference is undecidable in the presence of polymorphic recursion [Hen93, KTU93], even though it is tractable in practice. Haskell sidesteps this problem by allowing polymorphic recursion whenever the programmer provides an explicit type signature.

11
Implicit Recursive Slowdown

In Section 9.2.3, we saw how lazy redundant binary numbers support both increment and decrement functions in $O(1)$ amortized time. In Section 10.1.2, we saw how non-uniform types and polymorphic recursion afford particularly simple implementations of numerical representations such as binary random-access lists. In this chapter, we combine and generalize these techniques into a framework called *implicit recursive slowdown*.

Kaplan and Tarjan [KT95, KT96b, KT96a] have studied a related framework, called *recursive slowdown*, that is based on segmented binary numbers (Section 9.2.4) rather than lazy binary numbers. The similarities and differences between implementations based on recursive slowdown and implementations based on implicit recursive slowdown are essentially the same as between those two number systems.

11.1 Queues and Deques

Recall the binary random-access lists of Section 10.1.2, which have the type

datatype α RList =
    NIL | ZERO **of** $(\alpha \times \alpha)$ RList | ONE **of** $\alpha \times (\alpha \times \alpha)$ RList

To simplify later discussions, let us change this type to

datatype α Digit = ZERO | ONE **of** α
datatype α RList = SHALLOW **of** α Digit | DEEP **of** α Digit $\times$ $(\alpha \times \alpha)$ RList

A shallow list contains either zero or one elements. A deep list contains either zero or one elements plus a list of pairs. We can play many of the same games with this type that we played with binary random-access lists in Chapter 9. For example, we can support head in $O(1)$ time by switching to a zeroless representation, such as

171

datatype α Digit = ZERO | ONE **of** α | TWO **of** $\alpha \times \alpha$
datatype α RList = SHALLOW **of** α Digit | DEEP **of** α Digit $\times (\alpha \times \alpha)$ RList

In this representation, the digit in a DEEP node must be ONE or TWO. The ZERO constructor is used only in the empty list, SHALLOW ZERO.

Similarly, by suspending the list of pairs in each DEEP node, we can make either cons or tail run in $O(1)$ amortized time, and the other in $O(\log n)$ amortized time.

datatype α RList =
    SHALLOW **of** α Digit
    | DEEP **of** α Digit $\times (\alpha \times \alpha)$ RList susp

By allowing a choice of three non-zero digits in each DEEP node, we can make all three of cons, head, and tail run in $O(1)$ time.

datatype α Digit =
    ZERO | ONE **of** α | TWO **of** $\alpha \times \alpha$ | THREE **of** $\alpha \times \alpha \times \alpha$

Again, the ZERO constructor is used only in the empty list.

Now, extending this design to support queues and deques is simply a matter of adding a second digit to each DEEP node.

datatype α Queue =
    SHALLOW **of** α Digit
    | DEEP **of** α Digit $\times (\alpha \times \alpha)$ Queue susp $\times \alpha$ Digit

The first digit represents the first few elements of the queue, and the second digit represents the last few elements. The remaining elements are stored in the suspended queue of pairs, which we call the *middle* queue.

The exact choice of the digit type depends on what functions are to be supported on each end of the queue. The following table lists the allowable values for the front digit of a queue that supports the given combination of functions.

supported functions	allowable digits
cons	ZERO, ONE
cons/head	ONE, TWO
head/tail	ONE, TWO
cons/head/tail	ONE, TWO, THREE

The same choices apply to the rear digit.

As a concrete example, let us develop an implementation of queues supporting snoc on the rear end of the queue, and head and tail on the front end of the queue (i.e., ordinary FIFO queues). Reading from the above table, we choose to allow the front digit of a DEEP node to be ONE or TWO and the rear digit to be ZERO or ONE. We also allow the digit in a SHALLOW node to be ZERO or ONE.

To add a new element y to a deep queue using snoc, we look at the rear digit. If it is ZERO, then we replace the rear digit with ONE y. If it is ONE x, then we replace the rear digit with ZERO and add the pair (x, y) to the middle queue. We also need a few special cases for adding an element to a shallow queue.

```
fun snoc (SHALLOW ZERO, y) = SHALLOW (ONE y)
  | snoc (SHALLOW (ONE x), y) = DEEP (TWO (x, y), $empty, ZERO)
  | snoc (DEEP (f, m, ZERO), y) = DEEP (f, m, ONE y)
  | snoc (DEEP (f, m, ONE x), y) =
      DEEP (f, $snoc (force m, (x, y)), ZERO)
```

To remove an element from a deep queue using tail, we look at the front digit. If it is TWO (x, y), then we discard x and set the front digit to ONE y. If it is ONE x, then we "borrow" a pair (y, z) from the middle queue and set the front digit to TWO (y, z). Again, there are several special cases dealing with shallow queues.

```
fun tail (SHALLOW (ONE x)) = empty
  | tail (DEEP (TWO (x, y), m, r)) = DEEP (ONE y, m, r)
  | tail (DEEP (ONE x, $q, r)) =
      if isEmpty q then SHALLOW r
      else let val (y, z) = head q
           in DEEP (TWO (y, z), $tail q, r) end
```

Note that we force the middle queue in the last clause of tail. The complete code appears in Figure 11.1.

Next, we show that snoc and tail both run in $O(1)$ amortized time. Note that snoc ignores the front digit and tail ignores the rear digit. If we consider each function in isolation, then snoc is analogous to inc on lazy binary numbers and tail is analogous to dec on zeroless lazy binary numbers. By adapting the proofs for inc and dec, we can easily show that snoc and tail run in $O(1)$ amortized time as long as each is used without the other.

The key idea of implicit recursive slowdown is that, when functions like snoc and tail are *almost* independent, then we can combine their proofs by simply adding the debits required by each proof. The proof for snoc allows one debit if the rear digit is ZERO and zero debits if the rear digit is One. The proof for tail allows one debit if the front digit is Two and zero debits if the front digit is One. The following proof combines these debit allowances.

Theorem 11.1 snoc *and* tail *run in* $O(1)$ *amortized time.*

Proof We analyze this implementation using the banker's method. We assign debits to every suspension, each of which is the middle field of some deep queue. We adopt a debit invariant that allows each suspension a number of debits governed by the digits in the front and rear fields. The middle field of a

```
structure ImplicitQueue : QUEUE =
(* assumes polymorphic recursion! *)
struct
  datatype α Digit = ZERO | ONE of α | TWO of α × α
  datatype α Queue =
      SHALLOW of α Digit
    | DEEP of α Digit × (α × α) Queue susp × α Digit

  val empty = SHALLOW ZERO
  fun isEmpty (SHALLOW ZERO) = true | isEmpty _ = false

  fun snoc (SHALLOW ZERO, y) = SHALLOW (ONE y)
    | snoc (SHALLOW (ONE x), y) = DEEP (TWO (x, y), $empty, ZERO)
    | snoc (DEEP (f, m, ZERO), y) = DEEP (f, m, ONE y)
    | snoc (DEEP (f, m, ONE x), y) =
        DEEP (f, $snoc (force m, (x, y)), ZERO)

  fun head (SHALLOW ZERO) = raise EMPTY
    | head (SHALLOW (ONE x)) = x
    | head (DEEP (ONE x, m, r)) = x
    | head (DEEP (TWO (x, y), m, r)) = x
  fun tail (SHALLOW ZERO) = raise EMPTY
    | tail (SHALLOW (ONE x)) = empty
    | tail (DEEP (TWO (x, y), m, r)) = DEEP (ONE y, m, r)
    | tail (DEEP (ONE x, $q, r)) =
        if isEmpty q then SHALLOW r
        else let val (y, z) = head q
             in DEEP (TWO (y, z), $tail q, r) end
end
```

Figure 11.1. Queues based on implicit recursive slowdown.

deep queue may have up to $|f| - |r|$ debits, where $|f|$ is one or two, and $|r|$ is zero or one.

The unshared cost of each function is $O(1)$, so we must merely show that neither function discharges more than $O(1)$ debits. We describe only the proof for tail. The proof for snoc is slightly simpler.

We argue by debit passing, which is closely related to debit inheritance. Whenever a nested suspension has more debits than it is allowed, we pass those debits to the enclosing suspension, which is the middle field of the previous DEEP node. Debit passing is safe because the outer suspension must be forced before the inner suspension can be forced. Passing responsibility for discharging debits from a nested suspension to the enclosing suspension ensures that those debits will be discharged before the outer suspension is forced, and hence before the inner suspension can be forced.

We show that every call to tail passes one debit to its enclosing suspension, except the outermost call, which has no enclosing suspension. That call simply discharges its excess debit.

Each cascade of tails ends in a call to tail that changes f from TWO to ONE. (For simplicity of presentation, we ignore the possibility of shallow queues). This decreases the debit allowance of m by one, so we pass the excess debit to the enclosing suspension.

Every intermediate call to tail changes f from ONE to TWO and recurses. There are two subcases:

- r is ZERO. m has one debit, which must be discharged before m can be forced. We pass this debit to the enclosing suspension. We create one debit to cover the unshared cost of the suspended recursive call. In addition, this suspension is passed one debit by the recursive call. Since this suspension has a debit allowance of two, we are done.

- r is ONE. m has zero debits, so we can force it for free. We create one debit to cover the unshared cost of the suspended recursive call. In addition, this suspension is passed one debit by the recursive call. Since this suspension has a debit allowance of one, we keep one debit and pass the other to the enclosing suspension.

□

Exercise 11.1 Implement lookup and update functions for these queues. Your functions should run in $O(\log i)$ amortized time. You may find it helpful to augment each queue with a size field.

Exercise 11.2 Implement double-ended queues using the techniques of this section.

11.2 Catenable Double-Ended Queues

Finally, we use implicit recursive slowdown to implement catenable double-ended queues, with the signature shown in Figure 11.2. We first describe a relatively simple implementation that supports ++ in $O(\log n)$ amortized time and all other operations in $O(1)$ amortized time. We then describe a much more complicated implementation that improves the running time of ++ to $O(1)$.

Consider the following representation for catenable double-ended queues, or *c-deques*. A c-deque is either *shallow* or *deep*. A shallow c-deque is simply an ordinary deque, such as the banker's deques of Section 8.4.2. A deep c-deque is decomposed into three segments: a *front*, a *middle*, and a *rear*. The front and

```
signature CATENABLEDEQUE =
sig
   type α Cat

   val empty   : α Cat
   val isEmpty : α Cat → bool

   val cons    : α × α Cat → α Cat
   val head    : α Cat → α              (* raises EMPTY if deque is empty *)
   val tail    : α Cat → α Cat          (* raises EMPTY if deque is empty *)

   val snoc    : α Cat × α → α Cat
   val last    : α Cat → α              (* raises EMPTY if deque is empty *)
   val init    : α Cat → α Cat          (* raises EMPTY if deque is empty *)

   val ++      : α Cat × α Cat → α Cat
end
```

Figure 11.2. Signature for catenable double-ended queues.

rear are both ordinary deques containing two or more elements each. The middle is a c-deque of ordinary deques, each containing two or more elements. We assume that D is an implementation of deques satisfying the signature DEQUE, and that all of the functions in D run in $O(1)$ time (amortized or worst-case).

```
datatype α Cat =
      SHALLOW of α D.Queue
    | DEEP of α D.Queue × α D.Queue Cat susp × α D.Queue
```

Note that this definition assumes polymorphic recursion.

To insert an element at either end, we simply insert the element into the front deque or the rear deque. For instance, cons is implemented as

```
fun cons (x, SHALLOW d) = SHALLOW (D.cons (x, d))
  | cons (x, DEEP (f, m, r)) = DEEP (D.cons (x, f), m, r)
```

To remove an element from either end, we remove an element from the front deque or the rear deque. If this drops the length of that deque below two, then we remove the next deque from the middle, add the one remaining element from the old deque, and install the result as the new front or rear. With the addition of the remaining element from the old deque, the new deque contains at least three elements. For example, the code for tail is

fun tail (SHALLOW d) = SHALLOW (D.tail d)
  | tail (DEEP (f, m, r)) =
    let val f' = D.tail f
    in
      if not (tooSmall f') **then** DEEP (f', m, r)
      else if isEmpty (force m) **then** SHALLOW (dappendL (f', r))
      else DEEP (dappendL (f', head (force m)), \$tail (force m), r)
    end

where tooSmall tests if the length of a deque is less than two and dappendL appends a deque of length zero or one to a deque of arbitrary length.

Note that calls to tail propagate to the next level of the c-deque only when the length of the front deque is two. In the terminology of Section 9.2.3, we say that a deque of length three or more is *safe* and a deque of length two is *dangerous*. Whenever tail does call itself recursively on the next level, it also changes the front deque from dangerous to safe, so that two successive calls to tail on a given level of the c-deque never both propagate to the next level. We can easily prove that tail runs in $O(1)$ amortized time by allowing one debit per safe deque and zero debits per dangerous deque.

Exercise 11.3 Prove that both tail and init run in $O(1)$ amortized time by combining their respective debit allowances as suggested by implicit recursive slowdown. $\diamond$

Now, what about catenation? To catenate two deep c-deques c_1 and c_2, we retain the front of c_1 as the new front, the rear of c_2 as the new rear, and combine the remaining segments into the new middle by inserting the rear of c_1 into the middle of c_1, and the front of c_2 into the middle of c_2, and then catenating the results.

fun (DEEP (f_1, m_1, r_1)) ++ (DEEP (f_2, m_2, r_2)) =
    DEEP (f_1, \$(snoc (force m_1, r_1) ++ cons (f_2, force m_2)), r_2)

(Of course, there are also cases where c_1 or c_2 are shallow.) Note that ++ recurses to the depth of the shallower c-deque. Furthermore, ++ creates $O(1)$ debits per level, which must be immediately discharged to restore the debit invariant required by the tail and init. Therefore, ++ runs in $O(\min(\log n_1, \log n_2))$ amortized time, where n_i is the size of c_i.

The complete code for this implementation of c-deques appears in Figure 11.3.

To improve the running time of ++ to $O(1)$, we modify the representation of c-deques so that ++ does not call itself recursively. The key is to enable ++ at one level to call only cons and snoc at the next level. Instead of three segments, we expand deep c-deques to contain five segments: (f, a, m, b, r). f, m, and

```
functor SimpleCatenableDeque (D : DEQUE) : CATENABLEDEQUE =
    (* assumes polymorphic recursion! *)
struct
    datatype α Cat =
        SHALLOW of α D.Queue
      | DEEP of α D.Queue × α D.Queue Cat susp × α D.Queue

    fun tooSmall d = D.isEmpty d orelse D.isEmpty (D.tail d)

    fun dappendL (d₁, d₂) =
        if D.isEmpty d₁ then d₂ else D.cons (D.head d₁, d₂)
    fun dappendR (d₁, d₂) =
        if D.isEmpty d₂ then d₁ else D.snoc (d₁, D.head d₂)

    val empty = SHALLOW D.empty
    fun isEmpty (SHALLOW d) = D.isEmpty d
      | isEmpty _ = false

    fun cons (x, SHALLOW d) = SHALLOW (D.cons (x, d))
      | cons (x, DEEP (f, m, r)) = DEEP (D.cons (x, f), m, r)
    fun head (SHALLOW d) = D.head d
      | head (DEEP (f, m, r)) = D.head f
    fun tail (SHALLOW d) = SHALLOW (D.tail d)
      | tail (DEEP (f, m, r)) =
        let val f' = D.tail f
        in
            if not (tooSmall f') then DEEP (f', m, r)
            else if isEmpty (force m) then SHALLOW (dappendL (f', r))
            else DEEP (dappendL (f', head (force m)), $tail (force m), r)
        end

    ...snoc, last, and init defined symmetrically...

    fun (SHALLOW d₁) ⧺ (SHALLOW d₂) =
        if tooSmall d₁ then SHALLOW (dappendL (d₁, d₂))
        else if tooSmall d₂ then SHALLOW (dappendR (d₁, d₂))
        else DEEP (d₁, $empty, d₂)
      | (SHALLOW d) ⧺ (DEEP (f, m, r)) =
        if tooSmall d then DEEP (dappendL (d, f), m, r)
        else DEEP (d, $cons (f, force m), r)
      | (DEEP (f, m, r)) ⧺ (SHALLOW d) =
        if tooSmall d then DEEP (f, m, dappendR (r, d))
        else DEEP (f, $snoc (force m, r), d)
      | (DEEP (f₁, m₁, r₁)) ⧺ (DEEP (f₂, m₂, r₂)) =
        DEEP (f₁, $(snoc (force m₁, r₁) ⧺ cons (f₂, force m₂)), r₂)
end
```

Figure 11.3. Simple catenable deques.

r are all ordinary deques; f and r contain three or more elements each, and m contains two or more elements. a and b are c-deques of *compound elements*. A degenerate compound element is simply an ordinary deque containing two or more elements. A full compound element has three segments: (f, c, r), where f and r are ordinary deques containing at least two elements each, and c is a c-deque of compound elements. This datatype can be written in Standard ML (with polymorphic recursion) as

```
datatype α Cat =
    SHALLOW of α D.Queue
  | DEEP of α D.Queue            (* ≥ 3 *)
        × α CmpdElem Cat susp
        × α D.Queue              (* ≥ 2 *)
        × α CmpdElem Cat susp
        × α D.Queue              (* ≥ 3 *)
and α CmpdElem =
    SIMPLE of α D.Queue          (* ≥ 2 *)
  | CMPD of α D.Queue            (* ≥ 2 *)
        × α CmpdElem Cat susp
        × α D.Queue              (* ≥ 2 *)
```

Given c-deques $c_1 = \text{DEEP}\ (f_1,a_1,m_1,b_1,r_1)$ and $c_2 = \text{DEEP}\ (f_2,a_2,m_2,b_2,r_2)$, we compute their catenation as follows: First, we retain f_1 as the front of the result, and r_2 as the rear of the result. Next, we build the new middle deque from the last element of r_1 and the first element of f_2. We then combine m_1, b_1, and the rest of r_1 into a compound element, which we snoc onto a_1. This becomes the new a segment of the result. Finally, we combine the rest of f_2, a_2, and m_2 into a compound element, which we cons onto b_2. This becomes the new b segment of the result. Altogether, this is implemented as

```
fun (DEEP (f1, a1, m1, b1, r1)) ++ (DEEP (f2, a2, m2, b2, r2)) =
    let val (r'1, m, f'2) = share (r1, f2)
        val a'1 = $snoc (force a1, CMPD (m1, b1, r'1))
        val b'2 = $cons (CMPD (f'2, a2, m2), force b2)
    in DEEP (f1, a'1, m, b'2, r2) end
```

where

```
fun share (f, r) =
    let val m = D.cons (D.last f, D.cons (D.head r, D.empty))
    in (D.init f, m, D.tail r)
fun cons (x, DEEP (f, a, m, b, r)) = DEEP (D.cons (x, f), a, m, b, r)
fun snoc (DEEP (f, a, m, b, r), x) = DEEP (f, a, m, b, D.snoc (r, x))
```

(For simplicity of presentation, we have ignored all cases involving shallow c-deques.)

Unfortunately, in this implementation, tail and init are downright messy. Since the two functions are symmetric, we describe only tail. Given some c-deque $c = \text{DEEP}\ (f,a,m,b,r)$, there are six cases:

- $|f| > 3$.
- $|f| = 3$.
  - *a* is non-empty.
    - ○ The first compound element of *a* is degenerate.
    - ○ The first compound element of *a* is full.
  - *a* is empty and *b* is non-empty.
    - ○ The first compound element of *b* is degenerate.
    - ○ The first compound element of *b* is full.
  - *a* and *b* are both empty.

Here we describe the behavior of tail *c* in the first three cases. The remaining cases are covered by the complete implementation in Figures 11.4 and 11.5. If $|f| > 3$ then we simply replace *f* with D.tail *f*. If $|f| = 3$, then removing an element from *f* would drop its length below the allowable minimum. Therefore, we remove a new front deque from *a* and combine it with the remaining two elements of the old *f*. The new *f* contains at least four elements, so the next call to tail will fall into the $|f| > 3$ case.

When we remove the first compound element of *a* to find the new front deque, we get either a degenerate compound element or a full compound element. If we get a degenerate compound element (i.e., a simple deque), then the new value of *a* is $tail (force A). If we get a full compound element Cmpd (f',c',r'), then f' becomes the new *f* (along with the remaining elements of the old *f*), and the new value of *a* is

$$\$(\text{force } c' +\!\!+ \text{cons } (\text{SIMPLE } r', \text{tail (force } a)))$$

But note that the effect of the cons and tail is to replace the first element of *a*. We can do this directly, and avoid an unnecessary call to tail, using the function replaceHead.

```
fun replaceHead (x, SHALLOW d) = SHALLOW (D.cons (x, D.tail d))
  | replaceHead (x, DEEP (f, a, m, b, r)) =
        DEEP (D.cons (x, D.tail f), a, m, b, r)
```

The remaining cases of tail are similar, each doing $O(1)$ work followed by at most one call to tail.

Remark   This code can be written much more succinctly and much more perspicuously using a language feature called *views* [Wad87, BC93, PPN96], which allows pattern matching on abstract types. See [Oka97] for further details. Standard ML does not support views.   ◇

The cons, snoc, head, and last functions make no use of lazy evaluation,

functor ImplicitCatenableDeque (D : DEQUE) : CATENABLEDEQUE =
(∗ *assumes that* D *also supports a* size *function* ∗)
struct
  datatype α Cat =
    SHALLOW **of** α D.Queue
    | DEEP **of** α D.Queue $\times$ α CmpdElem Cat susp $\times$ α D.Queue
                          $\times$ α CmpdElem Cat susp $\times$ α D.Queue
  and α CmpdElem =
    SIMPLE **of** α D.Queue
    | CMPD **of** α D.Queue $\times$ α CmpdElem Cat susp $\times$ α D.Queue

  val empty = SHALLOW D.empty
  fun isEmpty (SHALLOW d) = D.isEmpty d
  | isEmpty _ = false

  fun cons (x, SHALLOW d) = SHALLOW (D.cons (x, d))
  | cons (x, DEEP (f, a, m, b, r)) = DEEP (D.cons (x, f), a, m, b, r)
  fun head (SHALLOW d) = D.head d
  | head (DEEP (f, a, m, b, r)) = D.head f

  ... snoc *and* last *defined symmetrically*...

  fun share (f, r) =
    let val m = D.cons (D.last f, D.cons (D.head r, D.empty))
    in (D.init f, m, D.tail r)
  fun dappendL (d_1, d_2) =
    if D.isEmpty d_1 **then** d_2
    else dappendL (D.init d_1, D.cons (D.last d_1, d_2))
  fun dappendR (d_1, d_2) =
    if D.isEmpty d_2 **then** d_1
    else dappendR (D.snoc (d_1, D.head d_2), D.tail d_2)

  fun (SHALLOW d_1) ⧺ (SHALLOW d_2) =
    if D.size d_1 < 4 **then** SHALLOW (dappendL (d_1, d_2))
    else if D.size d_2 < 4 **then** SHALLOW (dappendR (d_1, d_2))
    else let val (f, m, r) = share (d_1, d_2)
        in DEEP (f, \$empty, m, \$empty, r) **end**
  | (SHALLOW d) ⧺ (DEEP (f, a, m, b, r)) =
    if D.size d < 4 **then** DEEP (dappendL (d, f), a, m, b, r)
    else DEEP (d, \$cons (SIMPLE f, force a), m, b, r)
  | (DEEP (f, a, m, b, r)) ⧺ (SHALLOW d) =
    if D.size d < 4 **then** DEEP (f, a, m, b, dappendR (r, d))
    else DEEP (f, a, m, \$snoc (force b, SIMPLE r), d)
  | (DEEP (f_1, a_1, m_1, b_1, r_1)) ⧺ (DEEP (f_2, a_2, m_2, b_2, r_2)) =
    let val (r_1', m, f_2') = share (r_1, f_2)
      val a_1' = \$snoc (force a_1, CMPD (m_1, b_1, r_1'))
      val b_2' = \$cons (CMPD (f_2', a_2, m_2), force b_2)
    in DEEP (f_1, a_1', m, b_2', r_2) **end**

  ...

Figure 11.4. Catenable deques using implicit recursive slowdown (part I).

```
...
fun replaceHead (x, SHALLOW d) = SHALLOW (D.cons (x, D.tail d))
  | replaceHead (x, DEEP (f, a, m, b, r)) =
    DEEP (D.cons (x, D.tail f), a, m, b, r)
fun tail (SHALLOW d) = SHALLOW (D.tail d)
  | tail (DEEP (f, a, m, b, r)) =
    if D.size f > 3 then DEEP (D.tail f, a, m, b, r)
    else if not (isEmpty (force a)) then
      case head (force a) of
        SIMPLE d ⇒
          let val f' = dappendL (D.tail f, d)
          in DEEP (f', $tail (force a), m, b, r) end
        | CMPD (f', c', r') ⇒
          let val f'' = dappendL (D.tail f, f')
              val a'' = $(force c' ++ replaceHead (SIMPLE r', force a))
          in DEEP (f'', a'', m, b, r) end
    else if not (isEmpty (force b)) then
      case head (force b) of
        SIMPLE d ⇒
          let val f' = dappendL (D.tail f, m)
          in DEEP (f', $empty, d, $tail (force b), r) end
        | CMPD (f', c', r') ⇒
          let val f'' = dappendL (D.tail f, m)
              val a'' = $cons (SIMPLE f', force c')
          in DEEP (f'', a'', r', $tail (force b), r) end
    else SHALLOW (dappendL (D.tail f, m)) ++ SHALLOW r
...replaceLast and init defined symmetrically...
end
```

Figure 11.5. Catenable deques using implicit recursive slowdown (part II).

and are easily seen to take $O(1)$ worst-case time. We analyze the remaining functions using the banker's method and debit passing.

As always, we assign debits to every suspension, each of which is the *a* or *b* segment of a deep c-deque, or the middle (*c*) segment of a compound element. Each *c* field is allowed four debits, but *a* and *b* fields may have from zero to five debits, based on the lengths of the *f* and *r* fields. *a* and *b* have a base allowance of zero debits. If *f* contains more than three elements, then the allowance for *a* increases by four debits and the allowance for *b* increases by one debit. Similarly, if *r* contains more than three elements, then the allowance for *b* increases by four debits and the allowance for *a* increases by one debit.

Theorem 11.2 ++, tail, *and* init *run in* $O(1)$ *amortized time.*

Proof (++) The interesting case is catenating two c-deques DEEP (f_1,a_1,m_1,b_1,r_1) and DEEP (f_2,a_2,m_2,b_2,r_2). In that case, ++ does $O(1)$ unshared work and discharges at most four debits. First, we create two debits for the suspended snoc and cons onto a_1 and b_2, respectively. We always discharge these two debits. In addition, if b_1 or a_2 has five debits, then we must discharge one debit when that segment becomes the middle of a compound element. Also, if f_1 has only three elements but f_2 has more than three elements, then we must discharge a debit from b_2 as it becomes the new b. Similarly for r_1 and r_2. However, note that if b_1 has five debits, then f_1 has more than three elements, and that if a_2 has five debits, then r_2 has more than three elements. Therefore, we must discharge at most four debits altogether, or at least pass those debits to an enclosing suspension.

(tail and init) Since tail and init are symmetric, we include the argument only for tail. By inspection, tail does $O(1)$ unshared work, so we must show that it discharges only $O(1)$ debits. In fact, we show that it discharges at most five debits.

Since tail can call itself recursively, we must account for a cascade of tails. We argue by debit passing. Given some deep c-deque DEEP (f,a,m,b,r), there is one case for each case of tail.

If $|f| > 3$, then this is the end of a cascade. We create no new debits, but removing an element from f might decrease the allowance of a by four debits, and the allowance of b by one debit, so we pass these debits to the enclosing suspension.

If $|f| = 3$, then assume a is non-empty. (The cases where a is empty are similar.) If $|r| > 3$, then a might have one debit, which we pass to the enclosing suspension. Otherwise, a has no debits. If the head of a is a degenerate compound element (i.e., a simple deque of elements), then this becomes the new f along with the remaining elements of the old f. The new a is a suspension of the tail of the old a. This suspension receives at most five debits from the recursive call to tail. Since the new allowance of a is at least four debits, we pass at most one of these debits to the enclosing suspension, for a total of at most two debits. (Actually, the total is at most one debit since we pass one debit here exactly in the case that we did not have to pass one debit for the original a).

Otherwise, if the head of a is a full compound element CMPD (f',c',r'), then f' becomes the new f along with the remaining elements of the old f. The new a involves calls to ++ and replaceHead. The total number of debits on the new a is nine: four debits from c', four debits from the ++, and one newly created debit for the replaceHead. The allowance for the new a is either four or five, so we pass either five or four of these nine debits to the enclosing suspension.

Since we pass four of these debits exactly in the case that we had to pass one debit from the original *a*, we always pass at most five debits.   □

Exercise 11.4 Given an implementation D of non-catenable deques, implement catenable lists using the type

datatype α Cat =
  SHALLOW **of** α D.Queue
  | DEEP **of** α D.Queue × α CmpdElem Cat susp × α D.Queue
  and α CmpdElem = CMPD **of** α D.Queue × α CmpdElem Cat susp

where both the front deque of a DEEP node and the deque in a CMPD node contain at least two elements. Prove that every function in your implementation runs in $O(1)$ amortized time, assuming that all the functions in D run in $O(1)$ time (worst-case or amortized).

11.3 Chapter Notes

Recursive Slowdown Kaplan and Tarjan introduced recursive slowdown in [KT95], and used it again in [KT96b], but it is closely related to the regularity constraints of Guibas et al. [GMPR77]. Brodal [Bro95] used a similar technique to implement heaps.

Catenable Deques Buchsbaum and Tarjan [BT95] present a purely functional implementation of catenable deques that supports tail and init in $O(\log^* n)$ worst-case time and all other operations in $O(1)$ worst-case time. Our implementation improves that bound to $O(1)$ for all operations, although in the amortized rather than worst-case sense. Kaplan and Tarjan have independently developed a similar implementation with worst-case bounds [KT96a]. However, the details of their implementation are quite complicated.

Appendix A
Haskell Source Code

```
┌─────────┐
│ Queues  │
└─────────┘
```

```haskell
module Queue (Queue(..)) where
import Prelude hiding (head,tail)

class Queue q where
  empty   :: q a
  isEmpty :: q a → Bool

  snoc :: q a → a → q a
  head :: q a → a
  tail :: q a → q a
```

```haskell
module BatchedQueue (BatchedQueue) where
import Prelude hiding (head,tail)
import Queue

data BatchedQueue a = BQ [a] [a]

check [] r = BQ (reverse r) []
check f r = BQ f r

instance Queue BatchedQueue where
  empty = BQ [] []
  isEmpty (BQ f r) = null f

  snoc (BQ f r) x = check f (x : r)

  head (BQ [] _) = error "empty queue"
  head (BQ (x : f) r) = x

  tail (BQ [] _) = error "empty queue"
  tail (BQ (x : f) r) = check f r
```

```haskell
module BankersQueue (BankersQueue) where
import Prelude hiding (head,tail)
import Queue

data BankersQueue a = BQ Int [a] Int [a]

check lenf f lenr r =
  if lenr ≤ lenf then BQ lenf f lenr r
  else BQ (lenf+lenr) (f ++ reverse r) 0 []

instance Queue BankersQueue where
  empty = BQ 0 [] 0 []
  isEmpty (BQ lenf f lenr r) = (lenf == 0)

  snoc (BQ lenf f lenr r) x = check lenf f (lenr+1) (x : r)
```

```
head (BQ lenf [ ] lenr r) = error "empty queue"
head (BQ lenf (x : f') lenr r) = x

tail (BQ lenf [ ] lenr r) = error "empty queue"
tail (BQ lenf (x : f') lenr r) = check (lenf−1) f' lenr r
```

---

module PhysicistsQueue (PhysicistsQueue) **where**
import Prelude **hiding** (head,tail)
import Queue

data PhysicistsQueue a = PQ [a] Int [a] Int [a]

```
check w lenf f lenr r =
  if lenr ≤ lenf then checkw w lenf f lenr r
  else checkw f (lenf+lenr) (f ++ reverse r) 0 [ ]

checkw [ ] lenf f lenr r = PQ f lenf f lenr r
checkw w lenf f lenr r = PQ w lenf f lenr r
```

instance Queue PhysicistsQueue **where**
```
  empty = PQ [] 0 [] 0 []
  isEmpty (PQ w lenf f lenr r) = (lenf == 0)

  snoc (PQ w lenf f lenr r) x = check w lenf f (lenr+1) (x : r)

  head (PQ [ ] lenf f lenr r) = error "empty queue"
  head (PQ (x : w) lenf f lenr r) = x

  tail (PQ [ ] lenf f lenr r) = error "empty queue"
  tail (PQ (x : w) lenf f lenr r) = check w (lenf−1) (Prelude.tail f) lenr r
```

---

module HoodMelvilleQueue (HoodMelvilleQueue) **where**
import Prelude **hiding** (head,tail)
import Queue

data RotationState a =
      Idle
    | Reversing Int [a] [a] [a] [a]
    | Appending Int [a] [a]
    | Done [a]
data HoodMelvilleQueue a = HM Int [a] (RotationState a) Int [a]

```
exec (Reversing ok (x : f) f' (y : r) r') = Reversing (ok+1) f (x : f') r (y : r')
exec (Reversing ok [ ] f' [y] r') = Appending ok f' (y : r')
exec (Appending 0 f' r') = Done r'
exec (Appending ok (x : f') r') = Appending (ok−1) f' (x : r')
exec state = state

invalidate (Reversing ok f f' r r') = Reversing (ok−1) f f' r r'
invalidate (Appending 0 f' (x : r')) = Done r'
invalidate (Appending ok f' r') = Appending (ok−1) f' r'
invalidate state = state
```

```
exec2 lenf f state lenr r =
  case exec (exec state) of
    Done newf → HM lenf newf Idle lenr r
    newstate → HM lenf f newstate lenr r

check lenf f state lenr r =
  if lenr ≤ lenf then exec2 lenf f state lenr r
  else let newstate = Reversing 0 f [] r []
       in exec2 (lenf+lenr) f newstate 0 []

instance Queue HoodMelvilleQueue where
  empty = HM 0 [] Idle 0 []
  isEmpty (HM lenf f state lenr r) = (lenf == 0)

  snoc (HM lenf f state lenr r) x = check lenf f state (lenr+1) (x : r)

  head (HM _ [] _ _ _) = error "empty queue"
  head (HM _ (x : f') _ _ _) = x

  tail (HM lenf [] state lenr r) = error "empty queue"
  tail (HM lenf (x : f') state lenr r) =
    check (lenf−1) f' (invalidate state) lenr r
```

```
module BootstrappedQueue (BootstrappedQueue) where
import Prelude hiding (head,tail)
import Queue

data BootstrappedQueue a =
  E | Q Int [a] (BootstrappedQueue [a]) Int [a]

checkQ,checkF :: Int → [a] → (BootstrappedQueue [a]) → Int → [a]
                → BootstrappedQueue a
checkQ lenfm f m lenr r =
  if lenr ≤ lenfm then checkF lenfm f m lenr r
  else checkF (lenfm+lenr) f (snoc m (reverse r)) 0 []

checkF lenfm [] E lenr f = E
checkF lenfm [] m lenr r = Q lenfm (head m) (tail m) lenr r
checkF lenfm f m lenr r = Q lenfm f m lenr r

instance Queue BootstrappedQueue where
  empty = Q 0 [] E 0 []
  isEmpty E = True
  isEmpty _ = False

  snoc E x = q 1 [x] E 0 []
  snoc (Q lenfm f m lenr r) x = checkQ lenfm f m (lenr+1) (x : r)

  head E = error "empty queue"
  head (Q lenfm (x : f') m lenr r) = x

  tail E = error "empty queue"
  tail (Q lenfm (x : f') m lenr r) = checkQ (lenfm−1) f' m lenr r
```

```
module ImplicitQueue (ImplicitQueue) where
  import Prelude hiding (head,tail)
  import Queue

data Digit a = ZERO | ONE a | TWO a a
data ImplicitQueue a =
      SHALLOW (Digit a)
    | DEEP (Digit a) (ImplicitQueue (a, a)) (Digit a)

instance Queue ImplicitQueue where
  empty = SHALLOW ZERO
  isEmpty (SHALLOW ZERO) = True
  isEmpty _ = False

  snoc (SHALLOW ZERO) y = SHALLOW (ONE y)
  snoc (SHALLOW (ONE x)) y = DEEP (TWO x y) empty ZERO
  snoc (DEEP f m ZERO) y = DEEP f m (ONE y)
  snoc (DEEP f m (ONE x)) y = DEEP f (snoc m (x,y)) ZERO

  head (SHALLOW ZERO) = error "empty queue"
  head (SHALLOW (ONE x)) = x
  head (DEEP (ONE x) m r) = x
  head (DEEP (TWO x y) m r) = x

  tail (SHALLOW ZERO) = error "empty queue"
  tail (SHALLOW (ONE x)) = empty
  tail (DEEP (TWO x y) m r) = DEEP (ONE y) m r
  tail (DEEP (ONE x) m r) =
      if isEmpty m then SHALLOW r else DEEP (TWO y z) (tail m) r
      where (y,z) = head m
```

$$\boxed{\text{Deques}}$$

```
module Deque (Deque(..)) where
  import Prelude hiding (head,tail,last,init)

class Deque q where
  empty   :: q a
  isEmpty :: q a → Bool

  cons :: a → q a → q a
  head :: q a → a
  tail :: q a → q a

  snoc :: q a → a → q a
  last :: q a → a
  init :: q a → q a
```

```
module BankersDeque (BankersDeque) where
  import Prelude hiding (head,tail,last,init)
  import Deque
```

```
data BankersDeque a = BD Int [a] Int [a]

c = 3

check lenf f lenr r =
  if lenf > c*lenr + 1 then
    let i = (lenf+lenr) 'div' 2
        j = lenf+lenr−i
        f' = take i f
        r' = r ++ reverse (drop i f)
    in BD i f' j r'
  else if lenr > c*lenf + 1 then
    let j = (lenf+lenr) 'div' 2
        i = lenf+lenr−j
        r' = take j r
        f' = f ++ reverse (drop j r)
    in BD i f' j r'
  else BD lenf f lenr r

instance Deque BankersDeque where
  empty = BD 0 [] 0 []
  isEmpty (BD lenf f lenr r) = (lenf+lenr == 0)

  cons x (BD lenf f lenr r) = check (lenf+1) (x : f) lenr r

  head (BD lenf [] lenr r) = error "empty deque"
  head (BD lenf (x : f') lenr r) = x

  tail (BD lenf [] lenr r) = error "empty deque"
  tail (BD lenf (x : f') lenr r) = check (lenf−1) f' lenr r

  snoc (BD lenf f lenr r) x = check lenf f (lenr+1) (x : r)

  last (BD lenf f lenr []) = error "empty deque"
  last (BD lenf f lenr (x : r')) = x

  init (BD lenf f lenr []) = error "empty deque"
  init (BD lenf f lenr (x : r')) = check lenf f (lenr−1) r'
```

Catenable Lists

```
module CatenableList (CatenableList(..)) where
import Prelude hiding (head,tail,(++))

class CatenableList c where
  empty   :: c a
  isEmpty :: c a → Bool

  cons :: a → c a → c a
  snoc :: c a → a → c a
  (++) :: c a → c a → c a

  head :: c a → a
  tail :: c a → c a
```

```
module CatList (CatList) where
  import Prelude hiding (head,tail,(++))
  import CatenableList
  import Queue (Queue)
  import qualified Queue

data CatList q a = E | C a (q (CatList q a))

link (C x q) s = C x (Queue.snoc q s)

instance Queue q ⇒ CatenableList (CatList q) where
  empty = E
  isEmpty E = True
  isEmpty _ = False

  xs ++ E = xs
  E ++ xs = xs
  xs ++ ys = link xs ys

  cons x xs = C x Queue.empty ++ xs
  snoc xs x = xs ++ C x Queue.empty

  head E = error "empty list"
  head (C x q) = x

  tail E = error "empty list"
  tail (C x q) = if Queue.isEmpty q then E else linkAll q
    where linkAll q = if Queue.isEmpty q' then t else link t (linkAll q')
            where t = Queue.head q
                  q' = Queue.tail q
```

Catenable Deques

```
module CatenableDeque (CatenableDeque(..)) where
  import Prelude hiding (head,tail,last,init,(++))
  import Deque

class Deque d ⇒ CatenableDeque d where
  (++) :: d a → d a → d a
```

```
module SimpleCatenableDeque (SimpleCatDeque) where
  import Prelude hiding (head,tail,last,init,(++))
  import CatenableDeque

data SimpleCatDeque d a =
    SHALLOW (d a)
  | DEEP (d a) (SimpleCatDeque d (d a)) (d a)

tooSmall d = isEmpty d || isEmpty (tail d)
```

```haskell
dappendL d₁ d₂ = if isEmpty d₁ then d₂ else cons (head d₁) d₂
dappendR d₁ d₂ = if isEmpty d₂ then d₁ else snoc d₁ (head d₂)

instance Deque d ⟹ Deque (SimpleCatDeque d) where
  empty = SHALLOW empty
  isEmpty (SHALLOW d) = isEmpty d
  isEmpty _ = False

  cons x (SHALLOW d) = SHALLOW (cons x d)
  cons x (DEEP f m r) = DEEP (cons x f) m r

  head (SHALLOW d) = head d
  head (DEEP f m r) = head f

  tail (SHALLOW d) = SHALLOW (tail d)
  tail (DEEP f m r)
    | not (tooSmall f') = DEEP f' m r
    | isEmpty m = SHALLOW (dappendL f' r)
    | otherwise = DEEP (dappendL f' (head m)) (tail m) r
    where f' = tail f

  -- snoc, last, and init defined symmetrically...

instance Deque d ⟹ CatenableDeque (SimpleCatDeque d) where
  (SHALLOW d₁) ⧺ (SHALLOW d₂)
    | tooSmall d₁ = SHALLOW (dappendL d₁ d₂)
    | tooSmall d₂ = SHALLOW (dappendR d₁ d₂)
    | otherwise = DEEP d₁ empty d₂
  (SHALLOW d) ⧺ (DEEP f m r)
    | tooSmall d = DEEP (dappendL d f) m r
    | otherwise = DEEP d (cons f m) r
  (DEEP f m r) ⧺ (SHALLOW d)
    | tooSmall d = DEEP f m (dappendR r d)
    | otherwise = DEEP f (snoc m r) d
  (DEEP f₁ m₁ r₁) ⧺ (DEEP f₂ m₂ r₂) =
    DEEP f₁ (snoc m₁ r₁ ⧺ cons f₂ m₂) r₂
```

```haskell
module ImplicitCatenableDeque (Sized(..), ImplicitCatDeque) where
import Prelude hiding (head,tail,last,init,(⧺))
import CatenableDeque

class Sized d where
  size :: d a → Int

data ImplicitCatDeque d a =
    SHALLOW (d a)
  | DEEP (d a) (ImplicitCatDeque d (CmpdElem d a)) (d a)
         (ImplicitCatDeque d (CmpdElem d a)) (d a)

data CmpdElem d a =
    SIMPLE (d a)
  | CMPD (d a) (ImplicitCatDeque d (CmpdElem d a)) (d a)
```

```
share f r = (init f, m, tail r)
  where m = cons (last f) (cons (head r) empty)
```

```
dappendL d₁ d₂ =
  if isEmpty d₁ then d₂ else dappendL (init d₁) (cons (last d₁) d₂)
dappendR d₁ d₂ =
  if isEmpty d₂ then d₁ else dappendR (snoc d₁ (head d₂)) (tail d₂)
```

```
replaceHead x (SHALLOW d) = SHALLOW (cons x (tail d))
replaceHead x (DEEP f a m b r) = DEEP (cons x (tail f)) a m b r
```

```
instance (Deque d, Sized d) ⇒ Deque (ImplicitCatDeque d) where
  empty = SHALLOW empty
  isEmpty (SHALLOW d) = isEmpty d
  isEmpty _ = False
```

```
  cons x (SHALLOW d) = SHALLOW (cons x d)
  cons x (DEEP f a m b r) = DEEP (cons x f) a m b r
```

```
  head (SHALLOW d) = head d
  head (DEEP f a m b r) = head f
```

```
  tail (SHALLOW d) = SHALLOW (tail d)
  tail (DEEP f a m b r)
    | size f > 3 = DEEP (tail f) a m b r
    | not (isEmpty a) =
        case head a of
          SIMPLE d → DEEP f' (tail a) m b r
            where f' = dappendL (tail f) d
          CMPD f' c' r' → DEEP f'' a'' m b r
            where f'' = dappendL (tail f) f'
                  a'' = c' ++ replaceHead (SIMPLE r') a
    | not (isEmpty b) =
        case head b of
          SIMPLE d → DEEP f' empty d (tail b) r
            where f' = dappendL (tail f) m
          CMPD f' c' r' → DEEP f'' a'' r' (tail b) r
            where f'' = dappendL (tail f) m
                  a'' = cons (SIMPLE f') c'
    | otherwise = SHALLOW (dappendL (tail f) m) ++ SHALLOW r
```

```
  -- snoc, last, and init defined symmetrically...
```

```
instance (Deque d, Sized d) ⇒ CatenableDeque (ImplicitCatDeque d)
where
  (SHALLOW d₁) ++ (SHALLOW d₂)
    | size d₁ < 4 = SHALLOW (dappendL d₁ d₂)
    | size d₂ < 4 = SHALLOW (dappendR d₁ d₂)
    | otherwise = let (f, m, r) = share d₁ d₂ in DEEP f empty m empty r
  (SHALLOW d) ++ (DEEP f a m b r)
    | size d < 4 = DEEP (dappendL d f) a m b r
    | otherwise = DEEP d (cons (SIMPLE f) a) m b r
  (DEEP f a m b r) ++ (SHALLOW d)
    | size d < 4 = DEEP f a m b (dappendR r d)
    | otherwise = DEEP f a m (snoc b (SIMPLE r)) d
```

```
(DEEP f₁ a₁ m₁ b₁ r₁) ⧺ (DEEP f₂ a₂ m₂ b₂ r₂) = DEEP f₁ a'₁ m b'₂ r₂
  where (r'₁, m, f'₂) = share r₁ f₂
    a'₁ = snoc a₁ (CMPD m₁ b₁ r'₁)
    b'₂ = cons (CMPD f'₂ a₂ m₂) b₂
```

Random-Access Lists

```
module RandomAccessList (RandomAccessList(..)) where
import Prelude hiding (head,tail,lookup)

class RandomAccessList r where
  empty   :: r a
  isEmpty :: r a → Bool

  cons   :: a → r a → r a
  head   :: r a → a
  tail   :: r a → r a

  lookup :: Int → r a → a
  update :: Int → a → r a → r a
```

```
module BinaryRandomAccessList (BinaryList) where
import Prelude hiding (head,tail,lookup)
import RandomAccessList

data Tree a = LEAF a | NODE Int (Tree a) (Tree a)
data Digit a = ZERO | ONE (Tree a)
newtype BinaryList a = BL [Digit a]

size (LEAF x) = 1
size (NODE w t₁ t₂) = w
link t₁ t₂ = NODE (size t₁ + size t₂) t₁ t₂

consTree t [ ] = [ONE t]
consTree t (ZERO : ts) = ONE t : ts
consTree t₁ (ONE t₂ : ts) = ZERO : consTree (link t₁ t₂) ts

unconsTree [ ] = error "empty list"
unconsTree [ONE t] = (t, [ ])
unconsTree (ONE t : ts) = (t, ZERO : ts)
unconsTree (ZERO : ts) = (t₁, ONE t₂ : ts')
  where (NODE _ t₁ t₂, ts') = unconsTree ts

instance RandomAccessList BinaryList where
  empty = BL [ ]
  isEmpty (BL ts) = null ts

  cons x (BL ts) = BL (consTree (LEAF x) ts)
  head (BL ts) = let (LEAF x, _) = unconsTree ts in x
  tail (BL ts) = let (_, ts') = unconsTree ts in BL ts'

  lookup i (BL ts) = look i ts
```

```
  where
     look i [] = error "bad subscript"
     look i (ZERO : ts) = look i ts
     look i (ONE t : ts) =
       if i < size t then lookTree i t else look (i - size t) ts

     lookTree 0 (LEAF x) = x
     lookTree i (LEAF x) = error "bad subscript"
     lookTree i (NODE w t₁ t₂) =
       if i < w 'div' 2 then lookTree i t₁ else lookTree (i - w 'div' 2) t₂

  update i y (BL ts) = BL (upd i ts)
    where
       upd i [] = error "bad subscript"
       upd i (ZERO : ts) = ZERO : upd i ts
       upd i (ONE t : ts) =
         if i < size t then ONE (updTree i t) : ts
         else ONE t : upd (i - size t) ts

       updTree 0 (LEAF x) = LEAF y
       updTree i (LEAF x) = error "bad subscript"
       updTree i (NODE w t₁ t₂) =
         if i < w 'div' 2 then NODE w (updTree i t₁) t₂
         else NODE w t₁ (updTree (i - w 'div' 2) t₂)
```

```
module SkewBinaryRandomAccessList (SkewList) where
import Prelude hiding (head,tail,lookup)
import RandomAccessList

data Tree a = LEAF a | NODE a (Tree a) (Tree a)
newtype SkewList a = SL [(Int, Tree a)]

instance RandomAccessList SkewList where
  empty = SL []
  isEmpty (SL ts) = null ts

  cons x (SL ((w₁,t₁) : (w₂,t₂) : ts))
    | w₁ == w₂ = SL ((1+w₁+w₂, NODE x t₁ t₂) : ts)
  cons x (SL ts) = SL ((1,LEAF x) : ts)

  head (SL []) = error "empty list"
  head (SL ((1, LEAF x) : ts)) = x
  head (SL ((w, NODE x t₁ t₂) : ts)) = x

  tail (SL []) = error "empty list"
  tail (SL ((1, LEAF x) : ts)) = SL ts
  tail (SL ((w, NODE x t₁ t₂) : ts)) = SL ((w 'div' 2, t₁) : (w 'div' 2, t₂) : ts)

  lookup i (SL ts) = look i ts
    where
       look i [] = error "bad subscript"
       look i ((w,t) : ts) =
         if i < w then lookTree w i t else look (i−w) ts
```

```haskell
lookTree 1 0 (LEAF x) = x
lookTree 1 i (LEAF x) = error "bad subscript"
lookTree w 0 (NODE x t₁ t₂) = x
lookTree w i (NODE x t₁ t₂) =
    if i ≤ w' then lookTree w' (i−1) t₁ else lookTree w' (i−1−w') t₂
    where w' = w 'div' 2

update i y (SL ts) = SL (upd i ts)
  where
    upd i [] = error "bad subscript"
    upd i ((w,t) : ts) =
      if i < w then (w,updTree w i t) : ts else (w,t) : upd (i−w) ts

updTree 1 0 (LEAF x) = LEAF y
updTree 1 i (LEAF x) = error "bad subscript"
updTree w 0 (NODE x t₁ t₂) = NODE y t₁ t₂
updTree w i (NODE x t₁ t₂) =
    if i ≤ w' then NODE x (updTree w' (i−1) t₁) t₂
    else NODE x t₁ (updTree w' (i−1−w') t₂)
    where w' = w 'div' 2
```

```haskell
module AltBinaryRandomAccessList (BinaryList) where
import Prelude hiding (head,tail,lookup)
import RandomAccessList

data BinaryList a =
    Nil | ZERO (BinaryList (a,a)) | ONE a (BinaryList (a,a))

uncons :: BinaryList a → (a, BinaryList a)
uncons Nil = error "empty list"
uncons (ONE x Nil) = (x, Nil)
uncons (ONE x ps) = (x, ZERO ps)
uncons (ZERO ps) = let ((x,y), ps') = uncons ps in (x, ONE y ps')

fupdate :: (a → a) → Int → BinaryList a → BinaryList a
fupdate f i Nil = error "bad subscript"
fupdate f 0 (ONE x ps) = ONE (f x) ps
fupdate f i (ONE x ps) = cons x (fupdate f (i−1) (ZERO ps))
fupdate f i (ZERO ps) = ZERO (fupdate f' (i 'div' 2) ps)
    where f' (x,y) = if i 'mod' 2 == 0 then (f x, y) else (x, f y)

instance RandomAccessList BinaryList where
    empty = Nil
    isEmpty Nil = True
    isEmpty _ = False

    cons x Nil = ONE x Nil
    cons x (ZERO ps) = ONE x ps
    cons x (ONE y ps) = ZERO (cons (x,y) ps)

    head xs = fst (uncons xs)
    tail xs = snd (uncons xs)
```

```
lookup i Nil = error "bad subscript"
lookup 0 (ONE x ps) = x
lookup i (ONE x ps) = lookup (i−1) (ZERO ps)
lookup i (ZERO ps) = if i 'mod' 2 == 0 then x else y
   where (x,y) = lookup (i 'div' 2) ps

update i y xs = fupdate (λx → y) i xs
```

Heaps

```
module Heap (Heap(..)) where
  class Heap h where
    empty    :: Ord a ⇒ h a
    isEmpty  :: Ord a ⇒ h a → Bool

    insert   :: Ord a ⇒ a → h a → h a
    merge    :: Ord a ⇒ h a → h a → h a

    findMin   :: Ord a ⇒ h a → a
    deleteMin :: Ord a ⇒ h a → h a
```

```
module LeftistHeap (LeftistHeap) where
  import Heap

  data LeftistHeap a = E | T Int a (LeftistHeap a) (LeftistHeap a)

  rank E = 0
  rank (T r _ _ _) = r

  makeT x a b = if rank a ≥ rank b then T (rank b + 1) x a b
                else T (rank a + 1) x b a

  instance Heap LeftistHeap where
    empty = E
    isEmpty E = True
    isEmpty _ = False

    insert x h = merge (T 1 x E E) h

    merge h E = h
    merge E h = h
    merge h₁@(T _ x a₁ b₁) h₂@(T _ y a₂ b₂) =
      if x ≤ y then makeT x a₁ (merge b₁ h₂)
      else makeT y a₂ (merge h₁ b₂)

    findMin E = error "empty heap"
    findMin (T _ x a b) = x

    deleteMin E = error "empty heap"
    deleteMin (T _ x a b) = merge a b
```

```haskell
module BinomialHeap (BinomialHeap) where
import Heap

data Tree a = NODE Int a [Tree a]
newtype BinomialHeap a = BH [Tree a]

rank (NODE r x c) = r
root (NODE r x c) = x

link t₁@(NODE r x₁ c₁) t₂@(NODE _ x₂ c₂) =
  if x₁ ≤ x₂ then NODE (r+1) x₁ (t₂ : c₁) else NODE (r+1) x₂ (t₁ : c₂)

insTree t [] = [t]
insTree t ts@(t' : ts') =
  if rank t < rank t' then t : ts else insTree (link t t') ts'

mrg ts₁ [] = ts₁
mrg [] ts₂ = ts₂
mrg ts₁@(t₁:ts₁') ts₂@(t₂:ts₂')
  | rank t₁ < rank t₂ = t₁ : mrg ts₁' ts₂
  | rank t₂ < rank t₁ = t₂ : mrg ts₁ ts₂'
  | otherwise = insTree (link t₁ t₂) (mrg ts₁' ts₂')

removeMinTree [] = error "empty heap"
removeMinTree [t] = (t, [])
removeMinTree (t : ts) = if root t < root t' then (t, ts) else (t', t : ts')
  where (t', ts') = removeMinTree ts

instance Heap BinomialHeap where
  empty = BH []
  isEmpty (BH ts) = null ts

  insert x (BH ts) = BH (insTree (NODE 0 x []) ts)
  merge (BH ts₁) (BH ts₂) = BH (mrg ts₁ ts₂)

  findMin (BH ts) = root t
    where (t, _) = removeMinTree ts

  deleteMin (BH ts) = BH (mrg (reverse ts₁) ts₂)
    where (NODE _ x ts₁, ts₂) = removeMinTree ts
```

```haskell
module SplayHeap (SplayHeap) where
import Heap

data SplayHeap a = E | T (SplayHeap a) a (SplayHeap a)

partition pivot E = (E, E)
partition pivot t@(T a x b) =
  if x ≤ pivot then
    case b of
      E → (t, E)
      T b₁ y b₂ →
        if y ≤ pivot then
          let (small, big) = partition pivot b₂
          in (T (T a x b₁) y small, big)
```

```
        else
          let (small, big) = partition pivot b₁
          in (T a x small, T big y b₂)
    else
      case a of
        E → (E, t)
        T a₁ y a₂ →
          if y ≤ pivot then
            let (small, big) = partition pivot a₂
            in (T a₁ y small, T big x b)
          else
            let (small, big) = partition pivot a₁
            in (small, T big y (T a₂ x b))
```

```
instance Heap SplayHeap where
  empty = E
  isEmpty E = True
  isEmpty _ = False

  insert x t = T a x b
    where (a, b) = partition x t

  merge E t = t
  merge (T a x b) t = T (merge ta a) x (merge tb b)
    where (ta, tb) = partition x t

  findMin E = error "empty heap"
  findMin (T E x b) = x
  findMin (T a x b) = findMin a

  deleteMin E = error "empty heap"
  deleteMin (T E x b) = b
  deleteMin (T (T E x b) y c) = T b y c
  deleteMin (T (T a x b) y c) = T (deleteMin a) x (T b y c)
```

```
module PairingHeap (PairingHeap) where
import Heap

data PairingHeap a = E | T a [PairingHeap a]

mergePairs [ ] = E
mergePairs [h] = h
mergePairs (h₁ : h₂ : hs) = merge (merge h₁ h₂) (mergePairs hs)
```

```
instance Heap PairingHeap where
  empty = E
  isEmpty E = True
  isEmpty _ = False

  insert x h = merge (T x [ ]) h

  merge h E = h
  merge E h = h
  merge h₁@(T x hs₁) h₂@(T y hs₂) =
    if x < y then T x (h₂ : hs₁) else T y (h₁ : hs₂)
```

```
findMin E = error "empty heap"
findMin (T x hs) = x

deleteMin E = error "empty heap"
deleteMin (T x hs) = mergePairs hs
```

```
module LazyPairingHeap (PairingHeap) where
import Heap

data PairingHeap a = E | T a (PairingHeap a) (PairingHeap a)

link (T x E m) a = T x a m
link (T x b m) a = T x E (merge (merge a b) m)

instance Heap PairingHeap where
  empty = E
  isEmpty E = True
  isEmpty _ = False

  insert x a = merge (T x E E) a

  merge a E = a
  merge E b = b
  merge a@(T x _ _) b@(T y _ _) = if x ≤ y then link a b else link b a

  findMin E = error "empty heap"
  findMin (T x a m) = x

  deleteMin E = error "empty heap"
  deleteMin (T x a m) = merge a m
```

```
module SkewBinomialHeap (SkewBinomialHeap) where
import Heap

data Tree a = NODE Int a [a] [Tree a]

newtype SkewBinomialHeap a = SBH [Tree a]

rank (NODE r x xs c) = r
root (NODE r x xs c) = x

link t₁@(NODE r x₁ xs₁ c₁) t₂@(NODE _ x₂ xs₂ c₂) =
  if x₁ ≤ x₂ then NODE (r+1) x₁ xs₁ (t₂ : c₁)
  else NODE (r+1) x₂ xs₂ (t₁ : c₂)

skewLink x t₁ t₂ =
  let NODE r y ys c = link t₁ t₂
  in if x ≤ y then NODE r x (y : ys) c else NODE r y (x : ys) c

insTree t [] = [t]
insTree t ts@(t' : ts') =
  if rank t < rank t' then t : ts else insTree (link t t') ts'
```

```
mrg ts₁ [ ] = ts₁
mrg [ ] ts₂ = ts₂
mrg ts₁@(t₁:ts₁') ts₂@(t₂:ts₂')
  | rank t₁ < rank t₂ = t₁ : mrg ts₁' ts₂
  | rank t₂ < rank t₁ = t₂ : mrg ts₁ ts₂'
  | otherwise = insTree (link t₁ t₂) (mrg ts₁' ts₂')

normalize [ ] = [ ]
normalize (t : ts) = insTree t ts

removeMinTree [ ] = error "empty heap"
removeMinTree [t] = (t, [ ])
removeMinTree (t : ts) = if root t < root t' then (t, ts) else (t', t : ts')
  where (t', ts') = removeMinTree ts

instance Heap SkewBinomialHeap where
  empty = SBH [ ]
  isEmpty (SBH ts) = null ts

  insert x (SBH (t₁ : t₂ : ts))
    | rank t₁ == rank t₂ = SBH (skewLink x t₁ t₂ : ts)
  insert x (SBH ts) = SBH (NODE 0 x [ ] [ ] : ts)

  merge (SBH ts₁) (SBH ts₂) = SBH (mrg (normalize ts₁) (normalize ts₂))

  findMin (SBH ts) = root t
    where (t, _) = removeMinTree ts

  deleteMin (SBH ts) = foldr insert (SBH ts') xs
    where (NODE _ x xs ts₁, ts₂) = removeMinTree ts
          ts' = mrg (reverse ts₁) (normalize ts₂)
```

```
module BootstrapHeap (BootstrapHeap) where
  import Heap

  data BootstrapHeap h a = E | H a (h (BootstrapHeap h a))

  instance Eq a ⇒ Eq (BootstrapHeap h a) where
    (H x _) == (H y _) = (x == y)
  instance Ord a ⇒ Ord (BootstrapHeap h a) where
    (H x _) ≤ (H y _) = (x ≤ y)

  instance Heap h ⇒ Heap (BootstrapHeap h) where
    empty = E
    isEmpty E = True
    isEmpty _ = False

    insert x h = merge (H x empty) h

    merge E h = h
    merge h E = h
    merge h₁@(H x p₁) h₂@(H y p₂) =
      if x ≤ y then H x (insert h₂ p₁) else H y (insert h₁ p₂)

    findMin E = error "empty heap"
    findMin (H x p) = x
```

```
deleteMin E = error "empty heap"
deleteMin (H x p) =
  if isEmpty p then E
  else let H y p₁ = findMin p
           p₂ = deleteMin p
       in H y (merge p₁ p₂)
```

Sortable Collections

```
module Sortable (Sortable(..)) where
  class Sortable s where
    empty :: Ord a ⇒ s a
    add   :: Ord a ⇒ a → s a → s a
    sort  :: Ord a ⇒ s a → [a]
```

```
module BottomUpMergeSort (MergeSort) where
import Sortable

data MergeSort a = MS Int [[a]]

mrg [] ys = ys
mrg xs [] = xs
mrg xs@(x : xs') ys@(y : ys') =
  if x ≤ y then x : mrg xs' ys else y : mrg xs ys'

instance Sortable MergeSort where
  empty = MS 0 []

  add x (MS size segs) = MS (size+1) (addSeg [x] segs size)
    where addSeg seg segs size =
            if size 'mod' 2 == 0 then seg : segs
            else addSeg (mrg seg (head segs)) (tail segs) (size 'div' 2)

  sort (MS size segs) = foldl mrg [] segs
```

Sets

```
module Set (Set(..)) where
  -- assumes multi-parameter type classes!

  class Set s a where
    empty  :: s a
    insert :: a → s a → s a
    member :: a → s a → Bool
```

```haskell
module UnbalancedSet (UnbalancedSet) where
import Set

data UnbalancedSet a = E | T (UnbalancedSet a) a (UnbalancedSet a)

instance Ord a ⇒ Set UnbalancedSet a where
  empty = E

  member x E = False
  member x (T a y b) =
    if x < y then member x a
    else if x > y then member x b
    else True

  insert x E = T E x E
  insert x s@(T a y b) =
    if x < y then T (insert x a) y b
    else if x > y then T a y (insert x b)
    else s
```

```haskell
module RedBlackSet (RedBlackSet) where
import Set

data Color = R | B
data RedBlackSet a = E | T Color (RedBlackSet a) a (RedBlackSet a)

balance B (T R (T R a x b) y c) z d = T R (T B a x b) y (T B c z d)
balance B (T R a x (T R b y c)) z d = T R (T B a x b) y (T B c z d)
balance B a x (T R (T R b y c) z d) = T R (T B a x b) y (T B c z d)
balance B a x (T R b y (T R c z d)) = T R (T B a x b) y (T B c z d)
balance color a x b = T color a x b

instance Ord a ⇒ Set RedBlackSet a where
  empty = E

  member x E = False
  member x (T _ a y b) =
    if x < y then member x a
    else if x > y then member x b
    else True

  insert x s = T B a y b
    where ins E = T R E x E
          ins s@(T color a y b) =
            if x < y then balance color (ins a) y b
            else if x > y then balance color a y (ins b)
            else s
          T _ a y b = ins s    -- guaranteed to be non-empty
```

Finite Maps

```
module FiniteMap (FiniteMap(..)) where
-- assumes multi-parameter type classes!
  class FiniteMap m k where
    empty :: m k a
    bind  :: k → a → m k a → m k a
    lookup :: k → m k a → Maybe a
```

```
module Trie (Trie) where
import FiniteMap

data Trie mk ks a = TRIE (Maybe a) (mk (Trie mk ks a))

instance FiniteMap m k ⇒ FiniteMap (Trie (m k)) [k] where
  empty = TRIE NOTHING empty

  lookup [] (TRIE b m) = b
  lookup (k : ks) (TRIE b m) = lookup k m >>= λm' → lookup ks m'

  bind [] x (TRIE b m) = TRIE (JUST x) m
  bind (k : ks) x (TRIE b m) =
    let t = case lookup k m of
              JUST t → t
              NOTHING → empty
        t' = bind ks x t
    in TRIE b (bind k t' m)
```

```
module TrieOfTrees (Tree(..), Trie) where
import FiniteMap

data Tree a = E | T a (Tree a) (Tree a)
data Trie mk ks a = TRIE (Maybe a) (mk (Trie mk ks (Trie mk ks a)))

instance FiniteMap m k ⇒ FiniteMap (Trie (m k)) (Tree k) where
  empty = TRIE NOTHING empty

  lookup E (TRIE v m) = v
  lookup (T k a b) (TRIE v m) =
    lookup k m >>= λm' →
    lookup a m' >>= λm'' →
    lookup b m''

  bind E x (TRIE v m) = TRIE (JUST x) m
  bind (T k a b) x (TRIE v m) =
    let tt = case lookup k m of
               JUST tt → tt
               NOTHING → empty
```

```
t = case lookup a tt of
      JUST t → t
      NOTHING → empty
t' = bind b x t
tt' = bind a t' tt
in TRIE v (bind k tt' m)
```

Bibliography

[Ada93]   Stephen Adams. Efficient sets—a balancing act. *Journal of Functional Programming*, 3(4):553–561, October 1993.   (p. 29)

[AFM⁺95]   Zena M. Ariola, Matthias Felleisen, John Maraist, Martin Odersky, and Philip Wadler. A call-by-need lambda calculus. In *ACM Symposium on Principles of Programming Languages*, pages 233–246, January 1995.   (p. 37)

[And91]   Arne Andersson. A note on searching in a binary search tree. *Software—Practice and Experience*, 21(10):1125–1128, October 1991.   (p. 14)

[AVL62]   G. M. Adel'son-Vel'skiĭ and E. M. Landis. An algorithm for the organization of information. *Soviet Mathematics–Doklady*, 3(5):1259–1263, September 1962. English translation of Russian orginal appearing in *Doklady Akademia Nauk SSSR*, 146:263–266.   (p. 99)

[Bac78]   John Backus. Can programming be liberated from the von Neumann style? A functional style and its algebra of programs. *Communications of the ACM*, 21(8):613–641, August 1978.   (p. 1)

[BAG92]   Amir M. Ben-Amram and Zvi Galil. On pointers versus addresses. *Journal of the ACM*, 39(3):617–648, July 1992.   (p. 2)

[BC93]   F. Warren Burton and Robert D. Cameron. Pattern matching with abstract data types. *Journal of Functional Programming*, 3(2):171–190, April 1993.   (p. 180)

[Bel57]   Richard Bellman. *Dynamic Programming*. Princeton University Press, 1957.   (p. 37)

[BH89]   Bror Bjerner and Sören Holmström. A compositional approach to time analysis of first order lazy functional programs. In *Conference on Functional Programming Languages and Computer Architecture*, pages 157–165, September 1989.   (p. 82)

207

[BO96]   Gerth Stølting Brodal and Chris Okasaki. Optimal purely func-
            tional priority queues. *Journal of Functional Programming*,
            6(6):839–857, November 1996.   (pp. 140, 170)

[Bro78]   Mark R. Brown. Implementation and analysis of binomial queue
            algorithms. *SIAM Journal on Computing*, 7(3):298–319, August
            1978.   (pp. 20, 29)

[Bro95]   Gerth Stølting Brodal. Fast meldable priority queues. In *Work-
            shop on Algorithms and Data Structures*, volume 955 of *LNCS*,
            pages 282–290. Springer-Verlag, August 1995.   (pp. 170, 184)

[Bro96]   Gerth Stølting Brodal. Worst-case priority queues. In *ACM-SIAM
            Symposium on Discrete Algorithms*, pages 52–58, January 1996.
            (p. 170)

[BST95]   Adam L. Buchsbaum, Rajamani Sundar, and Robert E. Tar-
            jan. Data-structural bootstrapping, linear path compression, and
            catenable heap-ordered double-ended queues. *SIAM Journal on
            Computing*, 24(6):1190–1206, December 1995.   (p. 169)

[BT95]   Adam L. Buchsbaum and Robert E. Tarjan. Confluently persis-
            tent deques via data structural bootstrapping. *Journal of Algo-
            rithms*, 18(3):513–547, May 1995.   (pp. 113, 169, 184)

[Buc93]   Adam L. Buchsbaum. *Data-structural bootstrapping and caten-
            able deques*. PhD thesis, Department of Computer Science,
            Princeton University, June 1993.   (pp. 5, 141, 169)

[Bur82]   F. Warren Burton. An efficient functional implementation of
            FIFO queues. *Information Processing Letters*, 14(5):205–206,
            July 1982.   (p. 55)

[But83]   T. W. Butler. Computer response time and user performance. In
            Conference on Human Factors in Computing Systems, pages 58–
            62, December 1983.   (p. 83)

[BW88]   Richard S. Bird and Philip Wadler. *Introduction to Functional
            Programming*. Prentice Hall International, 1988.   (p. 29)

[CG93]   Tyng-Ruey Chuang and Benjamin Goldberg. Real-time deques,
            multihead Turing machines, and purely functional programming.
            In *Conference on Functional Programming Languages and Com-
            puter Architecture*, pages 289–298, June 1993.   (pp. 109, 113)

[CLR90]   Thomas H. Cormen, Charles E. Leiserson, and Ronald L. Rivest.
            Introduction to algorithms. MIT Press, 1990.   (p. 27)

[CM95]   Richard H. Connelly and F. Lockwood Morris. A generalization
            of the trie data structure. *Mathematical Structures in Computer
            Science*, 5(3):381–418, September 1995.   (p. 166)

[CMP88] Svante Carlsson, J. Ian Munro, and Patricio V. Poblete. An implicit binomial queue with constant insertion time. In *Scandinavian Workshop on Algorithm Theory*, volume 318 of *LNCS*, pages 1–13. Springer-Verlag, July 1988. (pp. 97, 140)

[Cra72] Clark Allan Crane. *Linear lists and priority queues as balanced binary trees*. PhD thesis, Computer Science Department, Stanford University, February 1972. Available as STAN-CS-72-259. (pp. 18, 29)

[CS96] Seonghun Cho and Sartaj Sahni. Weight biased leftist trees and modified skip lists. In *International Computing and Combinatorics Conference*, pages 361–370, June 1996. (p. 19)

[DGST88] James R. Driscoll, Harold N. Gabow, Ruth Shrairman, and Robert E. Tarjan. Relaxed heaps: An alternative to Fibonacci heaps with applications to parallel computation. *Communications of the ACM*, 31(11):1343–1354, November 1988. (pp. 97, 169)

[Die82] Paul F. Dietz. Maintaining order in a linked list. In *ACM Symposium on Theory of Computing*, pages 122–127, May 1982. (p. 169)

[Die89] Paul F. Dietz. Fully persistent arrays. In *Workshop on Algorithms and Data Structures*, volume 382 of *LNCS*, pages 67–74. Springer-Verlag, August 1989. (pp. 16, 81)

[DR91] Paul F. Dietz and Rajeev Raman. Persistence, amortization and randomization. In *ACM-SIAM Symposium on Discrete Algorithms*, pages 78–88, January 1991. (p. 97)

[DR93] Paul F. Dietz and Rajeev Raman. Persistence, randomization and parallelization: On some combinatorial games and their applications. In *Workshop on Algorithms and Data Structures*, volume 709 of *LNCS*, pages 289–301. Springer-Verlag, August 1993. (p. 97)

[DS87] Paul F. Dietz and Daniel D. Sleator. Two algorithms for maintaining order in a list. In *ACM Symposium on Theory of Computing*, pages 365–372, May 1987. (p. 113)

[DSST89] James R. Driscoll, Neil Sarnak, Daniel D. K. Sleator, and Robert E. Tarjan. Making data structures persistent. *Journal of Computer and System Sciences*, 38(1):86–124, February 1989. (pp. 2, 16, 37, 58, 81)

[DST94] James R. Driscoll, Daniel D. K. Sleator, and Robert E. Tarjan. Fully persistent lists with catenation. *Journal of the ACM*, 41(5):943–959, September 1994. (pp. 81, 169)

[FB97]   Manuel Fähndrich and John Boyland. Statically checkable pattern abstractions. In *ACM SIGPLAN International Conference on Functional Programming*, pages 75–84, June 1997.   (p. 26)

[FMR72]   Patrick C. Fischer, Albert R. Meyer, and Arnold L. Rosenberg. Real-time simulation of multihead tape units. *Journal of the ACM*, 19(4):590–607, October 1972.   (p. 113)

[FSST86]   Michael L. Fredman, Robert Sedgewick, Daniel D. K. Sleator, and Robert E. Tarjan. The pairing heap: A new form of self-adjusting heap. *Algorithmica*, 1(1):111–129, 1986.   (pp. 52, 53, 169)

[FT87]   Michael L. Fredman and Robert E. Tarjan. Fibonacci heaps and their uses in improved network optimization algorithms. *Journal of the ACM*, 34(3):596–615, July 1987.   (pp. 37, 169)

[FW76]   Daniel P. Friedman and David S. Wise. CONS should not evaluate its arguments. In *Automata, Languages and Programming*, pages 257–281, July 1976.   (p. 37)

[GMPR77]   Leo J. Guibas, Edward M. McCreight, Michael F. Plass, and Janet R. Roberts. A new representation for linear lists. In *ACM Symposium on Theory of Computing*, pages 49–60, May 1977. (pp. 140, 184)

[Gri81]   David Gries. *The Science of Programming*. Texts and Monographs in Computer Science. Springer-Verlag, New York, 1981. (p. 55)

[GS78]   Leo J. Guibas and Robert Sedgewick. A dichromatic framework for balanced trees. In *IEEE Symposium on Foundations of Computer Science*, pages 8–21, October 1978.   (pp. 24, 29, 99)

[GT86]   Hania Gajewska and Robert E. Tarjan. Deques with heap order. *Information Processing Letters*, 22(4):197–200, April 1986. (p. 113)

[Hen93]   Fritz Henglein. Type inference with polymorphic recursion. *ACM Transactions on Programming Languages and Systems*, 15(2):253–289, April 1993.   (p. 170)

[HJ94]   Paul Hudak and Mark P. Jones. Haskell vs. Ada vs. C++ vs. ... An experiment in software prototyping productivity, 1994.   (p. 1)

[HM76]   Peter Henderson and James H. Morris, Jr. A lazy evaluator. In *ACM Symposium on Principles of Programming Languages*, pages 95–103, January 1976.   (p. 37)

[HM81]   Robert Hood and Robert Melville. Real-time queue operations in pure Lisp. *Information Processing Letters*, 13(2):50–53, November 1981.   (pp. 55, 86, 97, 102, 113)

[Hoo82]   Robert Hood. *The Efficient Implementation of Very-High-Level Programming Language Constructs.* PhD thesis, Department of Computer Science, Cornell University, August 1982. (Cornell TR 82-503). (p. 113)

[Hoo92]   Rob R. Hoogerwoord. A symmetric set of efficient list operations. *Journal of Functional Programming*, 2(4):505–513, October 1992. (pp. 44, 109, 113)

[HU73]   John E. Hopcroft and Jeffrey D. Ullman. Set merging algorithms. *SIAM Journal on Computing*, 2(4):294–303, December 1973. (p. 37)

[Hug85]   John Hughes. Lazy memo functions. In *Conference on Functional Programming Languages and Computer Architecture*, volume 201 of *LNCS*, pages 129–146. Springer-Verlag, September 1985. (p. 37)

[Hug86]   John Hughes. A novel representation of lists and its application to the function "reverse". *Information Processing Letters*, 22(3):141–144, March 1986. (p. 169)

[Hug89]   John Hughes. Why functional programming matters. *The Computer Journal*, 32(2):98–107, April 1989. (pp. 1, 113)

[Jon86]   Douglas W. Jones. An empirical comparison of priority-queue and event-set implementations. *Communications of the ACM*, 29(4):300–311, April 1986. (p. 56)

[Jos89]   Mark B. Josephs. The semantics of lazy functional languages. *Theoretical Computer Science*, 68(1):105–111, October 1989. (p. 37)

[KD96]   Anne Kaldewaij and Victor J. Dielissen. Leaf trees. *Science of Computer Programming*, 26(1–3):149–165, May 1996. (p. 118)

[Kin94]   David J. King. Functional binomial queues. In *Glasgow Workshop on Functional Programming*, pages 141–150, September 1994. (pp. 29, 82)

[KL93]   Chan Meng Khoong and Hon Wai Leong. Double-ended binomial queues. In *International Symposium on Algorithms and Computation*, volume 762 of *LNCS*, pages 128–137. Springer-Verlag, December 1993. (p. 169)

[Knu73a]   Donald E. Knuth. *Searching and Sorting*, volume 3 of *The Art of Computer Programming*. Addison-Wesley, 1973. (pp. 18, 29)

[Knu73b]   Donald E. Knuth. *Seminumerical Algorithms*, volume 2 of *The Art of Computer Programming*. Addison-Wesley, 1973. (p. 116)

[KT95]   Haim Kaplan and Robert E. Tarjan. Persistent lists with catenation via recursive slow-down. In *ACM Symposium on Theory of*

Computing, pages 93–102, May 1995.   (pp. 5, 130, 169, 170, 171, 184, 212)

[KT96a]   Haim Kaplan and Robert E. Tarjan. Purely functional lists with catenation via recursive slow-down. Draft revision of [KT95], August 1996.   (pp. 171, 184)

[KT96b]   Haim Kaplan and Robert E. Tarjan. Purely functional representations of catenable sorted lists. In ACM Symposium on Theory of Computing, pages 202–211, May 1996.   (pp. 140, 171, 184)

[KTU93]   Assaf J. Kfoury, Jerzy Tiuryn, and Pawel Urzyczyn. Type reconstruction in the presence of polymorphic recursion. ACM Transactions on Programming Languages and Systems, 15(2):290–311, April 1993.   (p. 170)

[Lan65]   P. J. Landin.   A correspondence between ALGOL 60 and Church's lambda-notation: Part I. Communications of the ACM, 8(2):89–101, February 1965.   (pp. 37, 113)

[Lau93]   John Launchbury.   A natural semantics for lazy evaluation. In ACM Symposium on Principles of Programming Languages, pages 144–154, January 1993.   (p. 37)

[Lia92]   Andrew M. Liao. Three priority queue applications revisited. Algorithmica, 7(4):415–427, 1992.   (p. 56)

[LS81]   Benton L. Leong and Joel I. Seiferas. New real-time simulations of multihead tape units. Journal of the ACM, 28(1):166–180, January 1981.   (p. 113)

[MEP96]   Alistair Moffat, Gary Eddy, and Ola Petersson.   Splaysort: Fast, versatile, practical. Software—Practice and Experience, 26(7):781–797, July 1996.   (p. 52)

[Mic68]   Donald Michie. "Memo" functions and machine learning. Nature, 218:19–22, April 1968.   (pp. 3, 37)

[MS91]   Bernard M. E. Moret and Henry D. Shapiro. An empirical analysis of algorithms for constructing a minimum spanning tree. In Workshop on Algorithms and Data Structures, volume 519 of LNCS, pages 400–411. Springer-Verlag, August 1991.   (p. 56)

[MT94]   David B. MacQueen and Mads Tofte. A semantics for higher-order functors. In European Symposium on Programming, pages 409–423, April 1994.   (p. 160)

[MTHM97] Robin Milner, Mads Tofte, Robert Harper, and David MacQueen. The Definition of Standard ML (Revised). The MIT Press, Cambridge, Massachusetts, 1997.   (p. 31)

[Myc84]   Alan Mycroft. Polymorphic type schemes and recursive definitions. In International Symposium on Programming, volume 167 of *LNCS*, pages 217–228. Springer-Verlag, April 1984. (pp. 144, 170)

[Mye82] Eugene W. Myers. AVL dags. Technical Report TR82-9, Department of Computer Science, University of Arizona, 1982. (pp. 15, 29)

[Mye83] Eugene W. Myers. An applicative random-access stack. *Information Processing Letters*, 17(5):241–248, December 1983. (pp. 131, 140)

[Mye84] Eugene W. Myers. Efficient applicative data types. In *ACM Symposium on Principles of Programming Languages*, pages 66–75, January 1984. (pp. 15, 29, 169)

[NPP95] Manuel Núñez, Pedro Palao, and Ricardo Peña. A second year course on data structures based on functional programming. In *Functional Programming Languages in Education*, volume 1022 of *LNCS*, pages 65–84. Springer-Verlag, December 1995. (p. 29)

[Oka95a] Chris Okasaki. Amortization, lazy evaluation, and persistence: Lists with catenation via lazy linking. In *IEEE Symposium on Foundations of Computer Science*, pages 646–654, October 1995. (pp. 81, 169)

[Oka95b] Chris Okasaki. Purely functional random-access lists. In *Conference on Functional Programming Languages and Computer Architecture*, pages 86–95, June 1995. (pp. 131, 133, 140)

[Oka95c] Chris Okasaki. Simple and efficient purely functional queues and deques. *Journal of Functional Programming*, 5(4):583–592, October 1995. (pp. 81, 97, 113)

[Oka96a] Chris Okasaki. *Purely Functional Data Structures*. PhD thesis, School of Computer Science, Carnegie Mellon University, September 1996. (p. 34)

[Oka96b] Chris Okasaki. The role of lazy evaluation in amortized data structures. In *ACM SIGPLAN International Conference on Functional Programming*, pages 62–72, May 1996. (pp. 81, 82, 97)

[Oka97] Chris Okasaki. Catenable double-ended queues. In *ACM SIGPLAN International Conference on Functional Programming*, pages 66–74, June 1997. (p. 180)

[OLT94] Chris Okasaki, Peter Lee, and David Tarditi. Call-by-need and continuation-passing style. *Lisp and Symbolic Computation*, 7(1):57–81, January 1994. (p. 37)

[Ove83]   Mark H. Overmars. *The Design of Dynamic Data Structures*, volume 156 of *LNCS*. Springer-Verlag, 1983. (pp. 5, 98, 99, 101, 113)

[Pau96]   Laurence C. Paulson. *ML for the Working Programmer*. Cambridge University Press, 2nd edition, 1996. (p. x)

[Pet87]   Gary L. Peterson. A balanced tree scheme for meldable heaps with updates. Technical Report GIT-ICS-87-23, School of Information and Computer Science, Georgia Institute of Technology, 1987. (p. 169)

[Pip96]   Nicholas Pippenger. Pure versus impure Lisp. In *ACM Symposium on Principles of Programming Languages*, pages 104–109, January 1996. (p. 2)

[PPN96]   Pedro Palao Gostanza, Ricardo Peña, and Manuel Núñez. A new look at pattern matching in abstract data types. In *ACM SIGPLAN International Conference on Functional Programming*, pages 110–121, May 1996. (p. 180)

[Ram92]   Rajeev Raman. *Eliminating Amortization: On Data Structures with Guaranteed Response Times*. PhD thesis, Department of Computer Sciences, University of Rochester, October 1992. (pp. 81, 83, 97)

[Rea92]   Chris M. P. Reade. Balanced trees with removals: an exercise in rewriting and proof. *Science of Computer Programming*, 18(2):181–204, April 1992. (p. 29)

[San90]   David Sands. Complexity analysis for a lazy higher-order language. In *European Symposium on Programming*, volume 432 of *LNCS*, pages 361–376. Springer-Verlag, May 1990. (p. 82)

[San95]   David Sands. A naïve time analysis and its theory of cost equivalence. *Journal of Logic and Computation*, 5(4):495–541, August 1995. (p. 82)

[Sar86]   Neil Sarnak. *Persistent Data Structures*. PhD thesis, Department of Computer Sciences, New York University, 1986. (p. 113)

[Sch92]   Berry Schoenmakers. *Data Structures and Amortized Complexity in a Functional Setting*. PhD thesis, Eindhoven University of Technology, September 1992. (pp. 41, 55)

[Sch93]   Berry Schoenmakers. A systematic analysis of splaying. *Information Processing Letters*, 45(1):41–50, January 1993. (p. 82)

[Sch97]   Martin Schwenke. High-level refinement of random access data structures. In *Formal Methods Pacific*, pages 317–318, July 1997. (p. 166)

[SS90]   Jörg-Rüdiger Sack and Thomas Strothotte. A characterization of heaps and its applications. *Information and Computation*, 86(1):69–86, May 1990.   (p. 118)

[ST85]   Daniel D. K. Sleator and Robert E. Tarjan. Self-adjusting binary search trees. *Journal of the ACM*, 32(3):652–686, July 1985.   (pp. 46, 55, 59)

[ST86a]   Neil Sarnak and Robert E. Tarjan. Planar point location using persistent search trees. *Communications of the ACM*, 29(7):669–679, July 1986.   (p. 15)

[ST86b]   Daniel D. K. Sleator and Robert E. Tarjan. Self-adjusting heaps. *SIAM Journal on Computing*, 15(1):52–69, February 1986.   (pp. 37, 55, 59, 169)

[Sta88]   John A. Stankovic. Misconceptions about real-time computing: A serious problem for next-generation systems. *Computer*, 21(10):10–19, October 1988.   (p. 83)

[Sto70]   Hans-Jörg Stoß. K-band simulation von k-Kopf-Turing-maschinen. *Computing*, 6(3):309–317, 1970.   (p. 113)

[SV87]   John T. Stasko and Jeffrey S. Vitter. Pairing heaps: experiments and analysis. *Communications of the ACM*, 30(3):234–249, March 1987.   (p. 56)

[Tar83]   Robert E. Tarjan. *Data Structures and Network Algorithms*, volume 44 of *CBMS Regional Conference Series in Applied Mathematics*. Society for Industrial and Applied Mathematics, Philadelphia, 1983.   (p. 81)

[Tar85]   Robert E. Tarjan. Amortized computational complexity. *SIAM Journal on Algebraic and Discrete Methods*, 6(2):306–318, April 1985.   (pp. 40, 41, 55)

[TvL84]   Robert E. Tarjan and Jan van Leeuwen. Worst-case analysis of set union algorithms. *Journal of the ACM*, 31(2):245–281, April 1984.   (p. 37)

[Ull94]   Jeffrey D. Ullman. *Elements of ML Programming*. Prentice Hall, Englewood Cliffs, New Jersey, 1994.   (p. x)

[Vui74]   Jean Vuillemin. Correct and optimal implementations of recursion in a simple programming language. *Journal of Computer and System Sciences*, 9(3):332–354, December 1974.   (p. 37)

[Vui78]   Jean Vuillemin. A data structure for manipulating priority queues. *Communications of the ACM*, 21(4):309–315, April 1978.   (pp. 20, 29, 118)

[Wad71]   Christopher P. Wadsworth. *Semantics and Pragmatics of the Lamda-Calculus.* PhD thesis, University of Oxford, September 1971. (p. 37)

[Wad87]   Philip Wadler. Views: A way for pattern matching to cohabit with data abstraction. In *ACM Symposium on Principles of Programming Languages*, pages 307–313, January 1987. (p. 180)

[Wad88]   Philip Wadler. Strictness analysis aids time analysis. In *ACM Symposium on Principles of Programming Languages*, pages 119–132, January 1988. (p. 82)

[WV86]   Christopher Van Wyk and Jeffrey Scott Vitter. The complexity of hashing with lazy deletion. *Algorithmica*, 1(1):17–29, 1986. (p. 37)

Index

Printed in the United States
by Baker & Taylor Publisher Services